P9-DHZ-244

TESTING STUDENTS WITH DISABILITIES

CORWIN
PRESS

The Corwin Press logo—a raven striding across an open book—represents the happy union of courage and learning. We are a professional-level publisher of books and journals for K–12 educators, and we are committed to creating and providing resources that embody these qualities.

TESTING STUDENTS WITH DISABILITIES

Practical Strategies for Complying With District and State Requirements

MARTHA L. THURLOW
JUDY L. ELLIOTT
JAMES E. YSSELDYKE

NO LONGER
PROPERTY OF
JEFFERSON
COLLEGE
LIBRARY

JUNG-KELLOGG LIBRARY
MO. BAPTIST COLLEGE
ONE COLLEGE PARK DR.
ST. LOUIS, MO 63141-8698

LB
3051
.T526
1998
c. 2

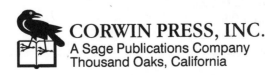
CORWIN PRESS, INC.
A Sage Publications Company
Thousand Oaks, California

Copyright ©1998 by Corwin Press, Inc.

All rights reserved. No part of this book may be reproduced or utilized in any form or by any means, electronic or mechanical, including photocopying, recording, or by any information storage and retrieval system, without permission in writing from the publisher.

For information:

Corwin Press, Inc.
A Sage Publications Company
2455 Teller Road
Thousand Oaks, California 91320
E-mail: order@corwin.sagepub.com

SAGE Publications Ltd.
6 Bonhill Street
London EC2A 4PU
United Kingdom

SAGE Publications India Pvt. Ltd.
M-32 Market
Greater Kailash I
New Delhi 110 048 India

Printed in the United States of America

Library of Congress Cataloging-in-Publication Data

Thurlow, Martha L.
  Testing students with disabilities: Practical strategies for
  complying with district and state requirements / by Martha L.
  Thurlow, Judy L. Elliott, James E. Ysseldyke.
       p.   cm.
    Includes bibliographical references.
    ISBN 0-8039-6551-6 (cloth: acid-free paper). — ISBN
  0-8039-6552-4 (pbk.: acid-free paper)
    1. Educational tests and measurements—United States.
  2. Handicapped children—United States—Ability testing.
  3. Education and state—United States.   I. Elliott, Judy L.
  II. Ysseldyke, James E.   III. Title.
  LB3051.T526   1997
  371.9′046—dc21   97-21048

This book is printed on acid-free paper.

  99 00 01 02 03 10 9 8 7 6 5 4 3

Production Editor: Astrid Virding
Editorial Assistant: Kristen L. Gibson
Production Assistant: Karen Wiley
Typesetter/Designer: Christina M. Hill
Cover Designer: Marcia M. Rosenburg

Contents

Preface

Just a few years ago, the topic of testing students with disabilities was relegated to books for school psychologists, diagnosticians, and other professionals who administer individualized assessments to these students, generally to determine their eligibility for special services. Today, the topic of testing students with disabilities is near the top of the list of district and state priorities. If it is not, it probably should be. Why? Because districts and states are being pushed to be accountable for the results of education, for how well students are performing. And states and districts are realizing that to have good educational accountability systems, it is important to be sure that all students are included—and this means students with disabilities.

The purpose of this book is to facilitate the meaningful assessment of students with disabilities in district and state assessments. The inclusion of students with disabilities in these assessments is required by the 1997 amendments to the Individuals With Disabilities Act (IDEA). It is the people in the schools who will have to make sure that the requirements are met. As they work toward meeting these requirements, many questions will arise. For example: How should good decisions be made about whether a student with a disability should take a test? What is the purpose of assessment accommodations, and who is eligible for them? How do you determine what accommodations a student needs? How do you decide that an assessment administered with accommodations is comparable to one administered without accommodations? What does all this have to do with a student's Individualized Educational Program (IEP)? How can the IEP process be blended with decisions about the district or state assessment? How can all levels of the educational system support the meaningful participation of students with disabilities in assessment and accountability systems? And, what do parents need to know to make the testing of students with disabilities in district and state assessments a valued experience? These are just some of the questions that this book answers.

Why did we write this book? Because we saw no one else addressing this critical information need. And, the need is rapidly increasing as states and districts set new policies that require the participation of all students in accountability systems.

Audience

We believe that this book is an essential resource for all district and school professionals, particularly as our schools move into educational accountability systems that include the performance of students as a key indicator of success. While we have directed the book primarily toward educators in schools, we hope that state-level personnel will read it also. Just as districts and schools must comply with state and district requirements, states also must be willing to learn about the impact of their requirements and the ways in which they might be implemented. They must be aware that practice can influence policy, just as it is assumed that policy will influence practice.

Overview

We have organized this book to provide you with not only needed information about testing students with disabilities to comply with district and state requirements but practical strategies for doing so. To help you implement these strategies, we have provided a variety of forms and checklists that you can use. Each of these appears in the chapter in which it is introduced and also in the Resource section at the end of the book, where it is in reproducible form for making copies to use.

To further facilitate the implementation, another resource provided at the end of the book is "Conducting Staff Development." This is designed to help in the delivery and dissemination of information about the what, why, how, and what-ifs of assessment programs and accommodations decisions for students with disabilities. This resource includes information on some of the most important points that need to be made about assessment and accountability, as well as some specific activities in which people can engage. Reproducible handouts and overheads are provided in this section as well.

As a final but no less important resource, we have created a list of technical assistance and dissemination networks that can provide information relevant to the topics covered in this book. Some of them are national resources; others are regional. Web sites offer a wealth of information on topics related to those addressed in this book, and we urge those who have not yet "surfed" to do so.

We have aimed to develop a book that is usable to the extreme, with both information and strategies and with materials to support both. We hope that as you use this book you will provide us with feedback on its usefulness in meeting your needs.

Acknowledgments

We have developed this book from our years of accumulated experience as practitioners, researchers, and staff developers. But, of course, we could not have completed it without the influence of many people and events. It was the initial work of the National Center on Educational Outcomes that pushed us to face the fact that practitioners, not just policy makers, need information on how best to test students with disabilities in district and state assessments. Numerous individuals from state departments of education and districts also urged us to continue to make information available to those most likely to bring about the changes toward which policy makers are striving.

We thank those individuals who took the time to review the text. They are Martha Hodgkins, Resident Teacher, Assessments and Accountability Branch, Delaware Department of Public Instruction; Lester Horvath, Education Consultant, Program Evaluation Unit, Connecticut State Department of Education; Stevan Kukic, Director of At-Risk and Special Education Services, Utah State Office of Education; Edward Roeber, Director, Student Assessment Program, Council of Chief State School Officers; Edward Wilkins, Director, Northeast Regional Resource Center, Burlington, Vermont; and Lynn Winters, Assistant Superintendent, Research, Planning, and Evaluation, Long Beach Unified School District. We hope that their approval of it reflects how you will react as you start your journey toward good assessment practices for students with disabilities in district and state assessments.

—Martha L. Thurlow
Judy L. Elliott
James E. Ysseldyke

About the Authors

Martha L. Thurlow is Associate Director at the National Center on Educational Outcomes. In this position, she addresses the implications of contemporary U.S. policy and practice for students with disabilities, including national and statewide assessment policies and practices, standards-setting efforts, and graduation requirements. She has worked with diverse groups of stakeholders to identify important outcomes for young children (ages 3-6), and for students in Grades 4, 8, and 12, and at the post-school level. She has conducted research involving special education for the past 25 years in a variety of areas, including assessment and decision making, learning disabilities, early childhood education, dropout prevention, effective classroom instruction, and integration of students with disabilities in general education settings. In 1995, she assumed the position of coeditor of *Exceptional Children*, the research journal of the Council for Exceptional Children.

Judy L. Elliott is Research Specialist at the National Center on Educational Outcomes. In this position, she assists state education departments in their efforts to update and realign curricular frameworks and assessments to include *all* students. As a former special education teacher of students with learning and behavioral disabilities and a school psychologist, she has worked with students and teachers from elementary through secondary levels. She also serves as a national consultant and staff development professional to school districts and organizations, with a focus on strategies and tactics for effective instruction, curriculum modification for students with mild to severe disabilities, intervention and teacher assistance teams, authentic and curriculum-based evaluation,

behavior management, and a variety of other topics. Her research has focused on IEPs, international studies of student performance, and translating information on standards and assessment for various audiences, including parents, teachers, school boards, and community groups.

 **James E. Ysseldyke** is Professor of Educational Psychology and Director of the National Center on Educational Outcomes. He has served as a special education teacher, school psychologist, and professor at the University of Minnesota. He has authored numerous books, including *Assessment in Special and Remedial Education, Critical Issues in Special Education, Special Education: A Practical Approach for Teachers, Strategies and Tactics for Effective Instruction, Tactics for Improving Parenting Skills,* and *The Instructional Environment System–II.* His research interests are in assessment, effective instruction, educational policy, school reform, and improving instructional results for all students.

Why Students With Disabilities Should Be in District and Statewide Accountability Systems

Topics

- Defining Accountability, Assessment, and Testing
- Reasons for Wanting Students With Disabilities in the Accountability System
- Overview of This Book

In this chapter, you will . . .

- review the definitions of accountability, assessment, and testing, and recognize the differences between them.
- learn some of the reasons for promoting an inclusive accountability system.
- gain a general overview of the content of the book.

We developed this book to help you comply with district and statewide testing requirements and at the same time meet the challenge of accountability for the diversity of students in our schools today. In this chapter, we summarize many of the reasons why it is important for students with disabilities to take district and state tests. For these reasons to make sense, you need to understand the distinctions between accountability, assessment, and testing. Thus, we start by defining these terms.

BOX 1.1

Myth or Truth? Do You Know?

Read each statement below and decide whether it is a myth or the truth about current practice.

- Assessment information on student performance is just one piece of evidence that might go into an accountability system.
- Assessment is a narrower term than testing.
- Standards-based reform emphasizes the results of education rather than the process.
- One reason for including students with disabilities in the accountability system, along with other special needs students, is that it gives us a more accurate picture of the status of education.
- There is amazing consistency from one place to the next in the high rates at which students with disabilities are excluded from assessments.
- Several new education laws emphasize the need to include all students in educational accountability systems.
- An unintended but documented consequence of exclusion of some students from accountability systems is increased rates of referral to special education.

Early in each chapter, we list topic-specific myths and truths that you will be able to identify when you finish the chapter. Those for Chapter 1 are presented in Box 1.1.

Along with providing the background information that you will need to answer questions about why students with disabilities should participate in district and statewide tests, this chapter outlines the framework for the rest of the book.

Defining Accountability, Assessment, and Testing

Accountability and assessment are not the same thing, and testing is just one type of assessment. It is important to keep the distinctions between these terms in mind as we talk about compliance with district and statewide testing. It is also important to realize that classroom assessments, with which we are most familiar, are related to district and state tests and the notion of accountability (National Forum on Assessment, 1995).

Accountability has been defined in many different ways. In relation to education, a respected definition is that "educational accountability" is a systematic method to assure those inside and outside the educational system that schools are moving in desired directions (Center for

---

BOX 1.2

Desired Evidence for Accountability Has Shifted From the Process and Context of Education to the Results of Education: Examples of Each Type of Evidence

Educational Process and Context	Educational Results
Student-teacher ratio	Student performance on district tests
Number of teachers with master's degrees and above	Student performance on statewide assessment
Adequacy of school buildings	Graduation rate
Per pupil expenditures	Dropout rate
Length of school day	Postschool status of graduates
Number of days in school year	SAT/ACT scores
Number of students in special education	GED completion rates
Number of students in compensatory education	
Parent involvement in schools	
Percentage of students taking advanced placement classes	

Policy Options, 1993). Although this definition is a bit academic, it simply means that accountability is evidence that schools are doing what they are supposed to be doing. We believe that

> a system is accountable for **all** students when it makes sure that all students **count** in the **evaluation program** of the education system.

The evidence that people want to see has changed over time (see Box 1.2). In the past, people accepted evidence about the educational process and the context of education. Examples of this type of evidence were student-teacher ratios, numbers of teachers with advanced degrees, and so on. Today, in part as a result of standards-based reform, the evidence that people demand is focused on the results of education. Have students achieved the skills that the public thinks are important for them to achieve? Can they read? Can they solve mathematical problems? For the most part, although not entirely, the evidence that people collect on the results of education is obtained from assessments.

Assessment refers to the collection of data (Salvia & Ysseldyke, 1995). Data can be collected in many different ways, one of which is testing. Most people think of testing when they think of assessment, but assessment also includes collections of student work, such as portfolios, interviews, and observations, to name a few. *Testing* typically refers just to multiple-choice, forced-choice (e.g., true, false), and open response (e.g., essay) types of assessments. All of these can contribute to accountability.

Testing is a narrower term than *assessment*, and *assessment* is a narrower term than *accountability*. As you read this book, you will learn why it is essential that all students be included in educational accountability systems. You also will find out why it is important to include more students with disabilities in current district and statewide testing.

Standards-based reform promotes the setting of high standards, identifying indicators of successfully meeting those standards, and ways to measure student progress toward the indicators. Associated with these are analyzing data and reporting the results. We have already alluded to one of the changes that has emerged as a result of standards-based reform—the shift from a focus on the process and context of education to a focus on the results of education. There has also been a narrowing of focus to academic kinds of results. Although not all policy-level people agree with these shifts, preferring instead to continue to collect process information, it remains true that the emphasis of standards-based reform is on students achieving high academic standards and that this achievement is documented by having students take tests to demonstrate what they know and can do.

Reasons for Wanting Students With Disabilities in the Accountability System

There are many good reasons why students with disabilities should be included in educational accountability systems. Some of these reasons are presented here.

Reason 1: For an Accurate Picture of Education

We do not obtain a fully representative, accurate picture of education, particularly of student performance in education, if we do not have all students in the accountability system. In most places, 10% or more of the population of students is not incorporated when our accountability system excludes students with disabilities. In some places, we are talking about a much greater percentage.

Nationwide, the number of students with disabilities is equivalent to the total populations of Idaho, Montana, Nevada, North Dakota, South Dakota, and Wyoming. The number of students with disabilities exceeds the population of 32 states. Those with disabilities are a significant portion of the student population and need to be included in that population if we are to obtain an accurate picture of education.

Reason 2: For Students With Disabilities to Benefit From Reforms

Today, more than in the past, educational reforms are being driven by the results obtained from accountability systems. When students with disabilities are not included in the district and statewide accountability systems on which reforms are based, it is likely that the reforms may not meet their needs. In essence, the saying "out of sight, out of mind" could be applied to what happens when policy and education reform decisions are made on the basis of accountability results that do not include all students.

Reason 3: To Make Accurate Comparisons

Increasingly, accountability information is used to make comparisons among states or among districts within a state. But, we know that the participation rates of students with disabilities may vary from one place to the next. For example, in the 1990 trial state administration of the National Assessment of Educational Progress (NAEP), also known as the nation's report card, the variation in the rates of exclusion of students with disabilities ranged from 33% to 87%. In other words, in one state 33% of all students with disabilities had been excluded from the assessment, and in another state 87% had been excluded. A more recent study (Zlatos, 1994) demonstrated similar variability among school districts across the United States in their rates of exclusion of students overall (see Box 1.3 for a sample of the Zlatos data). With these kinds of variability, comparisons become questionable. The only solution to unfair comparisons is for all students to be included in all accountability systems— always.

Reason 4: To Avoid Unintended Consequences of Exclusion

There are two very powerful unintended consequences of the exclusion of students from accountability systems. These usually occur when there are significant consequences associated with the test results (e.g., a school is accredited if students receive a certain score on an assessment that is administered at a specific grade level). First, it has been demonstrated that students are retained in the grades preceding the one in which the assessment is administered. As evidence of this, Allington and McGill-Franzen (1992) found that when a school accreditation assessment was administered in Grade 3, many of those students who should have been in Grade 3 had been retained in Grades 1 and 2, thus

BOX 1.3

**Students Tested in Selected School Districts
During 1992–1993 School Year**

District	Number of Students Tested	Number of Students Enrolled in Grades Tested	Percentage of Students Tested
Baltimore	51,602	57,517	90
Indianapolis	13,355	15,732	85
Detroit	139,941	169,439	83
Pittsburgh	30,182	36,960	82
Oklahoma City	8,599	12,534	69
Boston	32,866	49,948	66

SOURCE: From "Don't Test, Don't Tell," by Bill Zlatos, 1994, *American School Board Journal*, November, p. 26. Copyright 1994 by National School Boards Association. Reprinted with permission. All rights reserved.

delaying their entry into the grade at which they would be tested and affect scores.

A second unintended consequence is increased referral to special education. This outcome was found by Allington and McGill-Franzen and has been confirmed in states that have high school graduation exams coupled with policies that allow students with disabilities (on IEPs) to obtain a diploma without having to pass the test but by meeting their IEP goals. Dramatic increases have been noted in referral rates in the high school years in these places, an occurrence that is completely inconsistent with normal referral trends.

Reason 5: To Meet Legal Requirements

Legal requirements related to participation in assessment and assessment accommodations have existed for some time now through Section 504 of the Rehabilitation Act (1973) and continued through the Americans With Disabilities Act (ADA). New education legislation is recognizing the importance of having all students in the educational accountability system. The Improving America's Schools Act (IASA), which funds Title I programs, requires that program accountability be based on student performance on statewide tests and that students with limited English proficiency and students with disabilities be included in these systems. The reauthorization of the Individuals With Disabilities Education Act (IDEA), which funds special education programs, also requires that states report on the participation of students with disabilities in their state assessment programs and that an alternate assessment be used for those students who cannot be included in the statewide assessment program.

Reason 6: To Promote High Expectations

When students are excluded from testing it reflects an opinion that they are not able to meet the expectations represented in the test. For the majority of students with disabilities, parents and teachers tell us that they want these students to meet the same high standards that the rest are supposed to meet. Students with disabilities tell us that they want to be taught and tested on the same things as other students are. We are lowering the standards that students with disabilities must meet if we do not have them in the same accountability system as other students. For the majority of students with disabilities, this is a gross injustice. Only by holding high expectations can we expect students to meet them. And, when accountability is one part of our educational system's high expectations, then students must be in the accountability system.

Overview of This Book

To help you do what you need to do to comply with district and state-wide requirements and, at the same time, do what is best for the student, we have organized this book to first address what you need to know and then to address what you need to do. Thus, Chapters 2 through 6 address what you need to know about the participation of students with disabilities in assessments, what accommodations are, how to decide which accommodations are appropriate for use in assessments, the characteristics of alternate assessments, and the reporting of assessment results.

Chapters 7 through 10 address how you can move toward a fully inclusive accountability system. Included in these chapters are discussions on how the IEP can be restructured to promote greater participation in the accountability system, what teachers and parents can do to foster this participation and make it productive for all involved, and ideas for professional development in local districts and school buildings.

BOX 1.4

Myth or Truth Answers

TRUTH   Assessment information on student performance is just one piece of evidence that might go into an accountability system.

Explanation: In addition to student performance, an accountability system might include information on other educational results (e.g., graduation rate) and process data (e.g., student-teacher ratio, extent of parent involvement). [See page 3]

MYTH   Assessment is a narrower term than testing.

Explanation: Testing is narrower than assessment (assessment includes other methods, such as interviews and observations, in addition to testing), and assessment is narrower than accountability. [See page 4]

TRUTH   Standards-based reform emphasizes the results of education rather than the process.

Explanation: The emphasis of standards-based reform has corresponded to a shift away from process and toward educational results. Another trend has been a narrowing of focus to academics. [See page 4]

TRUTH   One reason for including students with disabilities in the accountability system, along with other special needs students, is that it gives us a more accurate picture of the status of education.

Explanation: The picture that we have of education is not fully representative and accurate if we do not include all students. [See page 4]

MYTH   There is amazing consistency from one place to the next in the high rates at which students with disabilities are excluded from assessments.

Explanation: There is tremendous variability in inclusion rates from one place to another. [See page 5]

TRUTH   Several new education laws emphasize the need to include all students in educational accountability systems.

Explanation: Besides Section 504 and the ADA, several new laws require that students with disabilities be afforded the opportunity to participate in educational accountability systems. [See page 6]

TRUTH   An unintended but documented consequence of exclusion of some students from accountability systems is increased rates of referral to special education.

Explanation: Evidence from research by Allington and McGill-Franzen (1992), as well as anecdotal information, indicates that referral to special education is a common consequence of exclusion of students on IEPs from the accountability system. [See page 6]

Summary

In this chapter, we introduced you briefly to the notion of accountability for *all* students. We distinguished between *testing* (a very narrow term), *assessment*, and *accountability*. While we are striving for accountability for all students, we also are striving to include almost all students with disabilities in the regular assessment system, taking the same tests (with and without accommodations) as given to other students. We also pointed out at least six reasons to avidly pursue including all students in the accountability system.

Now, check your knowledge about the myth/truth statements presented at the beginning of this chapter (see Box 1.4 for answers). Try to give an explanation for why each statement is correctly identified either as a myth or as the truth.

Resources for Further Information

Allington, R., & McGill-Franzen, A. (1992). Unintended effects of reform in New York. *Educational Policy, 6*(4), 397-414.

Center for Policy Options. (1993). *Outcomes-based accountability: Policy issues and options for students with disabilities.* Rockville, MD: Westat.

McGrew, K. S., Thurlow, M. L., Shriner, J. G., & Spiegel, A. (1992). *Inclusion of students with disabilities in national and state data collection systems* (Tech. Rep. 2). Minneapolis: University of Minnesota, National Center on Educational Outcomes.

National Forum on Assessment. (1995). *Principles and indicators for student assessment systems.* Cambridge, MA: National Center for Fair & Open Testing (FairTest).

Salvia, J., & Ysseldyke, J. E. (1995). *Assessment* (6th ed.). Boston: Houghton Mifflin.

Zlatos, B. (1994). Don't test, don't tell: Is "academic red-shirting" skewing the way we rank our schools? *American School Board Journal, 181*(11), 24-28.

Deciding Whether a Student Should Take the District or State Test

In this chapter, you will . . .

- learn some myths and truths about accountability systems and students with disabilities.

- review the purpose and need for assessment.

- think carefully about the goals of instruction for individual students.

- examine criteria for making decisions about a student's participation in assessment.

In Chapter 1, we summarized many of the reasons why it is important to have students with disabilities be part of the accountability system. Accountability for student learning, of course, is the primary reason, one that must be kept in mind when making participation decisions. But because educators are directly concerned with the welfare of students as well as the practical considerations of actually adminis-

---

BOX 2.1

Myth or Truth? Do You Know?

Read each statement below and decide whether it is a myth or the truth about current practice.

- Most states have accountability systems for the school performance of students with disabilities.
- Less than 50% of the students with disabilities in most states participate in the regular accountability system.
- It is unfair to students with disabilities to require them to participate in district and state assessments.
- All states but two now require that the IEP team be involved in the decision about whether students with disabilities participate in district or state assessments.
- The student's instructional goals comprise the primary factor in determining whether a student with disabilities should participate in a regular large-scale assessment.

---

tering the test, other considerations necessarily come into play. The purpose of this chapter is to address these considerations.

When you finish this chapter, you will be able to identify which of the statements in Box 2.1 are myths and which are the truth.

How do you decide about the way in which a student takes part in the accountability system? Should the student take the district or state test, or be part of an alternate accountability system? Answering these questions involves asking and answering other questions. The kinds of questions that need to be answered are these:

- How do you balance the need for accountability with the goals of the student's instruction?

- Who needs to be involved in making decisions about whether students participate in tests, and what do they need to know?

- What criteria should guide decisions about the participation of students with disabilities in a district or state test?

In this chapter, we begin to answer each of these questions. This provides you with the guidelines and rationale that you need to make the best decisions for educational accountability, on the one hand, and for the student, on the other.

Recognizing the Need for Accountability

Although we have already covered many of the reasons for wanting students in the educational accountability system, it is important to keep them in mind when thinking about individual students. It is important also to realize that education has been woefully negligent in promoting accountability for *all* students. Most states do not have accountability systems for the school performance of students with disabilities.

In those states with regular accountability systems, most include less than half of their students with disabilities in their state assessments. Because educational accountability is important for all students, educators need to take responsibility for finding ways to ensure the participation of students with disabilities in these accountability systems. Steps must be taken to recognize the need for accountability and to dispel myths about the negative effects of testing.

Documenting the Reasons Why Students With Disabilities Should Participate in the Accountability System and Why Most Should Be in the Existing Assessment System

It is helpful to keep available a list of the reasons for wanting students with disabilities in the accountability system and for wanting most of them in the existing assessment system. This list can be shared with those who may raise questions about the need for all students to be in the accountability system and for those who question their participation in existing tests. It also can help dispel myths about the negative effects of testing. Keeping a list of reasons, to which you might add over time, is especially helpful if the IEP team makes participation decisions, and the membership of the team changes. In Box 2.2, we list the major reasons why students should participate in the accountability system and in existing assessments. Add your own reasons, especially ones that are directly relevant to your own district or state.

Dispelling Myths About the Negative Effects of Testing and Confirming the Reality of Positive Effects

You should always have available a number of anecdotes to dispel myths about the negative effects of testing (e.g., extreme emotional stress for students with disabilities). Build a notebook of these anecdotes in your own district or state. Here are some that we have heard during visits to numerous states and districts:

- Students are being taught test-taking strategies to reduce the stress associated with testing. Both students with disabilities and

---

BOX 2.2

Reasons Why Students With Disabilities Should Participate in the Accountability System and in Existing Assessments

- Students are more likely to benefit from instructional changes and educational reforms when they are included in the accountability system.
- New legislation requires their participation.
- Students need to gain skills involved in taking tests.
- The possibility of corruption in accountability systems is reduced when all students are included in the accountability system.
- Participation in the accountability system provides an avenue for program monitoring and evaluation.
- Most students with disabilities have mild disabilities and should be pursuing the same educational goals as other students; these students should be taking the same assessments either with or without accommodations.
- Full participation in the accountability system facilitates making policy decisions that are applicable to all students.

---

students without disabilities are affected in varying degrees by the effects of stress at the time of testing. Students who experience stress can benefit from a variety of stress-reduction techniques. These strategies are being directed to all students who need them, not just students with disabilities, because all benefit from strategy instruction.

- In Kentucky, a state with an accountability system that provides cash awards to buildings for meeting targeted levels of improvement, all personnel in the building (including custodians and cooks as well as regular and special education teachers) assume responsibility for helping all children learn. This shared responsibility is a direct result of the fact that all students are included in the accountability system and count toward decisions about cash awards.

- Complaints that testing narrows the curriculum so that it focuses almost completely on the content of the tests are countered with the view that finally students are being taught what are considered the essential elements for them to learn.

- Parents of students with disabilities, and the students themselves, are asking for more opportunities for the experience of testing, so that work-related and postsecondary education assessments will not be a shock.

- When students with disabilities are exempted from tests that their peers are taking, they often feel "different" even though they usually see themselves as being like their peers. When these students are included in the tests, they feel part of the group.

It is also helpful to have strategies in mind for how you can turn an unsuccessful testing experience into a positive one. The most common concern about having students with disabilities participate in an assessment is that it will be too stressful for them. This is handled well in states that have a history of administering accountability assessments and including students with disabilities in them. First, it is recognized that all students experience some distress when faced with a test, particularly if the importance of it is emphasized by the teacher. Furthermore, there are some students whose past experiences have produced a lack of confidence and learned helplessness about taking tests.

Second, there is the realization that any additional distress experienced by students with disabilities is most often due to their lack of test-taking experiences. These students can be prepared to take tests by telling them what the test will be like, educating them in an array of test-taking skills, and making them aware of how to prepare physically for a test. This will decrease their feelings of stress about taking tests. More information on this is presented in Chapter 8.

These are just a few examples of strategies for dealing with potentially negative experiences when students with disabilities participate in accountability assessments. A good exercise is to have IEP team members (or other groups of personnel) identify common concerns about the participation of students with disabilities and then generate strategies for addressing them.

Involving Others in Decision Making

All but two states require that the IEP team be involved in the decision about whether students with disabilities participate in district or state assessments. Even when not required, parents, teachers, other school personnel, and students should be informed partners in decisions about participation in district and state assessments. To become informed, they need to know the following:

- Purposes of assessments
- Need for accountability assessments
- Nature of the district or state assessment being administered

This information is usually not common knowledge. Therefore, an effort must be made to ensure that this information is available to all parties

---

BOX 2.3

**Information on the Purposes of
Assessments Used in Schools**

Purpose	Explanation
Eligibility or Reevaluation	Assessment information is used along with other information to determine whether a student is eligible to receive or to continue to receive special education services.
Instructional	Assessment information is used to determine what to teach and how to teach it. Linked to this is information on the progress of students given what is being taught and how it is being taught. For example, if all students perform poorly on a classroom test, the decision might be to review the material or to teach it in a different way.
Accountability	Assessment information is used to provide a picture of the status of education. It can document how well an individual student is doing (student accountability), or how all students in a system are doing (system accountability). Consequences may be applied to either type of accountability (e.g., rewards for schools; earning a high school diploma for students).

---

who should contribute to decisions. Staff information sheets sometimes are adequate to convey information to school personnel. For parents, an option is to set up parent information teams, in which a knowledgeable parent of a student with disabilities conveys relevant information to other parents of students with disabilities.

It is also important to ensure that staff and students not directly involved in decision making understand the purposes for taking assessments and why some students may need accommodations in order to participate in district and state assessments. These topics are addressed in Chapter 7.

Purposes of Assessment

Most parents and teachers of students with disabilities think about assessments used for making eligibility or reevaluation decisions when they hear the term *assessment* or *testing*. Thus, it is critical to distinguish among assessments used for the following purposes:

- Eligibility and reevaluation decisions
- Classroom instructional decisions
- Accountability (either system-level or student-level)

Box 2.3 contains information that can be used to communicate the differences in purposes. This information communicates the basics of what parents, teachers, other school personnel, and students need to know. Additional information on the first two purposes of assessment presented in Box 2.3 can be found in most introductory textbooks on special education.

Conveying the Need for Accountability Assessments

Many parents and school personnel will not know about district or state assessments, much less about the roles of these as accountability tools. The information presented in Chapter 1 is relevant for everyone. These are the major points to make:

- We need to know how students are performing in school, not just whether they are in school.
- Schools are held accountable in different ways—through public reporting of scores of students in the school, by presenting awards and rewards to schools whose students perform well, and by imposing sanctions on schools whose students do not perform well.
- Educational reforms and instructional changes are driven by assessments when the performance on those assessments counts in some way (they are reported, or they are the basis for consequences).
- Students who do not participate in the assessments tend to be left out of the educational reforms and changes in instruction that accompany assessments used for accountability.

Other information on accountability that is directly relevant to your state or district should be discussed as well.

Describing the Current District or State Assessment

It is important for all individuals involved in making decisions about the participation of students with disabilities in an assessment to know more about the assessment. What kind of information do they need in addition to information on the purpose of the assessment? The more concrete and understandable the assessment can be made, the better. It is best to examine a copy of the assessment (or, if it is a secured test, a previous version of it). If this is not possible, the information that you need to know about the assessment, and that needs to be shared with others, includes the following:

- Name of the test
- Content areas covered by the test
- Grades tested
- How the test is administered (e.g., in classroom or other room, how many days, how long testing sessions are)
- Nature of the items (e.g., multiple-choice, extended response, writing sample, performance)
- What is done with student scores (e.g., individual reports, school reports, state report)

A copy of the test should be available from your district assessment and evaluation division (if one exists) or from the person responsible for setting up testing. It always helps decision making when people know more about what they are discussing.

Thinking About the Goals of Instruction

Tests are developed with different purposes in mind. These purposes may or may not be consistent with the desire for educational accountability. Thus, in making the decision about whether a student takes a specific district or state test, first make sure that you know why the test is being given. Then think about the goals of the student's instruction in relationship to this purpose.

Taking a Broad Perspective When Thinking About Instructional Goals

A broad perspective is one that involves thinking about where instruction is supposed to lead the student. For an individual student with disabilities, think about whether the student is working toward (a) the *same* instructional goals as students without disabilities, (b) *modified* goals, or (c) *functional* goals:

- *Same:* Goals that reflect preparation for participation in typical life experiences in the areas of education, employment, and social networks
- *Modified:* Goals that reflect preparation for participation in typical life experiences, with some modifications introduced to support the realization of these goals

BOX 2.4

**Instructional Goals for Three Students at
Three Points in Time**

Alice	Barbara	Carolyn
Alice is a student with a learning disability.	Barbara is a student with moderate mental retardation.	Carolyn is a student with a significant cognitive disability.
Grade 3: Alice's goals for instruction focus on reading, mathematics, and writing, the same as most students in the classroom. Her goals also focus on content area learning in social studies and science.	**Grade 3:** The goals of Barbara's instruction are the same as those of most students in the classroom—reading, mathematics, and writing are the primary focus.	**Grade 3:** Carolyn's instructional goals are focused on establishing relationships with her peers, developing beginning communication skills, and moving about the school building independently.
Grade 8: The goals of Alice's instruction continue to be the same as they are for the majority of students in the classroom.	**Grade 8:** Barbara's goals are basically the same as other students in the classroom, although she spends more time in instruction on employment-related skills.	**Grade 8:** The goals of Carolyn's instruction are focused on maintaining peer relationships and expanding communication skills. In addition, Carolyn's program is beginning to focus on developing community-based skills such as recreational activities, shopping, and getting about in the neighborhood.
Grade 11: Alice's instructional goals are like those of other students in the classroom, focusing on the coursework needed to meet diploma credit requirements.	**Grade 11:** Barbara's instructional goals now focus on transition and employment skills, with support on basic academic instruction in reading, mathematics, and writing.	**Grade 11:** Carolyn's goals now focus on community-based living and employment skills. She spends little time in the high school setting.

- *Functional:* Goals that reflect preparation for self-care and life skills, with support for engaging in training, employment, and social network building

Whenever thinking about the three types of goals as applied to an individual student, it is important to start with the first set and then change as circumstances require. The younger the student, the more important it is to think about that student as working toward the same instructional goals as other students. Identifying instructional goals is illustrated for three students in Box 2.4. Note how the instructional goals may change over time, as they do for Carolyn. Note also that while we have presented three illustrations here, the population of students with disabilities does not break down equally across these three alternatives. Rather, it is more likely that the greatest percentage of students with disabilities (probably 85% or more) fall within the first two kinds of instructional goals that we have described (same and modified), whereas only 15% or less of students with disabilities need to be working toward the third kind of instructional goals (functional).

Thinking More Carefully About Those Students With Functional Instructional Goals

Low expectations for students with disabilities is a serious concern. The concern is justified. There is a significant amount of evidence that low expectations are held for many students with disabilities. Therefore, whenever you identify a student for whom you have set functional instructional goals, it is important to rethink those goals and to make sure they do not reflect low expectations for the student. In a similar vein, of course, it is important to make sure that unrealistically low expectations are not the reason why a student is pursuing modified goals.

School personnel may work with a student, and parents may attend IEP meetings and visit their child's school regularly, yet they may not be able to verbalize the goals of the child's instruction and educational experiences. Thus, it is always important to revisit this topic, especially when the conversation is about participation in assessments.

Determining the Intent of the Test

There are many reasons why students take tests. Whenever the intent of a test is to inform the public and policy makers and whenever it is used to determine consequences for others than the student, there should be no question about the participation of nearly all students in the test. The only reason we use the phrase "nearly all" is that most district and state tests do not at this time have a form of assessment appropriate for those students working toward functional instructional goals. Considerations for developing alternate assessments are presented in Chapter 5.

When the purpose of a test is to assign consequences to the student (as in tests used to determine whether a student is promoted from one grade to the next or will receive a high school diploma), it is extremely critical that the decision-making process begin when the student first starts school, or when the student is first identified as having a disability. Then, very careful plans must be implemented and monitored throughout the transition through school to ensure that the student remains on target to participate successfully in and pass the tests administered. Parents must be involved in these decisions from the beginning.

Comparing the Intent of the Test With Students' Instructional Goals

The next step in making a decision about the participation of students with disabilities in a test is to compare the intent of the test with the students' instructional goals. As this is done, however, it should be kept in mind that almost all students with disabilities should be participating in the assessments; only in a few cases should the decision be that a student not participate in the assessment (see Box 2.5). A detailed checklist that combines participation and accommodations decisions is provided in Chapter 7.

Every effort should be made to have each student with a disability participate in the regular assessment. This approach, extended to some relatively rare cases (see Box 2.6), means that a student might participate in the regular mathematics assessment, even though most of that student's instructional goals lead to participation in an alternate assessment.

Participation in an alternate assessment and some parts of the regular assessment (sometimes referred to as partial participation) should be relatively rare. Students should never be pushed into the alternate assessment because they are not expected to do well on the regular assessment. However, they may be pushed into participation in the regular assessment because of unique abilities or skills in certain areas.

Meeting Test Preparation Needs

A student may not be prepared to take an assessment even though the appropriate decision is that the student participate in the assessment. When there is a history of excluding students with disabilities from assessments, it is likely that not enough thought has been given to preparing these students to participate in testing.

Many terms related to test preparation have been used, such as *test-wiseness* and *test-taking skills*. We have organized these into three areas:

BOX 2.5

Comparing Test Intent and Student Instructional Goals

Test Intent	Instructional Goals	Participation Decision
System accountability (e.g., for public reports or to determine staff, school, or district rewards)	Same	Participate in regular assessment with accommodation where needed
	Modified	Participate in regular assessment with accommodation where needed
	Functional	Participate in alternate assessment
Student accountability (e.g., for grades, promotion, or diploma)	Same	Participate in regular assessment with accommodation where needed
	Modified	Participate in regular assessment in early grades with accommodation where needed, but reconsider as student approaches graduation
	Functional	Participate in alternate assessment

- *Test approach skills* (e.g., good nutrition, adequate sleep, relaxation techniques): what students learn to do that will help in many situations other than test taking

- *Test-taking skills* (e.g., reading all options, knowing the meaning of phrases like "find the one that is different" and "which one comes next in the following sequence"): what general test strategy training programs teach students; they incorporate the skills most often referred to as "test-wiseness"

- *Test preparedness* (e.g., understanding the purpose of the test, knowing what kinds of items appear on the test, understanding directions and scoring procedures specific to the test): what stu-

---

BOX 2.6

**Billy's Participation in Both the
Regular and the Alternate Assessment**

Billy is a high school student who has mental retardation. He receives all of his content area instruction, except math, in a self-contained setting. Despite his mental retardation, Billy has good skills in the area of math and for this reason is enrolled in general education math classes. Billy is learning the same curriculum as other students in the class, takes the same tests (passing them), and is an active participant in class. He is earning a regular high school credit in math.

In the past, Billy would not have been in an accountability system at all. If his state had an alternate assessment, Billy would have been assigned to it because of his mental retardation and his focus on educational goals different from those of most students in the high school.

But Billy is one of a very few special students who could participate in both the regular assessment and the alternate assessment. His educational focus in mathematics qualifies him to participate in the regular math assessment even though he also participates in the alternate assessment.

---

dents learn through direct instruction, with examples and practice tests linked directly to the test to be taken

Of course, these aspects of test preparation are relevant to all students, but those with disabilities may be more likely to need direct instruction on these skills than those without disabilities. Further information on these is provided in Chapter 8.

Documenting Reasons for the Decision

The reasons for the decision that is made about a student's participation in an assessment should be documented on the student's IEP. It is imperative that documentation occur if the decision is that the student will *not* participate in the assessment.

The reasons that are documented should be monitored (see Chapter 7). Very few students should be excluded from the regular assessment. When exclusion occurs, the most common reason should be that the student is pursuing instructional goals that are not in alignment with the purpose of the assessment (e.g., self-help skills rather than traditional academic content).

BOX 2.7

Participation Decision-Making Form

1. Is the student working toward the same standards as other   [ ] YES   [ ] NO
   students in the classroom?

   (If answer to 1 is YES, student should participate in the regular assessment)

2. If NO, is the student working on a modified set of standards   [ ] YES   [ ] NO
   (many are the same, but some are modified slightly)?

   (If answer to 2 is YES, student should participate in the regular assessment)

3. If NO, is the student working on an alternate set of standards?   [ ] YES   [ ] NO

   (If answer to 3 is YES, student should participate in an alternate assessment)

4. If the student is working on an alternate set of standards, are   [ ] YES   [ ] NO
   there any areas of unique skills that could be assessed through
   the regular assessment?

   (If answer to 4 is YES, student should participate in both the regular and an alternate
   assessment)

Criteria for Good Participation Decisions

It is helpful to use a decision-making form to guide participation decisions. An example of a decision-making form is shown in Box 2.7. This form should be adjusted for the specifics of your district or state assessment. Take into consideration the purpose of the assessment as well as the student's instructional goals. Also, note the time at which the decision is being made, in relation to the time that the test is administered. There may be a need to reconsider the participation decision closer to the time that the test is administered. If so, note the need to reconsider the decision at another time.

The National Center on Educational Outcomes has developed a general set of criteria that districts and states can use to evaluate their guidelines on the participation of students with disabilities in assessments. These guidelines are easily translated into criteria that local decision makers can use to guide individual decisions about the participation of students in district and state assessments. The translated criteria are as follows:

MISSOURI BAPTIST COLLEGE LIBRARY

- Decision makers start from the premise that all students, including all students with disabilities, are to participate in the accountability system and, to the extent possible, in the regular assessment.

- Decisions are made by people who know the student, including the student's strengths and weaknesses.

- Decision makers take into account the student's instructional goals, current level of functioning, and learning characteristics.

- The student's program setting, category of disability, or percentage of time in the classroom does *not* influence the decision.

- The student is included in any part of the test for which the student receives *any* instruction, regardless of where the instruction occurs.

- Before a decision is made to have a student participate in an alternate assessment, decision makers reconfirm that only 1% to 2% of all students in their district or state are in the alternate assessment.

- Parents are informed of participation options and about the implications of their child *not* being included in a particular test or in the accountability system. They are encouraged to contribute to the decision-making process.

- The decision is written on the student's IEP, or on an additional form attached to the IEP, and the reason for the decision is documented.

Additional information on these criteria and their application is presented in Chapter 7.

Summary

In this chapter, we described the process of deciding whether a student with disabilities should take a district or state test. Because the topic of accountability assessments is new to most school personnel and parents, particularly in relation to students with disabilities, it is important to start by recognizing the need for accountability and then involving others in the decision-making process. We need to think about the goals of a student's instruction and follow some criteria for good participation decisions to round out the process described in this chapter.

Now, check your knowledge about the myth/truth statements presented at the beginning of this chapter (see Box 2.8 for answers). Try to give an explanation for why each statement is correctly identified either as a myth or as the truth.

MISSOURI BAPTIST COLLEGE LIBRARY

BOX 2.8

Myth or Truth Answers

MYTH   Most states have accountability systems for the school performance of students with disabilities.

Explanation: Most states do not have accountability systems for the school performance of students with disabilities. [See page 12]

TRUTH   Less than 50% of the students with disabilities in most states participate in the regular accountability system.

Explanation: In states with regular accountability systems, most include less than half of their students with disabilities in their state assessments. [See page 12]

MYTH   It is unfair to students with disabilities to require them to participate in district and state assessments.

Explanation: There are many reasons to want students with disabilities to participate in district and state assessments, among them access to the benefits of educational reforms, developing test-taking skills, and influencing policy decisions. The negative effects of assessment have been exaggerated. [See page 12 and Box 2.2]

TRUTH   All states but two now require that the IEP team be involved in the decision about whether students with disabilities participate in district or state assessments.

Explanation: Only two states do not have in their written guidelines that the IEP team is to be involved in decisions about participation in assessments. Even when not required, parents, teachers, other school personnel, and students should be involved, informed partners in decisions. [See page 14]

TRUTH   The student's instructional goals comprise the primary factor in determining whether a student with disabilities should participate in a regular large-scale assessment.

Explanation: When considering participation decisions, it is most important to think about the goals of a student's instruction in relation to the purpose of the assessment. [See page 17]

Resources for Further Information

Elliott, J., Thurlow, M., & Ysseldyke, J. (1996). *Assessment guidelines that maximize the participation of students with disabilities in large-scale assessments: Characteristics and considerations* (Synthesis Rep. 25). Minneapolis: University of Minnesota, National Center on Educational Outcomes.

McGrew, K. S., Thurlow, M. L., & Spiegel, A. (1993). An investigation of the exclusion of students with disabilities in national data collection programs. *Educational Evaluation and Policy Analysis, 15*(3), 339-352.

Thurlow, M., Olsen, K., Elliott, J., Ysseldyke, J., Erickson, R., & Ahearn, E. (1996). *Alternate assessments for students with disabilities* (NCEO Policy Directions 5). Minneapolis: University of Minnesota, National Center on Educational Outcomes.

Thurlow, M., Ysseldyke, J., Erickson, R., & Elliott, J. (1997). *Increasing the participation of students with disabilities in state and district assessments.* (NCEO Policy Directions 6). Minneapolis: University of Minnesota, National Center on Educational Outcomes.

Ysseldyke, J., Thurlow, M., & Olsen, K. (1996). *Self-study guide for the development of statewide assessments that include students with disabilities.* Minneapolis: University of Minnesota, National Center on Educational Outcomes.

Assessment Accommodations: Who Is Eligible? For What?

Topics

- Accommodations: What Are They?
- Accommodations: What Is the Controversy?
- What Happens During Instruction?
- Analyzing the Test's Requirements
- Knowing Your District or State Accommodations Policies
- Involving Others in Making Accommodations Decisions
- Criteria for Good Accommodations Decisions

In this chapter, you will . . .

- learn what accommodations are, their purpose, and the controversy that surrounds them.

- review the link and flow between instructional accommodations and assessment accommodations.

- examine considerations in providing assessment accommodations in relationship to what a test is attempting to measure.

- inspect criteria for making assessment accommodation decisions.

In Chapter 2, we suggested some of the many ways in which assessment accommodations are important for students with disabilities. Accommodations are changes in testing materials or procedures that enable the student with disabilities to participate in an

---

BOX 3.1

Myth or Truth? Do You Know?

Read each statement below and decide whether it is a myth or the truth about current practice.

- The most commonly used accommodations in state assessments are Braille and large-print editions of tests.
- The purpose of accommodations is to avoid measuring the student's disability.
- Norm-referenced assessments generally allow more accommodations than do criterion-referenced assessments.
- Most instructional accommodations should not be used during assessments.
- IEP teams always determine what accommodations students with disabilities will use during assessments.

---

assessment in a way that allows abilities to be assessed rather than disabilities.

In the past, Braille and large-print editions of exams, sign language presentation of oral directions, and individualized administrations were commonly accepted accommodations but not necessarily the ones used most often. Today, accommodations are viewed from a much broader perspective. This often makes it more difficult to decide whether a student should receive accommodations during assessment and, if so, what they should be. The purpose of this chapter is to address considerations in making these decisions.

When you finish this chapter, you will be able to identify which of the statements in Box 3.1 are myths and which are the truth.

How do you decide whether a student needs an accommodation in assessment? And, if a student needs an accommodation, how do you decide what it (or they) should be? These questions are intertwined with each other and lead to other questions. Here are the kinds of questions that this chapter will help you answer:

- What kinds of accommodations can be used during assessment?

- What do testing accommodations have to do with classroom instruction?

- Who should be involved in making decisions about assessment accommodations?

- What criteria should guide decisions about the use of testing accommodations in district and state assessments?

Specific accommodations that might be used and the ways in which they relate to student needs are addressed in Chapter 4. The purpose of this chapter is to provide you with the guidelines and rationale that you will need to make the best decisions about the use of testing accommodations for students with disabilities. The first step in moving forward is to know a little about what accommodations are and the controversy that surrounds them.

Accommodations: What Are They?

Most people think of Braille, large print, individualized testing, and extra time as accommodations, but there are many more accommodations that can be used for testing. One way to think about accommodations is in terms of what is changed—the *setting* in which the assessment is administered, the *timing* of the assessment, the *scheduling* of administration, the *presentation* of the assessment, or the *response* that the student makes to the assessment. There are also *other* kinds of changes. Box 3.2 lists examples of each of these types of accommodations. Many more examples are provided in Chapter 4.

Accommodations: What Is the Controversy?

Accommodations are provided to students with disabilities to "level the playing field" when they take an assessment. Without accommodations for their disabilities, an assessment may inaccurately measure what these students know and are able to do. The measure will reflect the disability rather than the student's knowledge and skills.

This premise about the purpose of accommodations in assessments is relatively easy to understand when thinking about common accommodations, ones that are used by most of society today. Take eyeglasses, for example. Glasses are an accommodation for a visual disability. Without glasses, many of us would not be able to read the words in assessments, and many of us would not be able to demonstrate our skills during the most common of all performance assessments—the driver's license test. Glasses help "level the playing field" for those of us who need them so that the test can measure our *ability* rather than our *disability*.

Little controversy surrounds accommodations for sensory and physical disabilities. In part, this is due to the visibility of these disabilities. The public can easily see that these disabilities exist and that without some adjustments those with sensory and physical disabilities will not be able to participate in the assessment at all, or if they can participate, it is likely to be less meaningful without accommodations than with them.

BOX 3.2

Examples of Six Types of Assessment Accommodations

Setting	Presentation
Study carrel	Repeat directions
Special lighting	Larger bubbles on multiple-choice questions
Separate room	Sign language presentation
Individualized or small group	Magnification device
Timing	**Response**
Extended time	Mark answers in test booklet
Frequent breaks	Use reference materials (e.g., dictionary)
Unlimited time	Word process writing sample
Scheduling	**Other**
Specific time of day	Special test preparation techniques
Subtests in different order	Out-of-level test

The controversy generally arises for those accommodations that are used with less visible disabilities, such as learning disabilities and emotional disabilities. Because these disabilities may be directly related to the content or procedures of assessments, their use becomes controversial. For example, a reading disability is directly related to the content of reading tests and tests that rely on reading skills to test other content areas. Making accommodations for needs that arise related to the reading disability may seem to give the student an advantage when reading is a part of the assessment.

It is often argued that accommodations allowed only for students with disabilities are ones that all students could use to their benefit. This may be true, but in most cases it is not. Many of our assumptions about what accommodations might be beneficial to students are incorrect.

Legally, accommodations must be provided to students with disabilities. But the law does not say which accommodations are acceptable and which ones are not. Most states now have written guidelines to indicate which accommodations are acceptable for use during specific assessments. Some districts also have produced guidelines.

Unfortunately, most of these guidelines are not easily applied when making decisions about an individual student and that student's accommodations needs.

To make good decisions, together with other pieces of information you need to think about what happens during instruction. Then, you need to compare these decisions with existing guidelines to make a final recommendation on the accommodations the student will use when participating in a specific assessment.

What Happens During Instruction?

There should be a direct link between what happens during instruction and what happens during assessment. Accommodations should not be introduced for the first time during an assessment. Also, consideration of what the district or state assessment requires must be linked with what happens during instruction. Finally, it is important to know what accommodations your district or state allows.

Classroom Accommodations

There should be a link between accommodations a student uses during instruction (to help learning take place) and during classroom tests (to accurately reflect what the student has learned) and the accommodations recommended for the student when taking a district or state assessment. But how do you know what kinds of accommodations should be used during classroom instruction?

There are going to be some accommodations used during instruction that may not be appropriate for use during assessment. For example, a student who requires multiple prompts to complete a task might not be provided this during a test, or a student who uses a calculator to complete mathematical problem-solving tasks might not be allowed to use it on an assessment that measures the ability to calculate math facts. It is important to delineate and clarify these exceptions.

Virtually no preservice or inservice training is provided on instructional accommodations, although some training is provided on accommodations for classroom testing. Surveys of teachers have revealed that there are many possible accommodations that might be used. For example, a national sample of general education teachers perceived the most helpful testing accommodations to be "(a) giving individual help with directions during tests, (b) reading test questions to students, and (c) simplifying wording of test questions" (Jayanthi, Epstein, Polloway, & Bursuck, 1996, p. 99).

Some common instructional accommodations, taken from higher education materials, are listed in Box 3.3.

BOX 3.3

Common Instructional Accommodations

Materials/Curriculum	Methods/Strategies
Alternative assignments	Highlight key points to remember
Substitute materials with lower reading levels	Eliminate distractions by using a template to block out other items
Fewer assignments	Have student use a self-monitoring sheet
Decrease length of assignments	Break task into smaller parts to do at different times
Copy pages so student can mark on them	Use study buddies whenever reading or writing is required
Provide examples of correctly completed work	Secure papers to work areas with tape or magnets
Early syllabus	Present information in multiple ways
Advance notice of assignments	Use listening devices
Tape-recorded versions of printed materials	

The multitude of accommodations that could be used should not be applied haphazardly to individual students. The underlying theme to remember is that instructional accommodations must be related to the student's unique learning needs.

It is important also to remember that just because a student needs an accommodation does not mean that the student will be able to use it. Students may need both training and practice to appropriately use accommodations they need during instruction. For example, there is evidence that students with spelling disabilities do not perform better, and may even perform more poorly, when allowed to use a spell checker during a writing assignment. This may be because they have not been taught how to use the spell checker, so it provides them no help at all, or because they have not had enough practice using it, so it actually interferes with their performance.

Thus, accommodations are not something that should be considered for the first time just before the assessment is to occur. Nor should they be considered for the first time during the school year in which the student will be assessed. There is a need for systematic consideration of accommodations from the beginning of the student's educational career (best), or from the onset of IEP services.

Another approach that has great potential is to incorporate more accommodating test procedures during the development of test items. For example, Delaware developed a grid to help its test developers view items in terms of students' strengths and weaknesses so that they could develop items that would enhance strengths and reduce the barriers created by areas of weakness. Thus, for students with strengths in the areas of speaking, reciting, and debating, task administration procedures would allow the use of recorded directions, and students could respond via spoken avenues, including the use of voice recognition technology. For students with challenges in the areas of visual and spatial relationships, task administration might provide step-by-step directions, perhaps tape-recorded, and allow extra time, or on the response end, the students could respond in their first language (if other than English), point to the answer, or respond in the test booklet rather than on a separate answer sheet. Much additional thought needs to be given to how to develop assessments that reduce the need for external accommodations.

Analyzing the Test's Requirements

Preparation is a key element in the successful and meaningful participation of a student with disabilities in assessments. Preparation depends on a good analysis of the test's requirements and matching these requirements to the student. Making good decisions about needed accommodations is a fundamental part of this analysis.

School personnel and parents need to be vigilant in carrying out these analyses during the early and middle school years, but by the time students are in high school, they need to be learning these analysis skills as well. Why? So that when these students enter a postsecondary education or employment situation they are able to advocate for themselves about the need for accommodations and the kinds of accommodations needed.

In Box 3.4 we provide some ideas of questions that might be used when analyzing a test's requirements. The questions are designed to ask about **what the test requires the student to be able to do** to take the test. Answers to these questions should help determine the kinds of accommodations the student might need to participate in the assessment. Consideration of the kinds of accommodations used for classroom instruction should come into play here because if it looks as though a student will need an accommodation to perform on the assessment, the accommodation should be one that the student is getting for classroom instruction and testing.

BOX 3.4

Analyzing the Test:
Questions to Ask

Requirement	Sampling of Questions to Ask
Setting	• Can the student focus on his or her own work with 25 to 30 other students in a quiet setting?
	• Does the student display behaviors that are distracting to other students?
	• Can the student take the test in the same way as it is administered to other students?
Timing	• Can the student work continuously for the entire length of a typically administered portion of the test (e.g., 20 to 30 minutes)?
	• Does the student use accommodations that require more time to complete individual test items?
Scheduling	• Does the student take a medication that dissipates over time, so that optimal performance might occur at a certain time of day?
	• Does the student's anxiety level increase dramatically when working in certain content areas, so that these should be administered after all other content areas are assessed?
Presentation	• Can the student listen to and follow oral directions given by an adult or an audiotape?
	• Can the student see and hear?
	• Can the student read?
Response	• Can the student track from a test booklet to a test response form?
	• Is the student able to manipulate a pencil or other writing instrument?
Other	• Is this the first time that the student will be taking a district or state assessment?

Add your own questions to those in Box 3.4; the ones provided serve only as a guide to the types of questions that might be asked. This decision-making tool will be most useful if it is generated by you and your colleagues, based on what you know about the test's requirements of students. It would also be beneficial to have parents participate in the process of generating questions that should be asked when considering accommodations. As students get older, they are also an excellent source of information on needed accommodations.

Most district and state tests are criterion-referenced tests. They measure the student's performance against a specific criterion. In many ways, these types of tests create the fewest challenges for accommodations. On the other hand, both norm-referenced assessments and graduation exams (even though they are typically criterion-referenced tests) create special challenges for providing accommodations to students who need them.

Norm-Referenced Tests

Norm-referenced tests create special challenges for thinking about accommodations because most of these tests have been developed without consideration of students with disabilities, and usually only a few students with disabilities are included in the normative sample. Those who are included typically do not use accommodations (even if they need them).

Almost always, a key aspect of norm-referenced testing is that individuals in the normative sample all take the test under the same "standard" conditions. Anything that deviates from the standard conditions is not included when calculating normative scores. This means that if a student does use an accommodation, that student's scores cannot be compared with scores of the normative sample. Essentially, the result is that the student's score does not count.

Some tests do allow for certain accommodations (usually Braille and large-print editions of the test). Sometimes when they do so, special norming studies are conducted so that the scores can be used. Often, this is not the case, however, so that even when students take the Braille version of the test, for example, their scores are not aggregated with those of other students. Examples of accommodations allowed by some of the more commonly used norm-referenced assessments are provided in Box 3.5. It is evident from this table that many issues must be addressed if students with disabilities are to be assessed appropriately in norm-referenced tests.

What should you do if your district is using a norm-referenced test that does not allow the accommodations a student needs? There are several principles to follow:

BOX 3.5

Selected Norm-Referenced Tests and Accommodations Allowed

Norm-Referenced Test	Accommodations Allowed
California Achievement Test (CAT)	None
Iowa Test of Basic Skills (ITBS) Iowa Test of Educational Development (ITED)	Extended time, individual administration, large-print book, magnifier, oral administration, answers recorded in test booklet, out-of-level testing
Metropolitan Achievement Test	None
Stanford Achievement Test (SAT, 9th ed.)	None; currently developing Braille version of the test

---

- Take the position that the student needs to be included in the assessment. Remember, the criteria for participation should be linked to the goals of the student's instruction.

- Determine what accommodations the student needs and whether any of them might be eliminated without causing significant changes in the student's performance.

- Identify minimal accommodations that others will agree do not significantly change the nature of a standard administration (e.g., taking the assessment individually, marking in the test booklet rather than on an answer sheet).

- If there are accommodations that the student needs but that do not meet standard conditions, allow the student to take the assessment using those accommodations.

- Insist that the scores of students who take the assessment using nonapproved accommodations be reported separately, at a minimum by reporting the number (or percentage) doing so and, more ideally, by reporting aggregate scores for these students (see Chapter 10 for considerations in reporting scores).

These, of course, are interim steps until test developers include students with disabilities in normative samples, using the accommodations that are needed to participate in assessments.

Promotion/Graduation Tests

Tests with high stakes for students, such as determining whether they move from one grade to the next or whether they earn a diploma, create special difficulties for students with disabilities because states have differing guidelines about the use of accommodations during these assessments. Although most states do allow accommodations to be used, these are not always the ones that individual students need.

Because of the high stakes for students, there is generally some procedure for making special accommodations requests. This should be done for individual students when it is evident that the use of an accommodation is essential to the accurate measurement of a student's skills. If approval is not possible, and if passing the test is the only way to be promoted or to graduate, it is essential that the student's instruction be focused on ways to compensate for the unavailable accommodation.

Knowing Your District or State Accommodations Policies

Districts and states often have written policies about the use of accommodations during district or state assessments. Sometimes, these policies are quite general (e.g., allowing whatever the student uses during instruction) and other times quite specific (e.g., extended time may be used during one assessment but not during another, and if used, the student's score will not be included in summaries of performance). Often, they are in between.

Selected state-level assessment accommodation policies for graduation exams in those states that had them in 1995 are shown in Box 3.6. It is obvious from this table that policies often vary tremendously. When other kinds of assessments are entered into the mix (e.g., those used for school accountability purposes), policies vary even more. Thus, it is important to be familiar with the policies that guide your own district or state assessment.

The information in Box 3.6 very likely is already out of date. That is because policies are changing all the time. For this reason, it is critical to be alert for changes in policies in your district and state. It is also important to be looking for hidden consequences of using accommodations. Districts and states may allow certain accommodations to be used but not allow the scores from assessments in which these accommodations were used to be included with the scores of others. This has important negative consequences, which were highlighted in Chapter 2.

How do you make a decision about an accommodation if it is one the student needs but whose use invalidates the score, resulting in that assessment not being counted? This is a difficult question for which

BOX 3.6
Selected Accommodations Policies for High School Graduation Exams

State	Setting		Timing		Scheduling		Presentation		Response	
	Individually	Separate Room	Extended Time	With Breaks	Special Time	Multiple Days	Braille Edition	Read Aloud	Proctor/ Scribe	Answer on Test
Alabama	X			X	X		X	X	X	X
Florida	X		X	X			X	X	X	X
Georgia	X	X	X	X	X	X	X	X	X	X
Hawaii		X				X				
Louisiana	X		X				X	X	X	X
Maryland	X	X	X	X	X	X	X	X	X	X
Mississippi	X		X	X	X		X	X	X	X
Nevada	X	X	X	X	X		X	X	X	X
New Jersey	X	X	X	X		X	X		X	X
New York	X	X	X	X		X	X	X	X	X
North Carolina		X	X	X			X	X	X	X
Ohio			X				X	X	X	
South Carolina	X		X	X			X	X		X
Tennessee	X			X		X	X		X	X
Texas	X	X	X	X		X	X	X	X	X
Virginia	X	X		X		X	X	X	X	X

there is no precise answer. It requires that the individual situation and consequences be examined. For example, if it means that a student's score on a graduation exam is judged invalid, a special appeal will have to be lodged, or the student might participate in the assessment without the accommodation. Another choice is participating in the exam with the accommodation but realizing that the student is ineligible to receive a diploma. Different types of assessments very likely will lead to different decisions. Such decisions are difficult to make and should be documented, with parents and students (when appropriate) signing off on them.

Involving Others in Making Accommodations Decisions

Involving others in making decisions about accommodations is the first step in making good decisions about the use of accommodations in assessments. Although nearly all states require that the IEP team be involved in the decision about whether a student participates in a district or state assessment, only about two-thirds have the same requirement for the decision about accommodations. If your state has this requirement, it is imperative that the team contributes to decisions about, or at least knows about, instructional accommodations. Also, make sure that any accommodations decision made involves input into the decision, not just signing off on the recommendation made by an individual member of the team (see Chapter 7).

Those who make decisions about accommodations need to know about the following:

- Nature and purpose of the assessment
- Instructional accommodations the student uses
- State or district accommodations guidelines
- Needed preparation for optimal use of accommodations
- How accommodations might change over time

Each of these topics plays a role in making final decisions about accommodations that a student might use during district and state assessments.

Nature and Purpose of the Assessment

To some extent, the way an assessment is designed can have an influence on the need for accommodations. For example, presenting items both graphically and in plain text can reduce the need for reading accommodations. This is why Delaware is attempting to develop assessments from the beginning, taking these considerations into account and thereby reducing the need for external accommodations.

The purpose of the assessment (graduation exam, accountability measure) and whether it is a norm-referenced or criterion-referenced one also will have an impact on the need for accommodations. Typically, norm-referenced tests are less amenable to the use of accommodations because the norms developed are based only on standard administrations of the assessment.

People familiar with the assessment for which accommodations decisions are being made should provide information to decision makers, even if they are not going to be involved in the decision. If you are asked to be involved in decision making without knowing about the nature and purpose of the assessment, it is critical that you obtain this information. It should be available from your local assessment coordinator or the state assessment division.

Instructional Accommodations the Student Uses

Teachers are generally the ones who know best the kinds of accommodations a student needs during instruction. But certainly they are not the only ones. Many parents observe their children making accommodations for themselves as they carry out household tasks, interact with others, and do their homework. This information can be valuable in determining accommodations that the child needs, even though the accommodations may not have been implemented at school. Of course, the time to have this discussion with parents is during initial IEP meetings so that the accommodations can be used during instruction and then implemented for the district or state assessment.

When making decisions about accommodations, IEP team members need to have not only information on the reasons why students should be provided with them during assessments but also a copy of the questions to help determine needed accommodations for individual students. Again, the questions in Box 3.3 are a good start; your own version is apt to be even better.

A list of possible accommodations is also helpful for the IEP team to have when making accommodations decisions. The lists provided in Chapter 4 are useful for this purpose. It is important, however, that these lists serve as mind ticklers rather than constraints on possible accommodations that the IEP team might consider.

Students themselves can offer valuable insights about needed accommodations. Heightening their awareness of needed accommodations, in fact, should be a goal of their instruction, so that by the time they are into high school and approaching postsecondary education or the work world, they will know which accommodations they need to request.

State or District Accommodations Guidelines

Nearly all states now have written guidelines about the use of accommodations, usually detailed for each test that is administered.

When districts have their own tests, they also may have written guidelines about the kinds of accommodations that are allowed. After identifying the accommodations that a student needs, compare these with what the written guidelines say. It is especially important to note the following:

- Whether the needed accommodation is allowed to be used for the test under consideration

- If the accommodation is not allowed, whether there are alternative avenues for gaining approval for its use (e.g., Department of Education approval)

- What happens to the student's score if the accommodation is used (is it treated the same as other scores, or is it considered an invalid score?)

All these factors contribute to the ultimate decision about recommended accommodations.

Preparation for Optimal Use of Accommodations

Use of accommodations during instruction is a key element in preparing students for the optimal use of accommodations during assessment. However, consideration must also be given to whether there are ways to assist the student in using accommodations during assessment. The example of students who do not use extended time as an accommodation is a case in point. Students who have directions read to them in class but who must listen to a tape cassette for the assessment (usually for security purposes) will need to have some experience with managing the tape player before the test.

How Accommodations Might Change Over Time

Accommodations that a student uses may change over time. Two kinds of changes in accommodations are likely to occur. First, different kinds of accommodations might be needed as the child gets older. For example, a young child with disabilities may need directions read, but as the child matures and gains reading skills, this accommodation may no longer be necessary.

Second, the way in which decisions are made about accommodations should change over time, with the student taking more responsibility for knowing what kinds of accommodations are needed. This helps the student make the transition through high school into postsecondary settings, be they additional training or work.

Criteria for Good Accommodations Decisions

Just as criteria were developed for states to use to evaluate their guidelines on the participation of students with disabilities in assessments, criteria also have been developed for states to use to evaluate their guidelines on accommodations that are allowed during assessments (Elliott, Thurlow, & Ysseldyke, 1996). These accommodations guidelines are easily translated into criteria that local decision makers can use to guide individual decisions about accommodations that students need when they participate in district and state assessments. The translated criteria are as follows:

- Decisions are made by people who know the student, including the student's strengths and weaknesses.

- Decision makers consider the student's learning characteristics and the accommodations currently used during classroom instruction and classroom testing.

- The student's category of disability or program setting does *not* influence the decision.

- The goal is to identify accommodations that the student is using in the classroom during instruction and in classroom testing situations; new accommodations should not be introduced for the district or statewide assessment.

- The decision is made systematically, using a form that lists questions to answer or variables to consider in making the accommodation decision. On this form, the decision about recommended accommodations and the reasons for the decision are documented.

- Parents (or students at an appropriate age) are involved in the decision by either participating in the decision-making process or at least being given the analysis of the need for accommodations and by signing the form that indicates accommodations that are to be used.

- The decision is documented on the student's IEP.

Additional information about these criteria and their application is included in Chapter 6.

Summary

In this chapter, we discussed some of the general considerations in making decisions about the use of accommodations during assessments. De-

---

BOX 3.7

Myth or Truth Answers

MYTH   The most commonly used accommodations in state assessments are Braille and large-print editions of tests.
Explanation: Braille and large print are among the most frequently allowed accommodations, but there are many others that are used more frequently. [See pages 29-32]

TRUTH   The purpose of accommodations is to avoid measuring the student's disability.
Explanation: The purpose of accommodations is to level the playing field, which means assessing a student's abilities rather than the student's disabilities. [See page 29]

MYTH   Norm-referenced assessments generally allow more accommodations than do criterion-referenced assessments.
Explanation: Since most norm-referenced tests have been developed without consideration of students with disabilities, and without including them in the standardization sample, these types of assessments generally allow fewer accommodations than criterion-referenced assessments. [See page 35]

MYTH   Most instructional accommodations should not be used during assessments.
Explanation: There should be a link between accommodations used during instruction and during classroom tests and the accommodations recommended for the student when taking a district or statewide assessment. [See page 40]

MYTH   IEP teams always determine what accommodations students with disabilities will use during assessments.
Explanation: Only about two-thirds of states require that IEP teams be involved in decisions about accommodations a student will use during statewide assessments; we do not have estimates of requirements for IEP involvement in decisions about accommodations for district assessments. [See page 39]

---

cision makers should be individuals who know the student, and they need to take into consideration the purpose and characteristics of the test, the accommodations that are allowed in state or district policies, needed preparation for using the accommodations, and what the consequences are of deciding to use an accommodation.

Check your knowledge now about the myth/truth statements presented at the beginning of this chapter (see Box 3.7 for answers). Give an explanation for why each statement is correctly identified either as a myth or as the truth.

Resources for Further Information

Elliott, J., & Roeber, E. (1996). *Assessment accommodations for students with disabilities* (videotape recording). Alexandria, VA: National Association of State Directors of Special Education.

Elliott, J., Thurlow, M., & Ysseldyke, J. (1996). *Assessment guidelines that maximize the participation of students with disabilities in large-scale assessments: Characteristics and considerations* (Synthesis Rep. 25). Minneapolis: University of Minnesota, National Center on Educational Outcomes.

Elliott, J., Ysseldyke, J., Thurlow, M., & Erickson, R. (1997). *Providing accommodations for students with disabilities in state and district assessments* (NCEO Policy Directions 7). Minneapolis: University of Minnesota, National Center on Educational Outcomes.

Jayanthi, M., Epstein, M. H., Polloway, E. A., & Bursuck, W. D. (1996). A national survey of general education teachers' perceptions of testing adaptations. *Journal of Special Education, 30*(1), 99-115.

King, W. L., Baker, J., & Jarrow, J. E. (n.d.). *Testing accommodations for students with disabilities.* Columbus, OH: Association on Higher Education and Disability.

Accommodations to Consider

In this chapter, you will . . .

- examine six categories of assessment accommodations.
- review the do's and don'ts in testing accommodations.
- become familiar with the issue of upholding assessment integrity.
- learn what research says about the effects of assessment accommodations.

■ In Chapter 3, we discussed the philosophy behind assessment accommodations for students with disabilities and identified general guidelines for making good accommodations decisions. In this chapter, we provide information on possible accommodations for a stu-

---

BOX 4.1

Myth or Truth? Do You Know?

Read each statement below and decide whether it is a myth or the truth about current practice.

- Most states allow setting accommodations and presentation accommodations in their statewide testing programs.
- The most controversial accommodations fall within the areas of timing, scheduling, and response accommodations.
- Most national college admissions exams allow a variety of accommodations with no penalty to the student.
- Out-of-level testing is an appropriate accommodation for students with mental retardation in accountability assessments.
- Computer adaptive testing has tremendous potential for making assessments more accessible and meaningful for the full range of students in today's schools.
- Research findings are now available that define which accommodations invalidate test scores.

---

dent to use during assessments. We also give you just a hint of some of the technical issues that require consideration and what the research tells us.

When you finish this chapter, you will be able to identify which of the statements in Box 4.1 are myths and which are the truth.

What are the kinds of accommodations that might be considered for district and state assessments? Should accommodations be used one at a time, or will students need more than one accommodation? Here are the kinds of questions this chapter will help you answer:

- What are the major kinds of accommodations, and specific examples, that can be used during assessment?
- What are the do's and don'ts that should be considered when making decisions about recommending accommodations for specific students?
- How can one determine what accommodations invalidate test scores?

As noted in Chapter 3, there are several types of accommodations and many different accommodations within each type. Different types of accommodations have different levels of acceptance. For example, timing, scheduling, and response accommodations generally are contro-

```
┌─────────────────────────────────────────────────────────────────────┐
│                                                                       │
│                              BOX 4.2                                  │
│                                                                       │
│                 Examples of Setting Accommodations                    │
│  ───────────────────────────────────────────────────────────────     │
│   Conditions of Setting              Location                         │
│  ───────────────────────────────────────────────────────────────     │
│   Minimal distractive elements (e.g.,   Study carrel                  │
│      books, artwork, window views)      Separate room (including      │
│   Special lighting                         special education          │
│   Special acoustics                        classroom)                 │
│   Adaptive or special furniture         Seat closest to test          │
│   Individual student or small group        administrator              │
│      of students rather than large         (teacher, proctor, etc.)   │
│      group                              Home                          │
│                                         Hospital                      │
│                                         Correctional institution      │
│                                                                       │
└─────────────────────────────────────────────────────────────────────┘
```

versial because they raise the issues of whether the accommodations (a) provide an unfair advantage and (b) change what is being measured.

Setting Accommodations

Setting accommodations are changes in the place in which an assessment is given. They can include changes in the conditions of the assessment setting as well as changes in the location of the assessment (see Box 4.2).

The most common reason why students may need setting accommodations is that they have difficulty focusing attention when in a group setting. This may be exhibited either by a student who engages in behaviors other than attending to the test (e.g., tapping pencil and watching other students) or by a student disturbing other students in a group setting. Setting accommodations may be needed in conjunction with others. For example, when a student needs extended time for an assessment or needs frequent breaks during an assessment, it often is useful also to have the student take the assessment in a separate setting or in a small group, where the special timing requirements will not complicate the assessment of those students who will take the assessment under regular timing conditions. The need for setting adjustments also may arise when a student uses special equipment that may take extra time to use (such as a Brailler to produce a response, or a tape recorder to give oral directions that can be repeated according to student needs).

States differ in the types of setting accommodations allowed in statewide assessments (see Box 4.3, which is a summary of information from Thurlow, Seyfarth, Scott, & Ysseldyke, 1997). Sometimes, states allow different setting accommodations depending on the specific assessment

BOX 4.3

Examples of Setting Accommodations Allowed by States

State	Condition			Location						
	Light-ing	Acous-tics	Adap. Furni-ture	Indi-vidu-ally	Small Group	Study Carrel	Sep-arate Room	Seat Loca-tion	Hos-pital	Stu-dent Home
Alabama				X	X	X		X		X
Alaska					X		X			
Arkansas				X	X	X		X		
Connecticut				X		X	X			
Delaware	X	X	X	X	X					
Florida				X	X					
Georgia	X	X		X	X	X	X	X	X	X
Hawaii				X			X	X		
Illinois	X	X	X	X	X		X			
Kansas	X		X	X	X		X			
Louisiana	X			X	X			X		
Maine				X	X	X		X		X
Maryland				X	X	X	X	X	X	X
Michigan	X	X	X	X	X		X		X	X
Minnesota				X	X					
Mississippi			X	X	X	X		X		X
Montana					X					
Nevada	X	X		X	X	X	X			
New Hampshire				X	X	X		X		X
New Jersey	X	X		X	X		X	X		
New York	X	X		X	X	X	X		X	X
North Carolina							X		X	X
Oregon			X	X	X	X	X			
Pennsylvania	X		X		X	X	X	X		
Rhode Island				X	X		X	X		
South Carolina				X	X				X	X
Tennessee				X	X		X			
Texas	X			X	X					
Washington				X	X					
Wisconsin			X	X	X	X	X	X		

NOTE: Only those states that allow at least one of the above setting accommodations are listed.

BOX 4.4

Examples of Setting Accommodations Allowed in National Tests

ACT	GED	SAT
None identified in ACT materials	None identified in GED materials	Separate testing room

---

being administered. Although the information in Box 4.3 gives a general picture, it is important to be aware of your own state's guidelines. Realize also that they do change, and states are not always able to get the information out to those who really need to be familiar with it.

National exams (e.g., ACT, GED, and SAT) also have specific setting accommodations that are allowed. These are summarized in Box 4.4.

As students progress through school, begin to familiarize them with the kinds of accommodations allowed in different assessments. Increasingly, they should be helped to consider what accommodations they need during assessments, so that when they enter postsecondary settings or employment they can identify and request accommodations they might need in assessment situations.

Timing Accommodations

Timing accommodations are changes in the duration of testing. They can include changes in how much time is allowed as well as how the time is organized (see Box 4.5).

Accommodations in the timing of a test are among the most frequently requested. There are many valid reasons for timing accommodations, but there are also cautions that must be observed in selecting them.

As mentioned previously, there are a wide variety of accommodations used that may require the addition of timing accommodations. For example, certain equipment takes more time to use, thus requiring extended time. There are some accommodations that create fatigue, such as the use of magnification equipment or tape recorders and earphones, thus requiring additional breaks during assessment.

Processing disabilities are often cited as a reason for needing timing accommodations. Students who have difficulty processing written text may need extended time to read and comprehend directions and item text. Students with dysgraphia (difficulty writing) or motor disabilities may need more time to write their responses.

BOX 4.5

Examples of Timing Accommodations

Duration	Organization
Changes in duration can be applied to selected subtests of an assessment or to the assessment overall	Frequent breaks, even during parts of the assessment (e.g., during subtests)
Extended time (i.e., extra time)	Extended breaks between parts of the assessment (e.g., between subtests) so that assessment is actually administered in several sessions
Unlimited time	

Timing accommodations should be used with caution because there is some evidence that they tend to be overly requested and actually may work to the detriment of some students. Overrequesting an accommodation suggests that it is being recommended even though the student does not use it. Nonuse by a student could be due to not needing the accommodation (e.g., it doesn't help to have more time) or embarrassment about it. Being allowed more time than other students may not be viewed positively by the student, especially as the student gets older (middle school and high school). There is an important need for instruction (both for those using accommodations and for other students) about the need for accommodations and the concept of "leveling the playing field" rather than providing "unfair advantages."

There are several reasons why timing accommodations may work to the detriment of a student, and these should be considered and balanced against the extent to which the accommodations might "level the playing field." For example, providing a student with additional breaks opens up the possibility of breaking concentration or interrupting a sequence of items or section of the test. Extending the time allowed to finish an assessment may encourage nonproductive guessing or changing answers when they should not be changed. It is important to try to balance the potential positive and negative effects of all timing accommodations under consideration. If the student is old enough, the student should be encouraged to signal when a break is needed.

States differ in the extent to which they allow timing accommodations and the nature of those allowed (see Box 4.6, which is based on Thurlow et al., 1997). Again, be aware that the information in Box 4.6 is a static representation of information that changes frequently as states revise their guidelines. Check your own district and state guidelines.

BOX 4.6

Examples of Timing Accommodations Allowed by States

State	Duration		Organization	
	Extended Time	Student Determined	Breaks During Testing	Multiple Sessions
Alabama	X	X	X	X
Alaska			X	
Arkansas			X	X
Connecticut	X		X	X
Delaware				X
Florida	X		X	
Georgia	X	X	X	X
Hawaii	X			
Idaho	X			
Illinois	X		X	X
Indiana	X			
Kansas	X		X	
Louisiana	X		X	
Maine		X	X	
Maryland	X		X	X
Michigan	X		X	
Minnesota	X			X
Mississippi	X		X	
Montana	X			
Nevada	X		X	
New Hampshire		X	X	
New Jersey	X		X	X
New York	X		X	X
North Carolina	X			X
Ohio	X			
Oregon	X		X	X
Pennsylvania	X		X	
Rhode Island	X	X	X	X
South Carolina	X			X
Tennessee				X
Texas	X		X	X
Wisconsin	X		X	X

NOTE: Only those states that allow at least one of the above timing accommodations are listed.

TESTING STUDENTS WITH DISABILITIES

BOX 4.7

Examples of Timing Accommodations Allowed in National Tests

ACT	GED	SAT
Extended testing time	Extra testing time (usually 1½ times standard amount)	Additional testing time

---

National exams also allow some timing accommodations. These are summarized in Box 4.7. Be aware that when timing accommodations are used in the ACT and the SAT they are looked on as producing a nonstandard administration. Nonstandard administrations of these assessments are "flagged," which means that institutions receiving the students' scores also are given the following "caution":

> One or more of the tests administered on this date were taken under nonstandard testing conditions. . . . The degree of comparability of the resulting scores with those achieved under standard conditions is not known. Final responsibility for interpreting the examinees' scores rests with the score recipients.

Scheduling Accommodations

Scheduling accommodations are changes in when testing occurs. They can include changes in the time of administration as well as changes in how the administration of the assessment is organized (see Box 4.8). The list of scheduling accommodations again makes it evident how accommodations often are intertwined. For example, when an assessment is given at a specific time of the day that is different from the time when other students take the test, setting accommodations necessarily are being used also as the test probably will be administered to the student individually in a separate setting.

There are many reasons for the use of scheduling accommodations for students with disabilities. Some reasons reflect the need to coordinate assessment with the effects of medication; others relate to using an optimal order to reduce frustration effects. Again, an interaction with another accommodation might be reflected in the need for scheduling accommodations.

As with other types of accommodations, states differ in their policies about the use of scheduling accommodations (see Box 4.9, which is

---

BOX 4.8

Examples of Scheduling Accommodations

Time	Organization
Specific time of day (e.g., morning, midday, afternoon, after ingestion of medication)	In a different order from that used for most students (e.g., longer subtest first, shorter later; math first, English later)
Specific day of week	
Over several days	Omit questions that cannot be adjusted for an accommodation (e.g., graph reading for student using Braille) and adjust for missing scores

---

based on Thurlow et al., 1997). Scheduling accommodations are less common than other types of accommodations. Again, be alert to your own district and state guidelines.

National exams typically do not recognize scheduling accommodations. They do generally provide different days to take the assessment, but this is provided as a convenience for the test administrators, not as an accommodation for the test taker.

Presentation Accommodations

Presentation accommodations are changes in how an assessment is given to a student. The main types of presentation accommodations are format alterations, procedure changes, and use of assistive devices (see Box 4.10). These may overlap when accommodations are actually administered, but for our purposes here, it helps to think about them as three distinct types.

Clearly, there are many more presentation accommodations than there are other types that we have listed here, and those presented in Box 4.10 are not all that might be provided. Furthermore, it is within the presentation accommodations that most controversy arises. Questions are raised about the comparability of scores from an assessment in which the directions are clarified for the student or in which the assessment is read to the student. These issues and ways to address them in decision making are discussed later in this chapter.

The variability in student need for presentation accommodations is great, as is evident in the list of possible accommodations provided here.

BOX 4.9

Examples of Scheduling Accommodations Allowed by States

	Time		Organization	
State	Over Several Days	Specific Time of Day or Week	Best Time for Student	Subparts in Different Order
Alabama			X	
Arkansas	X			
Delaware			X	
Florida		X		
Georgia	X		X	
Illinois	X			
Maine			X	
Maryland	X		X	
Minnesota	X		X	
Mississippi			X	
Nevada			X	
New Hampshire			X	
New Jersey	X		X	
New York	X		X	
Oregon	X		X	
Rhode Island	X		X	
Tennessee	X			
Texas	X	X	X	
Washington				X
Wisconsin	X		X	

NOTE: Only those states that allow at least one of the above scheduling accommodations are listed.

Students with sensory disabilities (hearing and visual impairments) may need a large-print or Braille version (format alterations), an interpreter to sign directions or a reader to read directions (procedure changes), or magnification or amplification devices (assistive devices). Students with learning or emotional disabilities also may need presentation accommodations. Perhaps the most typically requested presentation accommodations for these students are procedure changes, particularly reading the test, rereading directions, and answering questions about directions and items. Like timing accommodations, some of the presentation accommo-

---

BOX 4.10

Examples of Presentation Accommodations

Format Alterations	Procedure Changes	Assistive Devices
Braille edition	Use sign language to give directions to student	Audiotape of directions
Large-print version		Computer reads directions and/or items
Larger bubbles on answer sheet	Reread directions	Magnification device
One complete sentence per line in reading passages	Write helpful verbs in directions on board or on separate piece of paper	Amplification device (e.g., hearing aid)
Bubbles to side of choices in multiple-choice exams	Simplify language, clarify or explain directions	Noise buffer
Key words or phrases highlighted	Provide extra examples	Templates to reduce visible print
Increased spacing between lines	Prompt student to stay focused on test, move ahead, read entire item	Markers or masks to maintain place
Fewer number of items per page	Explain directions to student anytime during test	Dark or raised lines
Cues on answer form (e.g., arrows, stop signs)	Answer questions about items anytime during test without giving answers	Pencil grips
		Magnets or tape to secure papers to work area

---

dations are considered controversial. These are discussed later in this chapter.

Presentation accommodations allowed by states are highly variable (see Box 4.11, based on Thurlow et al., 1997). This variability reflects the differing perspectives on their appropriateness. On the other hand, several of the presentation accommodations are widely accepted, such as Braille and large-print editions of assessments.

The policies of national assessments (e.g., ACT, GED, and SAT) related to presentation accommodations are similar to those for timing accommodations (see Box 4.12). Note again that use of these accommodations results in scores that are "flagged," which may have significant implications for how a student's scores are viewed by a receiving institution.

BOX 4.11

Examples of Presentation Accommodations Allowed by States

State	Format		Procedure				Assistive Device			
	Braille Edition	Large Print	Read Test	Sign Direc-tions	Reread Direc-tions	Clarify Direc-tions	Mag-nify-Equip.	Ampli-fication Equip.	Noise Buffer	Tem-plates
Alabama	X	X	X	X			X	X	X	X
Alaska	X	X		X		X				
Arkansas	X	X	X	X			X		X	
Connecticut	X	X	X	X						
Delaware	X	X	X	X	X		X	X	X	X
Florida	X	X	X	X		X	X			X
Georgia	X	X	X				X	X	X	X
Hawaii	X	X		X						
Illinois	X	X	X	X		X	X	X		X
Indiana	X	X		X						
Kansas	X	X	X	X	X	X	X			X
Louisiana	X	X	X	X						
Maine	X	X	X	X		X	X	X	X	X
Maryland	X	X	X	X	X			X		
Michigan	X	X	X	X		X		X		
Minnesota	X	X		X	X	X	X	X		X
Mississippi	X	X	X				X	X		
Montana			X							
Nevada	X	X	X	X	X		X	X		X
New Hampshire	X	X	X			X	X	X	X	X
New Jersey	X	X		X		X				X
New York	X	X	X	X			X	X		X
North Carolina	X	X	X	X			X			
Ohio	X	X	X							
Oklahoma		X								
Oregon	X	X	X	X	X	X	X	X	X	X
Pennsylvania	X	X	X	X		X	X	X		X
Rhode Island	X	X	X	X			X	X		
South Carolina	X	X	X	X		X	X	X	X	X
Tennessee	X	X		X			X			X
Texas	X	X	X	X			X			
Washington	X	X		X			X		X	X
Wisconsin	X	X	X	X		X	X			

NOTE: Only those states that allow at least one of the above presentation accommodations are listed.

BOX 4.12

Examples of Presentation Accommodations Allowed in National Tests

ACT	GED	SAT
Braille edition	Audiocassette edition	Braille
Large-print version		Large print
Audiocassette		Cassette with large print or Braille figure supplement
		Test reader
		Interpreter

Response Accommodations

Response accommodations are changes in how a student responds to an assessment. The main types of response accommodations are format alterations, procedure changes, and use of assistive devices (see Box 4.13). As with presentation accommodations, these types may overlap when accommodations are actually administered, but for our purposes here it helps to think about them as three distinct types.

Even though response accommodations are relatively few in number, there is much controversy about some of them. Generally, it is questions about the "fairness" of some of these accommodations that are raised. These issues and ways to address them are presented later in this chapter.

The primary reason for providing response accommodations is to meet needs related to physical and sensory disabilities that limit the student's ability to respond. However, processing difficulties that limit the ability to get to a response also may be a reason for requesting such accommodations as using a calculator or spell checker when the target skill is math problem solving (not calculation) or written composition (excluding mechanics).

As with other types of accommodations, states vary in the response accommodations that are allowed (see Box 4.14, which is based on Thurlow et al., 1997). Like presentation accommodations, some response accommodations are widely accepted, such as use of a scribe or marking

---

BOX 4.13

Examples of Response Accommodations

Format Alterations	Procedure Changes	Assistive Devices
Mark responses in test booklet rather than on separate page Respond on different paper, such as graph paper, wide-lined paper, paper with wide margins	Use reference materials (e.g., dictionary, arithmetic tables) Give response in different mode (e.g., pointing, oral response to tape recorder, sign language)	Word processor or computer to record responses Amanuensis (proctor/scribe writes student responses) Slantboard or wedge Calculator or abacus Brailler Other communication device (e.g., symbol board) Spell checker

---

in the test booklet rather than on an answer sheet with bubbles, whereas others are highly controversial, such as use of a spell checker.

National exams do allow some response accommodations (see Box 4.15). As with other accommodations, their use raises the "flagging" issue.

Other Accommodations

There are a few accommodations that do not fit within the five types of accommodations described above. Some of these are appropriate, and others are not.

Out-of-Level Testing

Out-of-level testing is an "other" accommodation considered inappropriate for accountability assessments. In out-of-level testing, the third-grade version of the test might be administered to a fifth-grade student. Although testing at a level below the student's actual grade level may be appropriate for making instructional decisions, it is not appropriate for accountability purposes. Testing at a lower grade level does not reflect the student's performance at the standard being assessed for the majority of students.

BOX 4.14

Examples of Response Accommodations Allowed by States

State	Format		Procedure		Assistive Device		
	Mark on Test	Special Paper	Point to Response	Dictate to Tape	Computer or Machine	Proctor/ Scribe	Communication Device
Alabama	X	X			X	X	
Alaska				X			
Arkansas	X					X	
Connecticut					X	X	
Delaware		X		X	X	X	X
Florida	X				X	X	
Georgia	X	X	X			X	
Hawaii						X	
Illinois	X			X	X	X	X
Indiana						X	
Kansas	X		X	X	X		X
Louisiana	X					X	
Maine		X			X	X	
Maryland	X		X	X	X	X	X
Michigan	X			X	X	X	X
Minnesota	X		X	X	X	X	
Mississippi	X				X	X	X
Montana						X	X
Nevada	X	X			X	X	
New Hampshire					X	X	
New Jersey	X		X		X	X	
New York	X		X	X	X	X	X
North Carolina	X					X	
Ohio						X	
Oregon	X	X	X	X	X	X	X
Pennsylvania	X		X	X	X	X	X
Rhode Island			X	X	X	X	
South Carolina	X	X	X	X	X		X
Tennessee	X				X	X	
Texas	X				X	X	
Washington						X	
Wisconsin			X	X	X	X	X

NOTE: Only those states that allow at least one of the above response accommodations are listed.

BOX 4.15

Examples of Response Accommodations Allowed in National Tests

ACT	GED	SAT
None listed	Scribe	Recorder of answers Interpreter

Motivational Accommodations

These comprise a set of accommodations that less clearly fits within the broad categories presented in this book. Motivational accommodations encourage slow-to-begin students to start the test and also encourage "quitters" to continue working on the test and to refocus attention. It is our belief that these activities are indeed accommodations and as such should be discussed and noted on the IEPs of students needing them. They also comprise a need, however, that should be addressed through students' training. For example, self-monitoring techniques and other self-regulation interventions might be taught to students with attention or motivation difficulties.

Test Preparation

Another type of accommodation is test preparation. We have included test preparation as an accommodation here because it is often forgotten. Students without disabilities usually gain test-taking skills on their own without the need for explicit instruction. That often is not the case for students with disabilities, who may be less likely to pick up the skills on their own and who have had less practice in taking district and state assessments. Ideas for test preparation are discussed in Chapter 8.

Computerized Testing

Computers have the potential to revolutionize district and state testing. They have not yet done so because of the real and perceived costs of making computers more widely accessible in general and accessible for testing purposes in particular.

The most broadly examined version of computerized testing is commonly referred to as computer adaptive testing, which allows an individual student's responses to influence which items are presented to the student, just as individualized testing does through basals and ceilings.

In other words, a student starts a test at the item difficulty assumed to be most appropriate for his or her grade. If the student gets most of the items incorrect at this level, the test administrator goes back to easier items. Computers can serve the same function, which allows the assessment to have a much broader difficulty range (from very easy to very difficult) than can be included in a test in which every student must complete every item.

Although not really an accommodation just for students with disabilities, computer adaptive testing has the potential to dramatically increase the participation of students with disabilities in large-scale assessments. Of course, there are also several drawbacks to this type of testing as it exists in current technology. For example, skipping items confuses the program that determines which items should be presented, and until recently, answers could not be changed.

There are several computer-based accommodations that are directly relevant for students with disabilities. One is a computer voice synthesizer, which allows any paper-and-pencil test to be translated easily and quickly by passing it through a scanner, so that the computer can read the test to the student. Another is a videodisc system that can show written text while it presents a corresponding inset showing a person translating the text into sign language. We expect that the potential for other computer-based accommodations will expand in the future.

Do's and Don'ts in Testing Accommodations

Most of the do's and don'ts of testing accommodations relate to the purposes of the assessment, what happens during instruction, and common sense. But it is a good idea to run through these lists every now and again. Here are some of the don'ts:

- *Don't* introduce a new accommodation for the first time for an assessment.

- *Don't* base the decision about what accommodations a student will use on the student's disability category.

- *Don't* start from the district or state list of approved accommodations when considering what accommodations a student will use in an upcoming test.

Add your own don'ts to this list. Keep it in view when making decisions about accommodations. Also, keep in view a list of the do's:

- *Do* systematically use accommodations during instruction and carry these into the assessment process.

- *Do* base the decision about accommodations, both for instruction and for assessment, on the needs of the student.

- *Do* consult the district or state list of approved accommodations after determining what accommodations the student needs. Then, reevaluate the importance of the accommodations that are not allowed. If they are important for the student, request their approval from the district or state.

It is a good idea to add your own ideas to the "do" list, just as you did for the "don't" list. Keep it at hand as you make accommodations decisions.

Considering the Integrity of an Assessment

As we have talked about accommodations, we have on occasion mentioned that controversy surrounds the use of certain accommodations. The controversy is about whether the scores that a student obtains when using accommodations mean the same things as scores obtained by students who do not use them. When scores do not mean the same thing, the integrity of the assessment is compromised. Often, it is said that the accommodation invalidates the test. These kinds of concerns are reasonable in some cases but not in others. How can you know the difference? You probably cannot—yet. Even the psychometricians working on these issues do not agree with each other. And, like many other issues, most people's views on the use of certain accommodations vary with their fundamental beliefs about the importance of being accountable for all students. As there is even disagreement on what criteria must be met for an assessment to retain its integrity, it may be some time before the controversy surrounding the use of accommodations abates. It is hoped that research on their effects may help reduce the controversy.

The issues related to the use of accommodations and threats to the integrity of a test will surface again as we consider the reporting of test scores. The way it plays out most typically is that students are allowed to use the accommodations they need, but their scores do not count in school or district assessments if there are consequences attached to the scores. Sometimes, this means that a student is required to take the assessment without accommodations so that the score can count. Sometimes, it means that a student is encouraged to use accommodations so that the score will not count, without the student or the student's parents knowing this. Chapter 6 contains additional information on the topic of accommodations and reporting.

What the Research Tells Us

Although research has been conducted to examine the effects of accommodations on test integrity, the "answers" are by no means simple or clear. As noted previously, test integrity can be defined in different ways, and the way in which it is defined influences the "answer" you get.

Until very recently, only two major research efforts looked at the effects of testing accommodations. Both were carried out by test development companies (American College Testing and Educational Testing Services), and both were conducted in the mid-1980s. Furthermore, both efforts focused on college admissions exams, which in most ways are not comparable to district and state assessments.

Several research efforts are now under way. One study, conducted by the National Center for Education Statistics, looked at the effects of using a limited number of accommodations on performance on the National Assessment of Educational Progress (NAEP). This study attempted to use sophisticated Item Response Theory analyses to determine whether accommodated and nonaccommodated assessments were comparable. Unfortunately, these analyses require large numbers of students for good results. Large enough numbers were not obtained for specific categories of students, leading the researchers to suggest that the results had to be interpreted with great caution.

States themselves, with special funding, are conducting research on how accommodations affect the results of their own state assessments. Some initial findings suggest that accommodations may not influence overall performance of all students as some would expect them to if they were providing students with advantages.

Clearly, much additional research is needed! It is important to be critical of decisions based on opinions, for recommendations about whether the integrity of tests is maintained when various accommodations are used are generally based on opinions and best guesses.

Summary

In this chapter, we identified types of accommodations and specific accommodations that might be used during assessments. Decision makers should become familiar with both the broad array of accommodations that might be used and the list that might be used by a district or state to indicate which accommodations are allowed. More important, they should identify the accommodations that an individual student needs. Box 4.16 lists student characteristics and possible accommodations for decision makers to use. It is by no means a complete list and is one that might be added to within the context of a specific school, district, or state. Be sure to refer also to the interview on student needs in Chapter 8.

Now, check your knowledge about the myth/truth statements presented at the beginning of this chapter (see Box 4.17 for answers). Try to give an explanation of why each statement is correctly identified either as a myth or as the truth.

BOX 4.16

Student Characteristics and Possible Accommodations

Student Characteristic	Possible Accommodations
Attention difficulties: Student has difficulty staying focused on the task at hand, frequently looking at other students, out the window, or at other areas away from the test.	Setting: Individual, small group Scheduling: Administer within 30 minutes of taking medication Timing: Provide frequent breaks during the usual time of administration, extend the administration time to compensate for the increased break time
Tracking and attention difficulties: Student has difficulty staying on the problem on which he or she is working, often looking at multiple-choice item responses for another question than the one on which working.	Presentation: Provide student with a template to reduce distraction from other items Response: Allow student to respond on the test booklet rather than having to track to a separate bubble sheet
Text processing difficulties: Student has difficulty decoding text at the same speed as other students.	Presentation: Orally present testdirections or both test directions and test items
Low vision: Student has a visual impairment that does not quite meet the definition of legal blindness.	Setting: Individual setting, where extra-bright light can be provided to shine directly on the test materials Scheduling: Administer in morning to avoid end of day eye strain from day's work Timing: Administer with frequent breaks because of fatigue to eyes created by extra-bright light and intense strain at deciphering text Response: Scribe records responses to avoid extra time and eye strain trying to find appropriate location for a response and to give the response

---

BOX 4.17

Myth or Truth Answers

TRUTH Most states allow setting accommodations and presentation accommodations in their statewide testing programs.
Explanation: Setting accommodations and presentation accommodations are among the more frequently allowed accommodations [See Boxes 4.3, 4.11, and 4.14]

TRUTH The most controversial accommodations fall within the areas of timing, scheduling, and response accommodations.
Explanation: Accommodations in the areas of timing, scheduling, and response are most controversial because they raise the issues of (1) whether the accommodations provide an unfair advantage, and (2) whether the accommodations change what is being measured. [See pages 46-47]

MYTH Most national college admissions exams allow a variety of accommodations with no penalty to the student.
Explanation: College admissions tests allow relatively few accommodations. And, those that are used usually result in flagging of the test scores. [See page 52 and Boxes 4.4, 4.7, 4.12, and 4.15]

MYTH Out-of-level testing is an appropriate accommodation for students with mental retardation in accountability assessments.
Explanation: Out-of-level testing is not an appropriate accommodation for any student when the assessment is being used for accountability purposes. This may be an appropriate accommodation for assessments used for instruction. [See page 58]

TRUTH Computer adaptive testing has tremendous potential for making assessments more accessible and meaningful for the full range of students in today's schools.
Explanation: Advances in computer adaptive testing may be the best way to increase accessibility and meaningfulness of district and state tests for many students with disabilities. [See page 61]

MYTH Research findings are now available that define which accommodations invalidate test scores.
Explanation: We do not yet have the research findings that we need to answer most questions about which accommodations invalidate test scores. [See pages 62-63]

Resources for Further Information

Anderson, N. E., Jenkins, F. F., & Miller, K. E. (1996). *NAEP inclusion criteria and testing accommodations: Findings from the NAEP 1995 field test in mathematics.* Washington, DC: National Center for Education Statistics.

Arllen, N. L., Gable, R. A., & Hendrickson, J. M. (1996). Accommodating students with special needs in general education classrooms. *Preventing School Failure, 41*(1), 7-13.

Elliott, J., Thurlow, M., & Ysseldyke, J. (1996). *Assessment guidelines that maximize the participation of students with disabilities in large-scale assessments: Characteristics and considerations* (Synthesis Rep. 25). Minneapolis: University of Minnesota, National Center on Educational Outcomes.

FairTest. (1992). *Computerized testing: More questions than answers.* Cambridge, MA: National Center for Fair & Open Testing.

Jayanthi, M., Epstein, M. H., Polloway, E. A., & Bursuck, W. D. (1996). A national survey of general education teachers' perceptions of testing adaptations. *Journal of Special Education, 30*(1), 99-115.

King, W. L., Baker, J., & Jarrow, J. E. (n.d.). *Testing accommodations for students with disabilities.* Columbus, OH: Association on Higher Education and Disability.

Laing, I., & Farmer, M. (1984). *Use of the ACT assessment by examinees with disabilities* (Research Rep. 84). Iowa City: American College Testing Program.

Thurlow, M. L., Seyfarth, A., Scott, D., & Ysseldyke, J. E. (1997). *Summary grids of state assessment guidelines on participation and accommodations* (Synthesis Rep.). Minneapolis: University of Minnesota, National Center on Educational Outcomes.

Willingham, W. W., Ragosta, M., Bennett, R. E., Braun, H., Rock, D. A., & Powers, D. E. (Eds.). (1988). *Testing handicapped people.* Boston: Allyn & Bacon.

The Ultimate Accommodation:
An Alternate Assessment

Topics

- □ What Is an Alternate Assessment?
- □ When Should a Student Take an Alternate Assessment?
- □ Guidelines for Developing an Alternate Assessment
- □ Examples of Alternate Assessments

In this chapter, you will . . .

- – find out what an alternate assessment is and who is eligible to take one.
- – examine the impact of broad versus narrow standards on inclusive accountability systems.
- – learn guidelines for developing an alternate assessment.
- – study a variety of states' examples of alternate assessments.

In Chapter 4, we examined possible accommodations for a student to use during assessments. We also gave you just a hint of some of the technical issues that require consideration and what the research tells us. In this chapter, we address the ultimate accommodation—what to do for students for whom none of the accommodations discussed in Chapter 4 provide the support needed to participate in the regular assessment. These are students who are unable to meaningfully participate in the regular assessment because they are working toward a different set of standards than are most students. The ultimate accommodation is

---

BOX 5.1

Myth or Truth? Do You Know?

Read each statement below and decide whether it is a myth or the truth about current practice.

- Alternate assessments are not currently being used in any state or district.
- The best alternate assessment for system accountability for student learning is one that is completely individualized and based on the IEP.
- Student portfolios, record reviews, and observations are examples of acceptable alternate assessments.
- Perhaps the biggest challenge in developing an alternate assessment system is deciding on a set of common domains in which all students are assessed.

---

to provide the student with an alternate assessment—a different way to demonstrate learning and remain in the educational accountability system of the district or state.

In this chapter, we examine the following questions: What should an alternate assessment look like? What specifically should it assess? When should a student participate in the alternate assessment? How can I get this kind of assessment implemented? When you finish this chapter, you will be able to identify which of the statements in Box 5.1 are myths and which are the truth.

What Is an Alternate Assessment?

An alternate assessment is a method of measuring the performance of students unable to participate in the typical district or state assessment. We have thus far identified several different ways in which students can participate in an accountability system: (a) in the regular assessment without accommodations, (b) in the regular assessment with accommodations, (c) in an alternate assessment, and (d) partially in an alternate assessment and partially in the regular assessment. It is estimated that approximately 10% of students with disabilities (about 1% of the total student population) would participate in the alternate assessment. For those students not in the regular assessment, the alternate assessment serves as a substitute way to gather information needed to measure and document the results of education.

There are many approaches to measurement that are appropriate for an alternate assessment system. For an accountability system, however, it is critical that the data be "aggregated" (i.e., combined) to produce an overall estimate of performance for all students participating in the alternate assessment. That means that whatever is used for the alternate assessment must measure common elements so that data can be combined across students in the alternate assessment.

Two states currently have an alternate assessment. Kentucky has the Alternate Portfolio System. Maryland has the Independence Mastery Assessment Program (IMAP).

Defining the common domains for which student data can be combined is critical. Kentucky did this by first identifying domains for all students and then selecting those most relevant for students with significant disabilities. Maryland did it by gaining consensus on the important domains for students with significant disabilities, regardless of the domains for other students.

There are a number of ways to think about what alternate assessments look like. Salvia and Ysseldyke (1995) identify several assessment approaches that provide a framework for thinking about what might work for an alternate assessment system. Using four general approaches (observation, interviews and checklists, testing, and record review) you can generate an array of methods for an alternate assessment (see Box 5.2).

An alternate assessment can be almost anything that has been agreed on beforehand by individuals who know what they want to measure and who can devise a way to aggregate the data.

When Should a Student Take an Alternate Assessment?

This is an appropriate time to revisit this question, which was first addressed in Chapter 2. In that chapter, the criterion that targeted a student for participation in an alternate assessment was that the student was working toward a different set of standards than other students. Thus, if a student is working on life skills standards at the same time the student's peers are working on content-focused standards in English, mathematics, and science, that student should be in an alternate assessment. In most cases, students will not be shifted into the alternate assessment until they are older.

The academic lifespan of students with disabilities will necessarily differ as they progress through their school years. The degree or severity of a student's disability will have a major impact on the academic path that student takes. The academic lifespan for students with more significant cognitive disabilities will differ from those with mild to moderate cognitive disabilities. Students with mild to moderate disabilities are typically those with learning disabilities, mild mental retardation,

---

BOX 5.2

Possible Measurement Approaches for an Alternate Assessment

Observation	Interviews and Checklists
Marking occurrence of specific behaviors	Interviews: teachers, peers, parents, employers
Written narrative of what is observed	Rating scales or checklists: mobility and community skills, self-help skills, daily living skills, adaptive behavior, social skills
Notation of the frequency, duration, and intensity of behavior	
Videotape	
Audiotape	Peer and/or adult rating scales or check-lists

Testing	Record Review
Performance events	School records
Portfolios	Student products
	IEP objectives and progress

---

emotional disabilities, or those with multiple disabilities who are able, with assistance, to participate in the same course requirements and assessments as students without disabilities. Students with more significant cognitive disabilities are those who, because of their disability, need an alternate or more individualized curriculum. Generally, students who participate in an alternate assessment are those not working toward a standard diploma. The decision to participate in it should not be made for most students until they are approaching the age of transition planning (14 to 16 years). However, for some students with disabilities, the need for an alternate assessment will be more apparent and appropriate early in their academic lifespan due to the significance of their cognitive disability and the highly individualized curriculum they are learning.

Gray Area Students

While it is easy to state that the alternate assessment is for students who are pursuing different standards from those pursued by the majority of students, distinctions like these are not always so clear-cut. There are a number of factors that complicate the situation, producing what we refer to here as gray area students.

The most common factor, one that is to be encouraged, is that things change over time. When a student first enters school, it is in most cases appropriate to assume that the student will be taught the same things as other students. Even recognizing tremendous diversity in the abilities and skills that children bring to school, it is still appropriate to be teaching the same skill areas to all children.

As children progress through school and begin to enter the years when transition to postschool environments is under consideration, it is time to rethink the goals of instruction and the standards toward which the student is working. At some point, for some small percentage of students, there is the recognition that life skills are more important to target than are traditional academic subjects.

Another factor is the nature of the assessment that has been developed to measure students' progress toward the standards. Assessments can be developed to be very broad in difficulty levels or quite narrow. The narrower the assessment, in general, the easier it is to administer in a short amount of time.

Most district and state tests are not developed to be broad in the difficulty levels they assess. The result is that, for many students, the tests do not have any items on which they can successfully perform. This is a major problem for accountability systems. Needless to say, it is also a major problem for those making decisions about whether a student should participate in the regular or the alternate assessment.

At this point, there is one avenue to follow when a student should take the regular assessment (because he or she is pursuing the same goals as other students), but it seems inappropriate to require participation (because the test is so difficult that the student is unlikely to get any items correct). The recommended approach is to have the student participate in the alternate assessment but produce scores and prepare reports for accountability purposes as though the student participated in the regular assessment. In this way, the system receives a score of zero for the student (an appropriate score for an inappropriate test) while information on the student's performance is still available for other reports (and, in some cases, the main accountability report).

Broad Versus Narrow Standards

The decision about participation in an alternate assessment is also complicated by the nature of the standards developed by the district or state. The broader the standards originally developed, the easier it is to include all students in the same accountability system. Examples of broad and narrow standards are provided in Box 5.3.

When standards are very broad, a student may be working toward those standards but still need to be in an alternate assessment. This is what has occurred in Kentucky, where quite broad standards were devel-

---

BOX 5.3

Examples of Broad and Narrow Standards

Broad Standards	Narrow Standards
Students compare patterns of change and constancy in systems.	Students describe the basic processes of photosynthesis and respiration and their importance to life.
Students represent and solve problems using geometric models.	Students differentiate between area and perimeter and identify whether the application of the concept of perimeter or area is appropriate for a given situation.

NOTE: These examples were adopted from some in the American Federation of Teachers' (1996) document *Making Standards Matter, 1996* (p. 16). AFT classifies them as "weak" and "strong" standards.

---

oped for all students. Teachers and others who worked with students with significant cognitive disabilities double-checked all standards for their appropriateness for these students and determined that 28 of the original 60 were the most appropriate and important (see Box 5.4 for a sample of these standards and the indicators that apply to students in the Alternate Portfolio System).

In Maryland, a slightly different approach underlies the state standards and thus the alternate assessment. Maryland started with a set of standards appropriate for the majority of students and then went back to identify desired educational outcomes for those students with significant cognitive disabilities (see Box 5.5 for a sample of these standards and indicators of them).

Both Kentucky and Maryland have developed accountability systems that include all students, but they have done so in different ways. The major advantage of having started from broad standards is that the merging of data for reporting may be easier (more on this in Chapter 6).

Guidelines for Developing an Alternate Assessment

Unless you happen to live in Iowa, Florida, Kentucky, Maryland, or Michigan, it is unlikely that you have available to you an alternate as-

---

BOX 5.4

**Examples of Kentucky's Academic Expectations and Indicators
for Students in the Alternate Portfolio System**

Academic Expectation	Indicator
Accessing Information: Students use research tools to locate sources of information and ideas relevant to a specific need or problem.	Requests assistance
Reading: Students construct meaning from a variety of printed materials for a variety of purposes through reading.	Reads environmental, pictorial print
Writing: Students communicate ideas and information to a variety of audiences for a variety of purposes through writing.	Constructs printed, pictorial messages Uses personal signature

---

sessment for those students unable to participate in typical district or state assessments. What do you do in this case?

General and special education teachers are in the best position to develop alternate assessments for students. It is imperative that teachers work with district personnel so that these efforts are recognized. Perhaps more important is the need to be sure that data on students who do not fit within the regular assessment system are collected, counted, and reported along with the results of the rest of the school, district, or state.

We suggest seven steps that need to be taken to establish an alternate assessment. These steps are based on information produced by the National Center on Educational Outcomes, which, in turn, gathered its information from states that currently have alternate assessments. The seven steps are as follows:

- Establishing an advisory group for the alternate assessment
- Defining the purpose of the alternate assessment system and who qualifies to participate in it
- Identifying the common core of learning for the alternate assessment

---

BOX 5.5

Examples of Maryland's Content-Domain Outcomes and Indicators for Students in the Independence Mastery Assessment Program

Content Domain	Indicator
Personal Management: Students demonstrate their ability in the following areas: personal needs, appropriate health and safety practices, managing household routines, and participating in transition planning with adult service providers.	Eating and feeding self Dressing appropriately for activities, season, and weather
Community: Students demonstrate their ability to access community resources and get about safely in the environment.	Shopping or browsing for variety of items Demonstrating safe pedestrian skills
Career/Vocational: Students demonstrate their ability to participate in transitioning to employment and invarious employment opportunities.	Arriving at work appropriately dressed and on time Completing assigned duties with appropriate productivity and quality
Recreation/Leisure: Students demonstrate their ability to participate in recreational and leisure activities.	Engaging in hobbies Participating in clubs or organizations

---

- Developing participation guidelines to determine who is eligible for the alternate assessment system

- Deciding how to measure performance

- Determining how the results from the alternate assessment will be aggregated across students in the alternate assessment system

- Determining whether to, and how to, integrate results from the alternate assessment with results from the regular assessment

Establishing an Advisory Group for the Alternate Assessment

A key part of all of these steps is having a stakeholder group that can discuss, debate, and decide on the issues that must be addressed. Selection of the members of the stakeholder group is very important. A guiding principle is that the group should not include only individuals who all have the same perspective. In fact, it is essential to include different perspectives so that the end products really do represent a consensus-building product.

Defining the Purpose and Deciding Who Qualifies

Defining the purpose of the alternate assessment and the criteria for deciding who participates in the alternate assessment should flow directly from, and complement, the purpose of the regular assessment and the criteria for participation in that assessment. It is critical, of course, that these be agreed on by all stakeholders and that they be developed and put into print in a very clear and concise manner. We believe that the alternate assessment should be reserved for those students working toward a different set of standards from those assessed by the regular assessment system. Determining whether your group of stakeholders agrees with this is a critical first step in developing the alternate assessment.

Identifying the Common Core of Learning for the Alternate Assessment

An alternate assessment system must have a set of domains (or goals) within which data can be aggregated. This is what we refer to as the "common core of learning." If data cannot be aggregated, they cannot be used for accountability purposes.

For example, in a district with two students with significant cognitive disabilities, each student might be working on different goals. Still, their data can be combined if the common core of learning is defined. For example, Sarah might be working on mobility skills that include moving from the classroom to the bathroom, the lunchroom, and the door to the bus. Related to these skills, she is working on communicating requests such as "May I go to the bathroom?", "Is it time for lunch?", and "Open the door." Associated instruction related to appropriate behavior, independence, and academics (e.g., "reading" girls' bathroom sign, identifying bus) fill out her instructional day. In another example, the focus of Jimmy's instruction is primarily on work skills. He is learning to maintain the cleanliness of the local health club. His job includes picking up old newspapers and magazines left near exercise equipment, vacuuming the carpet, and polishing exercise equipment. Along with his job responsibilities, he is learning to get to work and leave work on time, punch in and out properly, and greet clients appropriately.

Despite the differences in the focus of their instructional programs, both Sarah and Jimmy can be assessed against a common core of learning that includes (a) communication skills, (b) social skills, (c) personal skills, and (d) task completion skills. The common core of learning might also include reading skills (which only Sarah's instruction is addressing at this point), mathematical skills (which only Jimmy's instruction is addressing at this point), and physical health (which is not the focus of either student's instruction at this point). Both students can be assessed on this common core of learning even if their instructional programs do not yet address these skills.

The few states that have alternate assessments have taken different approaches to defining the common core of learning. One approach is to build off of existing state standards. Another approach is to start over. Even when starting over, however, there are several models that can be adapted, such as the National Center on Educational Outcomes (NCEO) model of educational outcomes (see Box 5.6). Whatever the approach, it is critical to gain the buy-in of a group of stakeholders. Extensive materials are available from the NCEO on indicators of each domain and sources of data for each domain and indicator.

Developing Participation Guidelines

Developing guidelines to help decision makers reach appropriate decisions about the participation of students with disabilities in the alternate assessment flows from the first step, which is the development of principles that determine the purpose of the alternate assessment and who qualifies for participation. This is the point at which the principles are put into words. It is important once again to develop these guidelines in conjunction with existing guidelines for the regular assessment. For example, the guidelines used in Kentucky demonstrate the limited access to the alternate assessment (see Box 5.7).

Deciding How to Measure Performance

Measuring performance is the critical element of the alternate assessment. You should select from among the possible methods for measurement listed in Box 5.2. You could decide to use a single method (e.g., development of a student portfolio) or several methods (e.g., observation and interviews).

The district with Sarah and Jimmy decided to use a combination of observation and interviews to measure these students' performance on the common core of learning. The procedures the district used for these assessments (see Box 5.8) demonstrate the variability and intensity that may be involved in an alternate assessment system.

As you identify how performance is measured, you also need to identify how performance is scored. Scores can either be quantitative, such

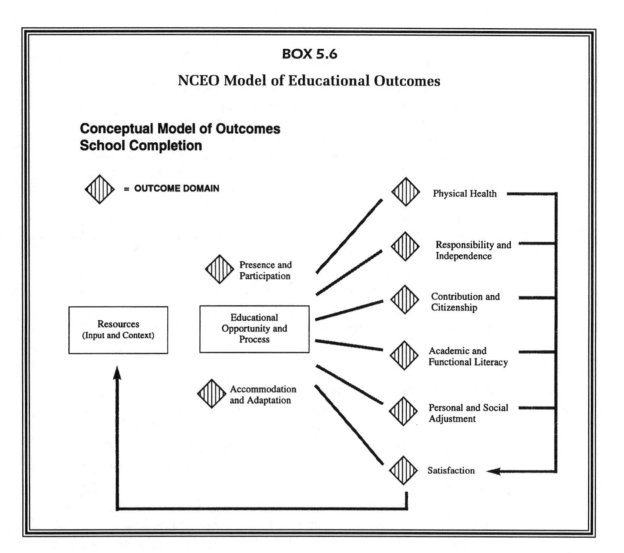

BOX 5.6

NCEO Model of Educational Outcomes

**Conceptual Model of Outcomes
School Completion**

as when a scale or checklist is used, or qualitative, such as when performance labels are assigned. One approach commonly used for alternate assessments is the use of rubrics with levels (e.g., 1 = basic, 2 = proficient, 3 = advanced) and descriptions of the nature of performance for each level. Another common approach is to use a "standard met" or "standard not met" distinction.

Determining How Results From the Alternate Assessment Will Be Aggregated

As noted previously, results from an alternate assessment can only be used for accountability if they can be aggregated across individual students to produce group information. Scores of students participating in the alternate assessment need to be combined into aggregate average scores (or some variant of an average score).

BOX 5.7

**Kentucky's Guidelines for Determining Eligibility
for Participation in Its Alternate Assessment
(based on KDE Program Advisory, May 1992)**

- The student's Admissions and Release Committee has determined and verified on the student's individual education plan (IEP) that the student meets all of the eligibility criteria for the KIRIS Alternate Portfolio Assessment.

- The student's Admissions and Release Committee has documented in writing in the student's record the basis for its decision, using current and longitudinal data (e.g., including performance data across multiple settings in the areas of academics, communication, cognition, social competence, recreation/leisure, domestic, community living, and vocational skills; behavior observations in multiple settings; adaptive behavior; and continuous assessment of progress on IEP goals and objectives). This will help ensure that the student meets all of the following criteria:

    (a) The student's demonstrated cognitive ability and adaptive behavior prevent completing the course of study even with program modification.

    (b) The student's current adaptive behavior requires extensive direct instruction in multiple settings to accomplish the application and transfer of skills necessary for functional application in domestic, community living, recreational/leisure, and vocational activities in school, work, home, and community environments.

    (c) The student's inability to complete the course of study may not be the result of excessive or extended absences; it may not be primarily the result of visual or auditory disabilities, specific learning disabilities, emotional-behavioral disabilities, and social, cultural, or economic differences.

    (d) The student is unable to apply or use academic skills at a minimal competency level in natural settings (e.g., home, community, or work site) when instructed solely or primarily through school-based instruction.

    (e) For 8th- and 12th-grade students with disabilities, the student is unable to

        − Complete a regular diploma program even with extended school services, schooling, program modifications, and adaptations

        − Acquire, maintain, and generalize skills and demonstrate performance without intensive, frequent, and individualized community-based instruction.

If the scores given to Sarah and Jimmy are qualitative, their performance could be compared with rubrics that define what performance should be. For example, it could be concluded and reported that both students achieved excellence in the area of communication skills but

BOX 5.8

Assessment Procedures Used for Sarah and Jimmy in an Alternate Assessment System

Common Core Area	Sarah's Procedures	Jimmy's Procedures
Communication skills	Observe Sarah three times (lunch, afternoon classes, bus departure) on three consecutive days, rating communications in mobility independence using a rubric Interview teachers about Sarah's communications related to her mobility needs Interview Sarah's parents about generalization of communications for mobility at other times and places	Interview Jimmy's employers about his communication with them and with health club clients
Social skills	Interview teachers about Sarah's interactions with school staff and other students	Interview Jimmy's employers and a sample of regular health club clients about his communication with them
Personal skills	Observe and rate the appropriateness of Sarah's requests to go to the bathroom	Observe the appropriateness of Jimmy's dress for work
Task-completion skills	Interview teachers about the extent to which Sarah is finishing requests that promote independence in mobility	Observe and rate the completeness of Jimmy's required work tasks each day Interview employers about Jimmy's task completion

only one of them achieved excellence in the social skills area. These are good data for accountability, and they have the added advantage of being based on information that can be used for instructional purposes as well.

Determining Whether to, and How to, Integrate Results From the Alternate and Regular Assessments

Eventually, the goal of an inclusive accountability system is to have a single set of scores for a school, district, or state that reflects the performance of all students. When some students take the regular assessment and other students take the alternate assessment, thought must be given to how all scores can be reported. The most obvious way is to report the scores from the regular and the alternate assessments separately but always to report both sets of scores. Kentucky combines the scores of students from the regular and the alternate assessment because all scores are on a 4-point rubric (novice, apprentice, proficient, distinguished). Rubrics hold equal weight for the general assessment and the alternate assessment. Thus, a 3 on the general assessment is counted the same as a 3 on the alternate assessment.

Examples of Alternate Assessments

Although we have talked almost exclusively about Kentucky and Maryland regarding alternate assessments, there are other states trying different approaches to accountability for students with significant disabilities. Our purpose here in presenting several of these is not to endorse them but, rather, to show the variety of approaches that might be taken.

Michigan

Many years ago, Michigan began its work on identifying common desired educational outcomes for students with disabilities. Building on the already established state assessment, the Michigan Educational Assessment Program (MEAP), the Center for Quality Special Education (working under a contract from the state) pulled together stakeholders to identify outcomes for students with disabilities. This was done for each category of disability (e.g., one set for students with learning disabilities, another set for students with emotional disabilities, yet another set for students with educable mental impairments, and so on). Examples of some of the identified outcomes are provided in Box 5.9. As is evident, the expectations for many categories of disabilities are that the student will meet other goals besides the basic academic goals set locally for all students. Michigan also devoted time to the development of assessments for local educators to measure progress toward achieving the category-specific outcomes.

BOX 5.9

Examples of Michigan's Outcomes for
Four Disability Categories

Learning Disabilities	**Visual Impairments**

Basic Academics:

1.1 Complete local school minimum general education graduation requirements.

Self-Esteem and Social Integration:

2.1 Approach decisions and challenges with competence and a positive and realistic attitude.

2.2 Proceed effectively in social situations and settings.

2.3 Work effectively to build relationships.

Personal Efficiency and Productivity:

3.1 Manage activities involving mathematical concepts efficiently.

3.2 Approach and complete tasks responsibly and efficiently.

3.3 Proceed systematically toward fulfillment of career and other life pursuits.

Language and Communication:

4.1 Facilitate the efficient interpretation and retrieval of information presented orally.

4.2 Express themselves effectively when communicating orally.

4.3 Facilitate the efficient interpretation and retrieval of information presented in print formats.

4.4 Express themselves effectively when communicating in print formats.

Basic Academics:

1.1 Complete local school minimum general education graduation requirements.

Math and English Language Effectiveness:

2.1 Complete daily living tasks requiring mathematical concepts and skills effectively.

2.2 Communicate effectively through the creation of written/print material.

2.3 Complete reading tasks efficiently.

Personal Management and Daily Living:

3.1 Move about and travel effectively within and beyond their communities.

3.2 Address personal and daily living needs through effective access of community and other resources and services.

3.3 Complete household routines and related tasks productively and efficiently.

3.4 Complete personal care and health related tasks effectively.

Life Role Orientation:

4.1 Proceed toward the fulfillment of realistic career, independent living, and other life pursuits.

4.2 Manage interpersonal interactions with facility, sensitivity, and personal confidence.

(Continued)

Florida

It has been relatively recent that Florida has systematically attempted to assess the performance of students with disabilities in a way that would produce aggregate state data. The model that Florida chose to follow was much like that of Michigan's, except that rather than being disability specific, it was designed for different disability levels. Outcomes were defined for students with mild disabilities, students with

---

BOX 5.9

Examples of Michigan's Outcomes for
Four Disability Categories (Continued)

Autism	Significant Mental Impairments
Personal Care and Productivity:	**Outcome 1:**
1.1 Complete personal care, health, and safety activities.	Engage in a typical pattern of leisure and productivity activities in homes and communities.
1.2 Complete domestic activities in their personal living environments.	**Outcome 2:**
1.3 Complete personal work assignments effectively.	Engage in a typical pattern of interactions.
Community Use and Integration:	**Outcome 3:**
2.1 Complete community transactions that meet daily living needs.	Participate in effective communication cycles.
2.2 Travel and move about effectively between and within community locations.	**Outcome 4:**
Interpersonal Effectiveness:	Participate in personal care, health, and safety routines.
3.1 Participate effectively in communication cycles.	**Outcome 5:**
3.2 Participate cooperatively in group situations.	Reach desired locations safely within familiar environments.
Time and Life Management:	
4.1 Manage unstructured time constructively.	
4.2 Proceed appropriately toward the fulfillment of personal desires.	
Basic Academics:	
[Depending on individual characteristics and circumstances, it may be appropriate to expect student to complete local district minimum graduation requirements.]	

---

moderate disabilities, and students with significant disabilities. Because Florida just completed the development of its expectancies, it has not yet developed its assessments.

Iowa

Use of the IEP as a basis for accountability for the results of education for students with disabilities has remained the focus of Iowa's state education department. To use the IEP as the basis for accountability, two things had to occur. First, outcome domains had to be established as a

---

BOX 5.10

Description of Judgments Used in Iowa's Pilot Study of Aggregating Data From IEPs for Accountability Purposes

Discrepancy Conclusion	**IEP Goal Progress Conclusion**
This reflects a comparison of the magnitude of the discrepancy before the intervention (baseline) and after the intervention (at the end of year or annual review). [Question to ask: After implementing the special education program, is the individual farther behind peers, about the same distance behind peers, or catching up to peers in the goal area?]	This is a judgment about the outcome of the intervention efforts as reflected by goal attainment. [Question to ask: Compared with the goal projected at the time of IEP planning, how did the individual perform in this goal area?]
	1 = Goal met or exceeded
L = Less discrepant from acceptable level of performance (indicates behavior is changing in a direction toward desired performance)	2 = Goal not met but performance improved
M = More discrepant from acceptable level of performance (indicates behavior is changing in a direction away from the desired performance)	3 = Goal not met and performance did not improve or got worse
	4 = Data are not available
S = Same amount of discrepancy from acceptable level of performance (indicates behavior remains unchanged when viewed compared with the performance standard)	5 = Data are not available, student has moved from school

---

basis for the accountability system. Second, IEPs had to be written to conform to the designated outcome areas.

Iowa chose to use the extensive work of the NCEO to identify its framework of outcomes (see Box 5.6). In developing its outcomes, the NCEO established several national stakeholder groups to reach consensus on critical domains and key indicators of these domains. Stakeholders included teachers, parents, administrators, legislators, business, and other relevant stakeholder groups.

The second step that Iowa took was to rethink its IEPs, so that each IEP goal is linked to one of the domain areas. For each goal, a standard is set for acceptable performance, and at the end of the year two kinds of judgment are recorded: discrepancy conclusion and IEP goal progress

---

BOX 5.11

Myth or Truth Answers

MYTH Alternate assessments are not currently being used in any state or district.
Explanation: Kentucky has a fully implemented alternate assessment in place. Other states are working on alternate assessments. Districts also may have such systems in place. [See page 69]

MYTH The best alternate assessment for system accountability for student learning is one that is completely individualized and based on the IEP.
Explanation: For system accountability, it is necessary for scores to be combined across students. An alternate assessment that is completely individualized (based on the IEP or not) does not meet this requirement. [See page 69]

TRUTH Student portfolios, record reviews, and observation are examples of acceptable alternate assessments.
Explanation: Possible procedures of measurement include many specific procedures within the areas of observation, interviews and checklists, testing, and record reviews. [See page 69 and Box 5.2]

TRUTH Perhaps the biggest challenge in developing an alternate assessment system is deciding on a set of common domains in which all students will be assessed.
Explanation: There are a number of challenges in developing alternate assessments, but the biggest one may be deciding on the set of common domains. If a common core is not identified, data cannot be aggregated. [See page 75]

---

conclusion. Descriptions of these judgments appear in Box 5.10. Iowa is now exploring ways in which these types of IEP data on discrepancy and goal attainment can be aggregated to produce data on the results of education at a variety of levels (regional, district, school, teacher).

Summary

In this chapter, we addressed a relatively new area of interest within the assessment arena but nevertheless one of extreme importance when talking about the participation of students with disabilities in accountability systems. Without some type of alternate assessment, it is impossible to have an accountability system that includes all students.

This chapter addressed this concept and provided a quick overview of the issues that surround it. Yet, despite defining the term and listing some steps for developing an alternate assessment, this chapter nevertheless leaves room for lots of work to be done. A key part of accomplishing that work is to establish a stakeholder group willing to work hard to sort through the issues and reach consensus on the purpose of the alternate assessment, who is to participate in it, what the assessment is to be like, and how its results are to be aggregated and integrated.

Now, check your knowledge about the myth/truth statements presented at the beginning of this chapter (see Box 5.11 for answers). Try to give an explanation for why each statement is correctly identified either as a myth or as the truth.

Resources for Further Information

American Federation of Teachers. (1996). *Making standards matter, 1996: An annual fifty-state report on efforts to raise academic standards.* Washington, DC: Author.

Center for Quality Special Education. (n.d.). *Special education outcomes.* (Contact Michigan Department of Education, Special Education, for further information)

Elliott, J., & Roeber, E. (1996). *Assessment accommodations for students with disabilities.* (Videotape recording). Alexandria, VA: National Association of State Directors of Special Education.

Olsen, K., & Ysseldyke, J. (1997). *Alternate assessment.* (Videotape recording). Alexandria, VA: National Association of State Directors of Special Education.

Salvia, J., & Ysseldyke, J. E. (1995). *Assessment* (6th ed.). Boston: Houghton Mifflin.

Thurlow, M., Olsen, K., Elliott, J., Ysseldyke, J., Erickson, R., & Ahearn, E. (1996). *Alternate assessments for students with disabilities: For students unable to participate in general large-scale assessments* (NCEO Policy Directions 5). Minneapolis: University of Minnesota, National Center on Educational Outcomes.

Thurlow, M., Ysseldyke, J., Erickson, R., & Elliott, J. (1997). *Increasing the participation of students with disabilities in state and district assessments* (NCEO Policy Directions 6). Minneapolis: University of Minnesota, National Center on Educational Outcomes.

Ysseldyke, J. E., & Olsen, K. (1997). *Putting alternate assessments into practice: Possible sources of data.* Minneapolis: University of Minnesota, National Center on Educational Outcomes.

Ysseldyke, J. E., Olsen, K., & Thurlow, M. (1997). *Issues and considerations in alternate assessments.* Minneapolis: University of Minnesota, National Center on Educational Outcomes.

Ysseldyke, J. E., & Thurlow, M. L. (1994). *Guidelines for inclusion of students with disabilities in large-scale assessments* (NCEO Policy Directions 1). Minneapolis: University of Minnesota, National Center on Educational Outcomes.

Ysseldyke, J. E., Thurlow, M. L., & Olsen, K. (1996). *Self-study guide for the development of statewide assessments that include students with disabilities.* Minneapolis: University of Minnesota, National Center on Educational Outcomes.

Reporting Accountability and Assessment Results

In this chapter, you will . . .

- – explore the issues of accounting for students with disabilities in accountability reports.

- – find out how and to whom the results of students with disabilities who take typical assessment are reported.

- – review criteria for making decisions about reporting assessment results.

In several of the chapters thus far, we have mentioned the reporting of scores. Reporting is an area that brings up lots of issues because even if educators are willing to have students with disabilities take assessments, with or without accommodations, they are less likely to want the scores of these students included within the scores that are reported. It is assumed that if the scores of students with disabilities are included, average scores will be pulled down. Questions are raised about the validity of merging scores from accommodated and nonaccommodated assessments. These and related topics are the focus of this chapter.

> **BOX 6.1**
>
> **Myth or Truth? Do You Know?**
>
> Read each statement below and decide whether it is a myth or the truth about current practice.
>
> - Most states require that if a student does not participate in the assessment, the score of that student, for reporting purposes, is zero.
> - If a student takes an assessment, that student automatically is included in average scores because of the way that test developers set up reporting programs.
> - There are ways to integrate the scores from alternate assessments with those from regular assessments so that the two can be reported together.
> - One reason for wanting to report the scores of students with disabilities is to produce data for program evaluation.

When you finish this chapter, you will be able to identify which of the statements in Box 6.1 are myths and which are the truth.

We think that reporting the scores of students with disabilities is an important element of a truly inclusive accountability system. This is reinforced by the 1997 amendments to IDEA, which require public reporting of scores of students with disabilities with the same frequency as for other students. Until we recognize that all students count, and back it up with data to evaluate the success of our programs for students with disabilities, we will continue to not be accountable for all students.

In this chapter, we clarify the issues involved in reporting. We also look at different options for reporting results and what we know about the performance of students with disabilities when they have participated in district and state assessments. Finally, we provide several criteria that you can use to make good reporting decisions.

Issues in Reporting for Students With Disabilities

Many issues surround the reporting of student performance results. Among these are how to communicate results clearly and what kinds of scores to report (e.g., average scores vs. percentages). Others arise because of educators' perceptions about the performance of these students or because educators are unsure what produces good data for reporting.

Who Is Included in Reports?

In explorations of reporting policies of states, the National Center on Educational Outcomes (NCEO; Thurlow et al., 1995) found that many states routinely exclude the scores of students with disabilities from their reports. Sometimes, the data are aggregated and put together in a separate report that may go back to the school or may go back to teachers or parents of individual students. In most states and districts, however, the scores simply are deleted from the files used to combine the data that will go into reports.

In other states, there is no way to tell whether students with disabilities have participated in the assessment. Sometimes, students are included in the assessment if they typically take part in classroom tests and are in the general education setting when the assessment is administered. But, they are not identified in any way, so those who pull together the data cannot report who participated in the assessment even if they wanted to do so.

Where Is Accountability Assigned in Reports?

Students with disabilities, usually more so than other students (unless you are in a district or state with a school choice program), may not be receiving educational services in their district of residence. This situation creates questions about where the scores of these students should be assigned—to their district of residence, or to the district in which they are receiving educational services? Either one of these approaches can be justified, and both approaches currently are being used.

For students with disabilities, there are several reasons to argue that accountability should be assigned to the home school and/or district and have scores reported there. A primary reason is that these students typically are sent away from the district or school of residence rather than choosing to go elsewhere for their education. Assigning scores to the home school and district ensures that, if a student has been moved to another location to receive services, it is because the home school or district believes that is the best way to maximize the learning and performance of the student. If the school or district is worried about being held accountable, it may give greater consideration before sending students away for reasons other than obtaining the best education for them.

Are Participation Rates Reported?

If it is known which of the students who participated in an assessment have a disability, it is possible to begin to calculate the assessment participation rates. This requires simply marking the assessment protocols in some way so that the data from students with disabilities can be pulled and reported separately. Reporting the number of students with disabilities participating in assessments is required in the 1997 IDEA reauthorization.

BOX 6.2

Data Elements and Coding Options That Facilitate the Development and Implementation of Appropriate Reporting Procedures

Data Element	Coding Option
How student participated in the accountability system	Whether student took the regular assessment
Student's primary disability	Name of the federal category for which student receives primary special education services
Student's related services	Type of related services a student receives (e.g., occupational therapy, physical therapy)
Student's placement	Placement of student's special education services (e.g., regular, resource, self-contained)
Student's functional learning characteristics (e.g., estimated reading level)	Any one of an array of variables that provides information about the student's learning and functional characteristics that goes beyond a mere categorical label
Accommodations used during the assessment (by category or by specific accommodation)	Indication of the accommodations used by a student during assessment

Is Other Information Available to Clarify Reporting?

Reporting of participation rates is important, if for no other reason than to keep track of whether desired participation policies are being carried out. It might also be relevant to collect, at the time of assessment, information on a student's disability and the accommodations that the student uses. This information then can be used later to look at the assessment results in different ways. In Box 6.2, we list each of the data elements that might prove useful in working toward an appropriate reporting system. These are elements that you could include in a demographic section of the answer sheet for each student.

Ways to Report Scores of Students With Disabilities

The scores of students with disabilities can be reported by combining them with the scores of other students (aggregated) or by separating them from the scores of other students (disaggregated). Both approaches can be used as well. In some places, more complicated (and usually less appropriate) approaches are used. For example, scores of only certain categories of students with disabilities (e.g., speech disabilities and physical disabilities) may be aggregated with those of other students. Students with mental impairments or emotional disabilities may be excluded from reporting altogether. Similarly, disaggregation may be completed only for students with certain types of disabilities, such as students with visual disabilities.

We think that it is important at this point to provide both aggregation and disaggregation of scores of students with disabilities. Aggregation is needed to further the notion that educators are responsible for all students with disabilities. Disaggregation is needed to have data available for evaluating the programs provided to students with disabilities.

Concerns about aggregation usually arise from the notion that including the scores of students with disabilities, those who are limited-English proficient (LEP), Title I students, and other potentially low-performing students will bring overall scores down. This is exacerbated by the reliance on single scores to reflect performance of a large and diverse group of students. Thus, a school with many LEP and Title I students performing below average compared with their peers lowers the overall school score. It is easy for these students to become the focus of blame and dissent. When these students do perform well, they are rarely recognized for their efforts because there are not enough of them to bring up the scores of an overall low-performing school population.

The aggregation of scores also becomes contested when people believe that the scores of students with disabilities mean something different from those of other students. This is most likely to occur when students with disabilities use accommodations during the assessment. As we indicated previously, there are certain accommodations that most people believe change the construct being tested. The most common of these is reading the reading test to the student. When the reading test is read to the student, the construct being tested should not be decoding. However, if the purpose of the assessment is to measure reading comprehension, then reading the test to the student may be an appropriate accommodation, and thus it would be appropriate to combine that score with the scores from all other students. The point to be gained from this discussion is that it is important to bring together groups of stakeholders to discuss these issues before the test is administered and before starting to prepare reports.

The aggregation of scores from alternate assessments with those from regular assessments (with or without accommodations) also raises issues about combining scores that mean different things. Kentucky does combine and weight equally the performance of students in the regular assessment and the performance of those in the alternate assessment. It does so by basing all performance on four rubrics (novice, apprentice, proficient, and distinguished), which can be assigned to any kind of task.

What We Know About How Students With Disabilities Perform on District or State Assessments

A common perception is that students with disabilities will bring down the scores of other students if the scores are combined. We do not yet have really good data to show what the effects of the scores of students with disabilities are, but we do have some indications.

First, we know that if state-level data are examined, the scores of students with disabilities span the same range of scores as is spanned by students without disabilities. In other words, some students with disabilities score as high as those without disabilities, and some students without disabilities score as low as some students with disabilities.

Overall, taking average scores, students with disabilities tend to perform lower than students without disabilities. The effect of this lower performance is probably negligible when data are aggregated at the state level. At the district level, it probably also has a minimal effect on the performance of one district compared with another, although the effect may be greater for smaller districts. At the school level, however, particularly if schools vary in the percentage of students with disabilities attending different schools, there is likely to be some effect of aggregating the scores of students with disabilities with those of students without disabilities. This is one reason to argue that accountability should be based on looking at change over time, starting with baseline performance for schools and districts.

Given the possible influence of scores of students with disabilities on aggregate performance, it is important to think about a basis for good reporting decisions. This is the focus of the next section.

Criteria for Good Reporting Decisions

The NCEO has developed a general set of criteria that districts and states can use to evaluate their guidelines on the reporting of performance of students with disabilities in assessments. Although these guidelines are most easily applied to district and state policies, they also are relevant for educators willing to advocate for truly inclusive accountability systems. The criteria are as follows:

- A written policy exists about who is included when calculating participation or exclusion rates.

- Rates of exclusion that are specific to students with disabilities, and reasons for the exclusion, are reported when assessment results are reported.

BOX 6.3

Myth or Truth Answers

MYTH   Most states require that if a student does not participate in the assessment, the score of that student, for reporting purposes, is zero.
Explanation: Analyses of states' written guidelines indicate that states routinely exclude the scores of students with disabilities from their reports. [See page 89]

MYTH   If a student takes an assessment, that student automatically is included in average scores because of the way that test developers set up reporting programs.
Explanation: Because most places do identify students with disabilities and specifically indicate that their scores are excluded from reports, this is a myth. However, even in those places where all students are included in reporting because it is not known whether any of the students had disabilities, usually they were excluded from participation. [See page 89]

TRUTH   There are ways to integrate the scores from alternate assessments with those from regular assessments so that the two can be reported together.
Explanation: Kentucky is an example of a state that does this. It has developed a set of rubrics that can be applied to all types of performance, whether from a regular assessment or from an alternate assessment. [See page 91]

TRUTH   One reason for wanting to report the scores of students with disabilities is to produce data for program evaluation.
Explanation: If the data from students with disabilities are merged with the data from other students, there is no way to examine their performance separately. Only by looking at performance separately and, ideally, over time is it possible to evaluate the effectiveness of programs for students with disabilities. The need for program evaluation data is a good justification for reporting the scores of students with disabilities. [See page 91]

- Data reports include information from all test takers.

- Records are kept so that data for students with disabilities could be reported separately, overall, or by other breakdowns.

- Records are kept of the use of accommodations by students with disabilities, by type of accommodation, so that the information could be reported separately either by individual student or in aggregate.

- Parents are informed about the reporting policy for their child's data.

Even if your state or district does not report on students with disabilities, you should consider ways to aggregate and report this information.

Summary

In this chapter, we described several considerations related to the reporting of the performance of students with disabilities. While reporting is more of a policy-level decision, it also has a critical impact on how other policies are carried out at the local level. Understanding the importance of reflecting accountability for all students through the reporting system is extremely important.

Now, check your knowledge about the myth/truth statements presented at the beginning of this chapter (see Box 6.3 for answers). Try to give an explanation for why each statement is correctly identified either as a myth or as the truth.

Resources for Further Information

Elliott, J., Thurlow, M., & Ysseldyke, J. (1996). *Assessment guidelines that maximize the participation of students with disabilities in large-scale assessments: Characteristics and considerations* (Synthesis Rep. 25). Minneapolis: University of Minnesota, National Center on Educational Outcomes.

Erickson, R., Ysseldyke, J., & Thurlow, M. (1996). *Neglected numerators, drifting denominators, and fractured fractions: Determining participation rates for students with disabilities in statewide assessment programs* (Synthesis Rep. 23). Minneapolis: University of Minnesota, National Center on Educational Outcomes.

Erickson, R., Ysseldyke, J., Thurlow, M., & Elliott, J. (1997). *Reporting the results of students with disabilities in state and district assessments* (NCEO Policy Directions 8). Minneapolis: University of Minnesota, National Center on Educational Outcomes.

McGrew, K. S., Thurlow, M. L., & Spiegel, A. (1993). An investigation of the exclusion of students with disabilities in national data collection programs. *Educational Evaluation and Policy Analysis, 15*(3), 339-352.

Thurlow, M., Olsen, K., Elliott, J., Ysseldyke, J., Erickson, R., & Ahearn, E. (1996). *Alternate assessments for students with disabilities* (NCEO Policy Directions 5). Minneapolis: University of Minnesota, National Center on Educational Outcomes.

Thurlow, M. L., Scott, D. L., & Ysseldyke, J. E. (1995). *A compilation of states' guidelines for including students with disabilities in assessments* (Synthesis Report 17). Minneapolis: University of Minnesota, National Center on Educational Outcomes.

Ysseldyke, J., Thurlow, M., & Olsen, K. (1996). *Self-study guide for the development of statewide assessments that include students with disabilities.* Minneapolis: University of Minnesota, National Center on Educational Outcomes.

Rethinking the IEP

Topics

- ☐ Overview of the IEP
- ☐ Tools for Making Inclusive Accountability Decisions for Assessment
- ☐ Rethinking the IEP Format
- ☐ Logistics, Training, and Implementation of Accountable Decision Making

---

In this chapter, you will . . .

- learn how the IEP facilitates the participation and accommodation of students with disabilities in assessment.

- learn what role the IEP team has in this process.

- examine checklists used during the IEP process to make informed decisions about participation and accommodations for instruction and assessment.

In Chapter 5, we discussed alternate assessments needed for a small percentage of students with disabilities unable to participate in the general assessment regardless of accommodation(s) given. Even when an alternate assessment exists, the challenge is how to make informed and documented decisions about who participates in what assessment and with what accommodations. We need a systematic decision-making process that is documented on the IEP. Most IEP forms do not provide for such documentation. In this chapter, we rethink the IEP so that it becomes a useful tool and process for *accounting* for all students' learning and progress.

BOX 7.1

Myth or Truth? Do You Know?

Read each statement below and decide whether it is a myth or the truth about current practice.

- The purpose of an assessment and what it sets out to measure is a critical variable in deciding assessment accommodations for a student.
- IEP forms require the same basic information from district to district.
- Most IEP formats allow for the documentation of accommodations needed for instruction and classroom tests but not district or state tests.
- IEP team members are fully informed decision makers about the process of making assessment accommodations decisions and the assessment process itself.
- If older and able, students can be helpful in making decisions on what accommodations are needed both for instruction and assessment.

When you finish this chapter, you will be able to identify which of the statements in Box 7.1 are myths and which are the truth.

Overview of the IEP

The Individualized Education Program (IEP) is a required document for all students receiving special education services. As part of the Individuals with Disabilities Education Act (IDEA), the IEP is a planning tool that commonly is built around four major areas. These areas reflect the need for instruction and service delivery. Most school districts have their own format for the IEP, and the information contained in them varies as well. Regardless, each student's IEP must be based on the least restrictive environment (LRE). LRE decisions must be made on an individual student basis.

Four Domains of the IEP

Among other mandated parts of any IEP are statements about a student's present level of educational performance including how the child's disability affects involvement and progress in the general curriculum. Present levels of educational performance typically fall in four domains: academic, social, physical, and management (see Box 7.2). Present levels of performance, strengths, and needs for each of these domains are considered individually for each child with special needs. For example, a student may have multiple instructional needs but none

BOX 7.2

Examples of Four IEP Domains

Academic Data

1. Strengths:

__x__Reading readiness   _____Inferential comprehension   _____Numeration

_____Math application

_____Word recognition   _____Spelling   _____Math computation

_____Written expression

__x__Literal comprehension   _____Other

2. Weaknesses:

Inferential weakness, math computation, math application, written language

3. Needs/Comments:

Julie requires some reinforcement with reading comprehension, money, and time skills. The development of internal motivation and initiative are currently being addressed within the classroom setting.

Social Data

1. Relationship With Peers: Inconsistent

2. Relationship With Adults: Inconsistent

3. Self-Esteem: Moderate

4. Needs/Comments:

Julie has difficulty verbalizing her feelings and engaging in effective problem solving. She is developing a better understanding of how her actions affect social situations.

Physical Data

1. Status:

__x__Student is in good health _____Student participates in adaptive physical education

2. History/Health Factors:

__x__Visual impairment: __x__does _____does not wear corrective lenses

_____Hearing loss _____Tourette's syndrome _____Seizure disorder _____Asthma

_____ADHD _____Other

3. Needs/Comments:

Appearance and hygiene need to be monitored for appropriateness.

(Continued)

Box 7.2

Examples of Four IEP Domains (Continued)

Management Data

1. On-Task Commitment:

_____Works independently   __x__Works inconsistently
__x__Easily distracted   __x__Works best with adult supervision

2. Organizational/Time Management Skills:

_____Well organized   _____Completes required work on time
__x__Organized with teacher assistance   __x__Completes required work on time,
_____Disorganized even with assistance   with monitoring
                                            _____Generally does not complete
                                                  required work on time, even with
                                                  monitoring

3. Needs/Comments:

Julie requires reinforcement and frequent monitoring to remain on task. Self-monitoring skills to remain focused may be beneficial.

---

within the physical domain. From these statements of current levels of performance, corresponding goals and objectives are then written to reflect needed instruction. The four domains may or may not be identified as separate categories on the IEP or may be organized under different categories.

The *academic* domain deals with any academic skill that may be in need of acquisition, remediation, or compensatory skill development. Students who have a reading disability, for example, may have several goals and objectives written specifically in the area of reading. Each of these reflects the student's current instructional need.

Any need that a student has in the areas of social skills, peer relations, adult relations, independence, ability to initiate conversation, and so on are listed in the *social* domain. Again, it is important to remember that the needs under each of these areas will vary widely and that the examples given in Box 7.2 are not exhaustive.

Physical needs or medical conditions that a student might have that may have an impact on the learning and instruction process are listed in the *physical* domain. For example, a student with Chronic Fatigue Syndrome may require a change in the daily schedule to allow late arrival to or early dismissal from school. This same student may be physically unable to sit for a test or exam that exceeds 30 minutes. Another student may have allergies that have a significant impact on learning and attendance during specific times of the year, and yet another student may need to avoid certain foods.

The *management* domain includes behavioral needs and structural considerations (e.g., ability to function in small and/or large group instruction, independent work habits) that the student may require to successfully participate in the educational process. For example, a student with a visual or hearing impairment or behavioral disability may need to be seated in close proximity to the teacher or board to learn best. For some students, teachers need to ascertain what instructional formats work best to facilitate and maintain engaged learning with the least behavioral interference. This may include providing incentives, contracts, or modified assignments.

Other Mandated Components of the IEP

Among these are the amount of time (duration and frequency) a student receives special education services or related services (e.g., speech/ language therapy, counseling, physical therapy, occupational therapy), date of service initiation, and anticipated duration of the service. Although needed modifications or accommodations should be included in a student's IEP, many IEPs do not provide a specific place for these to be recorded, and in some cases they do not exist on the IEP. In most cases, there is a general reference to the types of modifications a student requires for assignments and/or tests, but these accommodations are not specifically identified for the kind of test (classroom or district/state). Box 7.3 indicates state policies about the documentation of district or state testing accommodations on student IEPs. Few states require that this documentation occur. This will change with the 1997 reauthorization of IDEA, which states that individual modifications needed for students to participate in state and districtwide assessment must be documented on the IEP. In addition, if the student will not participate in the general assessment, the IEP must indicate why the assessment is not appropriate and how the student will be assessed.

A requirement to document accommodations for classroom assessments probably does exist in some locations even though it is not noted in state guidelines. For example, participation guidelines for the state of New York do not indicate that the IEP should document testing accommodations. But we know that there are many local districts in New York that require IEP teams to document what classroom testing accommodations are needed by a student. Still, in these same districts, these IEP forms do not require documentation of accommodations needed or provided for district and state assessments.

This note of caution highlights and provides a precise example of how states and local districts are all over the map in the depth, breadth,

---

BOX 7.3

States With Testing Accommodations Stated in IEPs

State	Accommodations Listed for District or State Assessments	State	Accommodations Listed for District or State Assessments	State	Accommodations Listed for District or State Assessments
Alabama	X	Louisiana	X	Ohio	X
Alaska		Maine	X	Oklahoma	X
Arizona	X	Maryland	X	Oregon	
Arkansas		Massachusetts	X*	Pennsylvania	
California		Michigan		Rhode Island	
Colorado		Minnesota	X*	South Carolina	X
Connecticut		Mississippi	X	South Dakota	
Delaware	X	Missouri	X	Tennessee	
Florida		Montana		Texas	X
Georgia		Nebraska		Utah	
Hawaii	X	Nevada	X	Vermont	
Idaho		New Hampshire	X	Virginia	X
Illinois		New Jersey	X	Washington	
Indiana	X	New Mexico	X	West Virginia	
Iowa		New York	X	Wisconsin	X
Kansas	X	North Carolina	X*	Wyoming	
Kentucky	X	North Dakota			

*Document implies but does not specifically state that accommodations *must* be included on the IEP.

---

and clarity on how students with disabilities should be accommodated in assessment, not to mention their participation.

There are at least three kinds of tests that students take throughout their education:

- Classroom (e.g., formative and summative)
- District (e.g., achievement)
- State (e.g., graduation, exit or competency tests)

The lack of specification leads to misinterpretation, implementation, and often exclusion from assessments in which many students with disabilities can meaningfully participate, some with and some without assessment accommodations. Often, decisions to exclude or exempt students with disabilities from assessments occur because the assessments are considered "too difficult" for these students. For the most part, those making the decisions are members of the IEP team. The IEP team, in coordination with a student's parents/guardians, is responsible for making eligibility decisions for special education services and programmatic decisions, and for development of the IEP itself. Members of this team include but are not limited to the student's parent/guardian, an administrator, someone who knows the student's learning strengths and needs, school psychologist or diagnostician, and specialists (reading, math, related service personnel, school nurse, and physicians). Team membership varies from state to state, from district to district, and among schools in a district.

Tools for Making Inclusive Accountability Decisions for Assessment

Student-centered decisions about program, service, and evaluation of students with disabilities are made by the IEP team. Clearly, the charge of this team is expansive and extremely important. Who makes the decision about which student with a disability takes an alternate assessment or a regular assessment with accommodations? Who decides what, if any, assessment accommodations are needed by a student with a disability to provide that student equal footing during a testing situation? Who decides what accommodation will be helpful and technically sound? Answer: Usually the IEP team. Having the tools to build a decision-making process that is accountable for all students, including those with disabilities, is necessarily the responsibility of the IEP team.

In Chapters 2, 3, and 6, we provided you with criteria to use in making thoughtful decisions around participation, accommodation, and reporting of test results for all students, regardless of disabilities. The first two areas are within the jurisdiction of IEP teams, but reporting the test results is a broader policy issue to be determined by school district administration and the state's Department of Education.

Using the criteria presented earlier, we constructed a checklist that integrates the issues of participation and accommodation (see Box 7.4). This checklist can be used during IEP development or review. While this certainly is not the only way to make decisions, it does provide a reliable framework from which accountable assessment decisions can be made. It is important to find out what guidelines and policies already exist in your state and district regarding assessment and accommodations. Some may exist but be broadly discussed and lend little information about

BOX 7.4

Checklist of Criteria for Making Decisions About Participation and Needed Accommodations for Classroom, District, and State Assessments

Participation and Accommodation Decisions

Student Name: **Grade:**

School/Program: **Date of Meeting:**

Our goal as the IEP team of _____ school is to include all students with disabilities in district and state assessments. The decisions for participation and accommodation of _____ (student's name) are based on the following process:

Use the checklist below to guide decisions about accommodations.

The following decisions were made by person(s) who know _____'s learning needs and skills. These decisions were based on _____'s current level of functioning and learning characteristics as follows:

Yes   No

       SETTING

____ ____ 1.   Can work independently

____ ____ 1a. Can complete tasks with assistance or with the following accommodation(s):

         ___One-to-one assistance to complete written tasks

         ___On-task reminders

         ___Directions repeated and/or clarified

         ___Other _____

____ ____ 2.   Can complete tasks within a large group but quiet setting

____ ____ 2a. Can complete tasks if provided the following accommodation(s):

         ___Test administered in a separate location with minimal distractions

         ___Test administered in a small group, study carrel, or individually (circle one)

         ___Special lighting

         ___Adaptive furniture—specify _____

         ___Noise buffer (e.g., earplugs, earphones, other) _____

         ___Other _____

BOX 7.4

Checklist of Criteria for Making Decisions (Continued)

Yes   No

TIMING

____ ____ 1. Can work continuously for 20- to 30-minute periods; if not, specify the average length of time student is able to work continuously.

____ ____ 1a. Can work in a group without distracting other test takers

SCHEDULING

____ ____ 1. Can complete tasks if provided periodic breaks or other timing consideration(s)/accommodation(s):

___Test administered over several sessions, time per session not to exceed _____ minutes

___Allowed to take breaks as needed, not to exceed _____ breaks per 20- to 30-minute period

___Test administered over several days, each session not to exceed _____ minutes in duration

___Test administered in the morning, early afternoon, late afternoon (circle one)

___Extended time to complete the test in one session

___Other _____

PRESENTATION

____ ____ 1. Can listen to and follow oral directions given by an adult or on audiotape

____ ____ 1a. Can listen to and follow oral directions with assistance or the following accommodation(s):

___Visual cues or printed material to facilitate understanding of orally given directions

___Directions repeated, clarified, or simplified

___Directions read individually

___Visual magnification device

___Auditory amplification device

___Other _____

____ ____ 2. Can read and comprehend written directions

____ ____ 2a. Can comprehend written directions with assistance or the following accommodation:

___Written directions read

___Directions repeated, clarified, or simplified

___Key words or phrases in written directions highlighted

___Visual prompts (e.g., stop signs, arrows) that show directions to start, stop, and continue working

___Written directions presented in larger and/or bold print

___Written directions presented with one complete sentence per line of text

(Continued)

BOX 7.4

Checklist of Criteria for Making Decisions (Continued)

PRESENTATION (Continued)

Yes   No

___Visual magnification device
___Auditory amplification device
___Other _____

_____ _____ 3.   Can read, understand, and answer questions in multiple-choice format

_____ _____ 3a.   Can understand and answer questions in multiple-choice format with assistance or the following accommodation(s):
___Reader to read the test*
___Pencil grip
___Access to prerecorded reading
___Test signed
___Test presented in Braille or large print
___Visual magnification device
___Auditory amplification device
___Increased spacing between items and/or limited items presented per page
___Templates or masks to reduce visible print
___Papers secured to desk (e.g., magnets, tape)
___Other _____

RESPONSE

_____ _____ 1.   Can use paper and pen/pencil to write short answer or paragraph-length responses to open-ended questions

_____ _____ 1a.   Can respond to open-ended questions when provided assistance or the following accommodation(s):
___Pencil grip
___Word processor
___Scribe (someone to record verbatim oral responses to questions)
___Brailler
___Copy assistance between drafts of writing
___Write an outline to a question and, using a tape recorder, dictate the body of the response, per the written outline
___Dictate answer into a tape recorder
___Visual magnification devices
___Touch Talker or other communication device
___Calculator*
___Abacus
___Arithmetic tables*
___Spell checker or spelling dictionary*
___Other _____

BOX 7.4

Checklist of Criteria for Making Decisions (Continued)

RESPONSE (Continued)

Yes   No

____ ____ 2.   Can use pencil to fill in bubble answer sheets

____ ____ 2a.   Can use pencil to fill in bubble answer sheets with assistance or the
following accommodation(s):

___Pencil grip

___Bubbles enlarged

___Bubbles presented on the test itself next to each question

___Bubbles enlarged and presented on the test itself next to each
question

___Scribe

___Calculator*

___Abacus

___Arithmetic tables*

___Spell checker or spelling dictionary*

___Other _____

Use the following section to guide decisions about participation in assessments.

LEVEL OF PARTICIPATION

____ ____ 1.   _____'s current level of skill and noted accommodations allow
him/her to meaningfully participate in all/part (circle one) of the
following assessments:

___Classroom

___District—specify which one(s)

___State/national—specify which one(s)

If partial participation is considered more appropriate, specify which part of the
assessment. The decision for partial participation on the assessment is based on the
following:

____ ____ 2.   _____ is incapable of meaningfully participating in the _____
assessment, regardless of accommodation. This decision is based on
the following:

(Continued)

BOX 7.4

Checklist of Criteria for Making Decisions (Continued)

____ ____ 3.   Consideration has been given to how _____'s learning will be
                assessed. A different or alternate assessment of learning will be
                conducted as follows:

____ ____ 4.   The consequences of exclusion and/or use of accommodations
                (if applicable) have been discussed with _____'s parent/guardian.

____ ____ 5.   Proactive planning is under way to provide _____ the opportunity to
                meaningfully participate in the assessment cycle (either entire or partial)
                next year as follows (specify who is involved in the planning process):

____ ____ 6.   _____'s parent/guardian is fully aware of these participation and
                accommodation decisions and has been a part of the process. Explain,
                if necessary.

Your signature on this form indicates that you were a part of the participation and
accommodation decision-making process for _____. You are in agreement with the
decisions.

_____   _____   _____
IEP Team Chair   Building Administrator   Student

_____   _____   _____
Parent/Guardian   Student's Teacher(s)   Others

_____   _____
Assessment Coordinator   Director of Special Education

Date of Meeting: _____

*Careful consideration must be given to the purpose of the test for which these accommo-
 dations are provided.

BOX 7.5

**Example of a Checklist for the
Participation Decision-Making Process**

Checklist for Deciding Assessment Type

Name: **School Year:**

School: **Special Education Teacher:**

Grade: **Date:**

The purpose of this checklist is to facilitate and justify what district or state assessment program _____ will be a part of. Three options are being considered: regular (or the name of the district/state assessment), alternate, or both (regular/alternate) assessments. The final decision must be justified and validated by several parties including, but not limited to _____ (student, if deemed appropriate), parent/guardian, special and general education teachers, and involved related personnel.

On _____ (date), the IEP team, after much discussion and consideration, has decided that _____ is a candidate for:

_____ 1.   Regular assessment (or the name of the district/state assessment)
           ____ a. Without accommodation
           ____ b. With the following accommodation(s):

_____ 2.   Alternate assessment (student is not working toward diploma)*

_____ 3.   Regular/Alternate.* List the content areas _____

*This decision is based on the following (list any and all factors that led to the above decision—be specific):

(Continued)

---

how building-level IEP teams are to operationalize them into day-to-day practice. The purpose of this and other checklists included in this book is to promote the participation of students with disabilities in assessment and accountability systems.

BOX 7.5

**Example of a Checklist for the
Participation Decision-Making Process (Continued)**

While this decision was made based on the above factors, we recognize that the decision is not a permanent one and may change, if warranted and appropriate, at another scheduled IEP meeting.

Parent/Guardian _____   Other _____

Administrator _____

IEP Chair _____

Special Educator _____

General Educator _____

Related Service Providers: _____

_____

_____

The tool for the participation decision-making process makes clear the thoughtful consideration needed for assessment decisions. Box 7.5 provides a form to guide your decision about which assessment a student takes. Each decision is an extensive one and may need to be tailored to the type and kind of assessment administered. As you make the participation decision, you should also be considering the accommodations that the student needs.

For some students, decisions about what assessment they will take can be made as early as elementary school. Those students with more significant cognitive disabilities will need an alternate assessment, which better reflects the individualized goals, objectives, and curriculum they are learning. We recognize that not all decisions are clearcut. If you are unsure of the academic path a student will take, regardless of age, have the student participate in the regular assessment with needed accommodations.

Where appropriate, include older, able students in these discussions. Such students need to be aware that these types of decisions are being made and should participate in them, for they can provide valuable input to the process. It is important to keep in mind that as these students move from the K-12 education system and into postsecondary settings they will be in charge of these kinds of decisions.

Rethinking the IEP Format

It is time to rethink the content and structure of the IEP. We know that the mandated parts of the IEP will remain intact. Additional areas are needed, however, to document assessment decisions about participation and accommodation on tests and to document accommodations needed during instruction. The key is to align accommodations provided during the instructional process with those needed for classroom, district, and state assessment. As discussed earlier in this chapter, not all accommodations provided during instruction are appropriate during an assessment process. However, some types of assessments—for example, performance tests—are more amenable to a wider range of accommodations. Again, consideration must be given to the purpose and goal of the assessment.

In Box 7.6, we identify those states suggesting that accommodations used on state assessments be consistent with those used in the classroom. This does not necessarily mean, however, that the accommodations are documented on a student's IEP in these states.

Additional IEP Components

At minimum, two sections must be added to IEPs for each assessment: instructional accommodations and testing accommodations. The formats will vary.

One possible IEP format would require that the IEP team create its own list of the student's needed instructional accommodations (see Box 7.7). Another possible format would provide a checklist of allowed instructional accommodations (see Box 7.8). In this format, it is important to provide an "Other" option as students' needs vary. This option allows for the provision of an accommodation that may not be listed on the checklist. Instructional accommodations may vary according to content area of instruction. Some students may require accommodations for one area but not for another. Regardless of format, the emphasis is on thinking about what is needed by individual students to actively participate in the instructional process and show what they know.

Teachers instruct many different students each day. Most have different individual needs, some more substantial than others. However, there are those students who, without instructional accommodations,

BOX 7.6

Making the Instruction to Assessment Accommodation Link:
The Instruction to Assessment Flow

State	Accommodations Include Those Used in Classroom Instruction	State	Accommodations Include Those Used in Classroom Instruction
Alabama	X	Montana	
Alaska		Nebraska	
Arizona		Nevada	
Arkansas		New Hampshire	X
California		New Jersey	
Colorado		New Mexico	
Connecticut		New York	
Delaware	X	North Carolina	
Florida		North Dakota	
Georgia	X	Ohio	X
Hawaii		Oklahoma	
Idaho		Oregon	
Illinois	X	Pennsylvania	
Indiana	X	Rhode Island	
Iowa		South Carolina	
Kansas		South Dakota	
Kentucky	X	Tennessee	
Louisiana	X	Texas	
Maine	X	Utah	
Maryland	X	Vermont	
Massachusetts		Virginia	X
Michigan		Washington	
Minnesota		West Virginia	
Mississippi	X	Wisconsin	X
Missouri		Wyoming	

BOX 7.7

Example of a Format in Which the IEP Team Creates Accommodations

IEP Form for Identifying Accommodations

Name: Grade: School/Teacher:

Date:

Instructional Accommodations:

List the accommodations needed for general instruction.

List instructional accommodations needed for each applicable content area.

---

will not learn or be able to participate fully in instruction. By documenting the instructional accommodations a student with special needs requires, teachers are kept informed of what needs to be done to include all students in the education process.

The examples in Boxes 7.7 and 7.8 are not meant to be exhaustive. Rather, they are a starting point for developing additional components of the IEP. These kinds of formats are necessary for inclusive accountability and assessment, not to mention good individualized instruction. The case study presented in Box 7.9 gives you some practice in generating instructional and assessment accommodations for an individual student.

Logistics, Training, and Implementation of Accountable Decision Making

Clearly, much learning, information exchange, and dissemination must take place among teachers, parents, administrators, students, and community members. Training IEP team members is a logical place to start. Do not assume that IEP teams understand inclusive assessment,

BOX 7.8

Example of an Instructional Accommodation Format to Add to the IEP

IEP Form for Identifying Accommodations

Name: **Grade:**   **Date:**

Use the following checklist to guide decisions about what instructional accommodations are needed by this student.

Instructional Accommodation Checklist:

Setting
____Distraction-free space within classroom (e.g., doorway, windows, other students, front of class, back of class)
____One-to-one assistance to complete written tasks
____On-task reminders
____Several verbal prompts to initiate a task
____Verbal encouragement, praise, or recognition to continue a task
____Directions repeated and/or clarified
____Small group or partner instruction, especially when learning or practicing new facts, concepts, and strategies
____Adaptive furniture
____Other _____

Timing
____Periodic breaks during work sessions (specify)
____Other _____

Scheduling
____Extended time to complete class/homework assignments
____Length of assignments shortened to complete as overnight homework assignments
____A daily assignment sheet
____A weekly quick strategic assignment meeting
____A weekly or monthly assignment calendar
____A weekly or monthly assignment calendar with check-in and due dates posted

Presentation
____Visual cues or printed material to facilitate understanding of orally given directions
____Directions repeated, clarified, or simplified
____Directions read individually
____Visual magnification device
____Auditory amplification device
____Written directions read
____Key words or phrases in written directions highlighted

BOX 7.8

Example of an Instructional Accommodation Format to Add to the IEP (Continued)

____ Visual prompts (e.g., stop signs, arrows) that show directions to start, stop, and continue working

____ Written directions presented in larger and/or bold print

____ Written directions presented with one complete sentence per line of text

____ Reader to read the text

____ Pencil grip

____ Access to a prerecorded reading

____ Test presented in sign language

____ Written information presented in Braille or large print

____ Increased spacing between items and/or limited items presented per page

____ Templates or masks to reduce visible print

____ Papers secured to desk (e.g., magnets, tape)

____ Calculator*

____ Abacus

____ Arithmetic tables*

____ Spell checker or spelling dictionary*

____ Manipulatives

____ Other _____

Response

____ Text-talker converter

____ Speech synthesizer

____ Pencil grip

____ Word processor

____ Scribe (someone to record verbatim oral responses to questions)

____ Brailler

____ Copying assistance between drafts of writing

____ Option to write an outline to a question and, using a tape recorder, dictate the body of the response, per the written outline

____ Option to dictate answer into a tape recorder

____ Visual magnification device

____ Touch Talker or other communication device

(Continued)

BOX 7.8

**Example of an Instructional Accommodation Format to Add to the IEP
(Continued)**

____ Calculator*
____ Abacus
____ Arithmetic tables*
____ Spell checker or spelling dictionary*
____ Other _____

*Based on the purpose of the assignment and what and how the skill(s) will be assessed.

Additional Instructional Accommodations Needed for Specific Content Areas

List content area and any additional instructional accommodations needed.

---

accountability, and issues for students with disabilities. The inclusion of students with disabilities in assessments at the school, district, and state levels requires a shift in thinking for all those involved in the IEP process. Consideration must be given to the purpose of the assessment or what it is trying to measure. Decisions to provide accommodations must be made while keeping the purpose of the assessment in mind. To avoid making accommodation decisions that could invalidate the test results, IEP teams must be able to answer some tough questions:

- What is the test measuring? Do some subtests measure different skills? For example, a reading test will test different skills in different subtests.

- What accommodations do students need in order to meaningfully participate and show what they know without the impediment of disability?

- Of the needed accommodations, which, if any, directly challenge what the test is attempting to measure?

- How will these same skills be measured validly if needed accommodations invalidate the test?

BOX 7.9

Case Study to Practice Generating Instructional and Assessment Accommodations

Student: Ima Tryun

Ima Tryun is an eighth grader who was retained in first grade. Ima has been identified as a student with a learning disability in the area of written communication/basic reading skills. Ima attends school regularly. Ima has an integrated special/regular instruction schedule. He receives resource room services and in-class support for mathematics. Science and social studies are taken in the general education classroom.

Ima reads on a third-grade level. His writing is hampered by his inability to spell. He has wonderful ideas and communicates them well. With the use of a tape recorder, Ima is able to record his ideas. His writing skills are improving with his reading skills. Ima shows excellent auditory comprehension, and his attention to task is above average. He actively participates in class activities and discussions.

Ima exhibits low self-esteem toward school. However, he will ask for and accept help from teachers. Ima is well accepted by his peers and is "looked up to" within the school context.

Instructional Accommodations

Using the above information, suggest instructional accommodations for Ima.

Assessment Accommodations

Now that you have identified possible instructional accommodations, suggest accommodations that would be needed for assessment.

Setting: **Presentation:**

Timing: **Response:**

Scheduling: **Other (specify):**

BOX 7.10

Try Your Skill:
Roberta's Case

Roberta is currently a seventh grader who has a significant reading disability. When provided a reader or someone to read and/or clarify written text, Roberta is able to complete work on assignments in an exemplary fashion. Throughout this year and next, Roberta will continue to receive accommodations during instruction and on classroom tests. A reader, usually her resource room teacher, will be provided for Roberta.

Next year, Roberta will be required to take and pass the eighth-grade benchmark reading test, which purports to measure decoding, comprehension, and ability to answer literal and inferential questions on the passages.

It is annual review time, and the IEP team is faced with the decision of making participation and accommodation decisions for Roberta's eighth-grade year, including the benchmark test. What should the IEP team do regarding the benchmark reading test? Should Roberta participate? If so, with what accommodations? If not, why not?

How skillfully you make decisions is an important part of accountable decision making. Try your skills on the example provided in Box 7.10 and then see Box 7.11 for an example of a supportable decision and an explanation of it.

Another shift is that needed by teachers. Providing students with instructional and assessment accommodations within the classroom may conflict with beliefs about what is fair and what will be required of students in society. The role of the IEP team is to embrace the practice of inclusive accountability and assessment and then disseminate and exchange information to parents and other staff. Chapter 9 provides an overview of what should be considered when designing a faculty meeting or staff development session on inclusive assessment and accountability systems.

Summary

In this chapter, we provided you with several resources for making decisions about participation and accommodations. We have provided frameworks to guide IEP team decisions for participation and accommodation, as well as examples of components to add to the IEP. The need to align instructional practices and accommodations with what a student

---

BOX 7.11

Decision and Explanation for Roberta's Case

Roberta should continue to receive reading accommodations during instruction and on classroom tests. The issue of the eighth-grade benchmark test is a more difficult decision. There should be a natural flow between what accommodations Roberta is receiving during instruction and what she is provided on tests. However, it appears that having a reader for the benchmark test may invalidate the test because decoding seems to be part of the skills measured.

More information is needed about the test. Often, reading tests measure different reading skills. Therefore, it may be that a reader could be provided for some parts of the test but not others. In addition, consideration needs to be given to the type of diploma Roberta is targeted for and the curriculum she is learning. Clearly, if she is on the same academic path as other students, she should participate in the benchmark test.

If in fact the entire test is attempting to measure Roberta's reading ability—both decoding and comprehension—then a decision about her participation must be made.

We believe it is better to include Roberta in the test with needed accommodations than to exclude her and have no data at all. If in fact the test results could be invalidated by the needed accommodations, it is the charge of the IEP team to decide on an alternate means of assessing the same skills, perhaps using a different or alternate test. Certainly, Roberta's scores may need to be disaggregated from the scores of other students to avoid introducing an inaccurate representation of results. In this case, the issue really becomes one of reporting.

---

is required to know and show on a test is of great importance and falls into the roles and responsibilities of the IEP team.

Now, check your knowledge about the myth/truth statements presented at the beginning of this chapter (see Box 7.12 for answers). Try to give an explanation for why each statement is correctly identified either as a myth or as the truth.

Resources for Further Information

Bateman, B. (1996). *Better IEPs: How to develop legally correct and educationally useful programs* (2nd ed.). Longmont, CO: Sopris West.

Parent Advocate Coalition for Educational Rights. (1995a). *Tips on attending a staff conference on the Individual Education Program.* Minneapolis, MN: PACER Center.

BOX 7.12

Myth or Truth Answers

TRUTH The purpose of an assessment and what it sets out to measure is a critical variable in deciding assessment accommodations for a student.
Explanation: To provide assessment accommodations that do not invalidate what the test is attempting to measure, it is critical to know what the test purports to measure. [See pages 111-114]

MYTH IEP forms require the same basic information from district to district.
Explanation: There are fundamental components that, by law, must be on all IEPs. However, over and above the mandated IEP components, both the format and the information vary tremendously. [See pages 96-101]

MYTH Most IEP formats allow for the documentation of accommodations needed for instruction and classroom tests but not district or state tests.
Explanation: IEP formats are all over the map. Most do not necessarily provide for the documentation of instructional accommodations, much less those for classroom assessment. [See pages 99-101]

MYTH IEP team members are fully informed decision makers about the process of making assessment accommodations decisions and the assessment process itself.
Explanation: To date, the primary responsibilities of IEP teams have been to make eligibility and programming decisions for special education students. [See page 99; also pages 111-114]

TRUTH If older and able, students can be helpful in making decisions on what accommodations are needed both for instruction and assessment.
Explanation: It is always good practice to involve students when they are able to participate in their educational program. [See pages 108-109]

Parent Advocate Coalition for Educational Rights. (1995b). *What makes a good Individual Education Program?* Minneapolis, MN: PACER Center

Parent Advocate Coalition for Educational Rights. (1996). *A guide for parents to the Individual Education Program.* Minneapolis, MN: PACER Center.

Collaboration for Success in Testing Students With Disabilities

In this chapter, you will . . .

- know the roles of general and special education teachers.
- know the roles of the paraeducator and related service providers.
- learn how to plan for the alignment and flow of instructional accommodations to assessment accommodations.
- learn how to plan for the logistics of implementing assessments for students with disabilities who need accommodations.
- know how to prepare students for different types of assessments.

In Chapter 7, the IEP and the role of the IEP team were examined. The need to rethink and revise the IEP to include information about participation in assessments and accommodations, in both

---

BOX 8.1

Myth or Truth? Do You Know?

Read each statement below and decide whether it is a myth or the truth about current practice.

- There should be a link between accommodations provided during instruction and those provided for classroom and district/state assessments.
- Special education teachers are in the best position to make decisions about what accommodations students with disabilities need.
- Paraprofessionals can be key players in the logistical planning and delivering instructional and assessment accommodations.
- Related services personnel (e.g., occupational and physical therapists, speech/language pathologists) can provide insight into what, if any, instruction/assessment accommodations are needed by a student they are delivering service to.
- In some places, all students are eligible for assessment accommodations.
- Students need to be taught test-taking skills for an assessment (e.g., format of test, time limits, directions).

---

instruction and assessment, is warranted. The IEP is the vehicle that affords students with disabilities a cohesive and consistent opportunity to learn and show what they know without being impeded by their disability.

In this chapter, we discuss how school personnel can collaborate in assessing students with disabilities, from making decisions about the type of assessment these students take to determining the accommodations needed. We also look at the roles of general and special educators and paraprofessional involvement and assistance. There are many factors involved in the assessment of all students, including those with disabilities. However, as discussed elsewhere in this book, students with disabilities have been excluded or left out of assessment and accountability systems in school buildings, school districts, and states. In this chapter we examine the planning and collaboration that need to take place among educators for schools, districts, and states to be accountable for all students enrolled in schools. When you finish this chapter, you will be able to identify which of the statements in Box 8.1 are myths and which are the truth.

Instructional and Assessment Accommodations

It is important to consider the alignment of accommodations used during instruction with those provided during assessment when preparing students for assessments (see Chapter 4). There should be a flow from instructional accommodations to assessment accommodations. While we recognize that some accommodations delivered during instruction will not be appropriate for assessment, it is important to identify those accommodations that students need to show what they know without being impaired by their disabilities. Many different types of school personnel need to contribute to this shift from the classroom to the assessment. Often, classroom teachers are in the best position to help do this because they work with students on a daily basis. For this reason, classroom teachers and other personnel need to understand why it is important that students with disabilities participate in district and state assessments. They also need to understand accommodations and their appropriateness.

The IEP team and administration play a big role in helping facilitate the necessary shift in thinking. For some people, it is the lack of information about the definition of inclusive accountability and assessment that creates resistance. It is important that all staff members have information on the reasons why students should be provided with accommodations during classroom, district, and state assessments. Providing a guideline or list of questions to ask in determining the need for accommodations, as well as a list of possible accommodations for individual students, will help (see Chapters 3 and 4 for questions and possible accommodations).

The process of providing instructional and assessment accommodations is a top-down, bottom-up process. Policy or guidance is set at the state and district level, which in turn is implemented at the local school level by teachers and administrators. Teachers and other staff members are key to this process. The roles of all team players cannot be underestimated.

Roles and Responsibilities

Role of the General Education Classroom Teacher

Depending on the service needs of a student with a disability, a general education classroom teacher may see a student with special needs more than the special educator does. For example, if a student is in need of resource room services one time per day, the remainder of the day is spent in general education classes and, depending on the grade level, with one or several general education teachers. In the same manner, if the student is mainstreamed for a few classes or is in a self-contained special education program, the special education teacher is in a better position to help make assessment and accommodation decisions. Finally, inclusive schooling is the option that affords students an education in the least restrictive environment for the entire day. This means that students with a variety and range of disabilities receive all their education while in the general education setting. Some services may be in the general education curriculum, and others will be tailored to the students' needs and IEPs and delivered in the general education setting. In this case, both the general and special education teachers are in the best position collaboratively to coordinate decisions about inclusive assessment and the accommodations these students will need to maintain an equal footing with peers without disabilities.

Even if students are mainstreamed for only a few classes, we recommend that teachers who teach students with special needs be involved in discussions on assessment and accommodations. After all, we are talking about our students—not yours, theirs, his, hers, or mine. Together with the special education teacher, the general educator can identify the needs of each special-needs student in the class. Together, the teachers can explore what instructional provisions or accommodations need to be considered, how they can be provided, and what assistance is necessary. Finally, teachers can examine how instructional accommodations naturally flow into the classroom assessments and district and state assessments.

Role of the Special Education Teacher

The role of the special education teacher is wide and varied. Depending on job responsibilities (e.g., resource room, self-contained, or consultant teacher), contact and collaboration with students and general education teachers will vary. The primary responsibility of a special education teacher is to make sure that students in special education are educated in the least restrictive environment (LRE) and are provided the instructional and behavior supports to achieve success. Special education is a service, not a place, and this fact has opened the doors for students with disabilities to participate in general education classes and activities.

Special education teachers are in the best position to support general education teachers and collaboratively plan for special education students' instruction, behavior management, and assessment. Although the focus of most of this book is on district and state assessments, collaboration really begins at the classroom level. Classroom teachers, especially special education teachers, are in the position to interpret a student's IEP and what it means in terms of classroom instruction. It is not uncommon to hear from general education teachers that "I have seven resource room students in my fifth-period class." Often, they may not know the needs or the IEP goals of these students or that they have mild disabilities, so mild in fact that they only require a 45-minute period of support once per day. (The time period and frequency may vary from student to student.) Best practice dictates that both general and special education teachers who share instructional responsibilities for the same students communicate to be sure that goals are being met with necessary supports and needed supplemental services.

Another role of a special education teacher is to advocate for special education students. At the classroom level, special educators must talk with general education teachers about the needs of enrolled students and the accommodations that may be needed to afford them success in class during both instruction and assessment. Here again is where the "fair argument" may be raised. For example, how often have you heard "Why should Betty get extended time limits when José could also use them but he does not have an IEP?" This argument is a valid one. Some states are addressing this by providing accommodation to any student who needs it both in instruction and in assessment. There are English-language learners, Section 504 students, and others who need accommodations. Yet, until now, the only students eligible for accommodations, by law, have been students with disabilities. Recently, some states have opened accommodations up to all students, at least for their performance assessments. It is important that special educators communicate the purpose of need versus benefit to those who raise the fairness argument. At the same time, this is a policy issue that needs to be dealt with at both the state and district levels.

Role of the Paraeducator

There are approximately 500,000 instructional paraeducators or paraprofessionals working in public schools across the country (Pickett, 1996). The recent surge of paraeducators can be attributed to several factors—ongoing collaborative efforts to integrate special-needs students into the general education system, the increasing enrollment of second-language learners or students with limited English, expanding remedial programs (e.g., Title I), and the increasing demands placed on the classroom teacher (e.g., site-based team involvement, co-teaching, collaboration).

The role of the paraeducator in the education and assessment of students with disabilities is important. Paraeducators are in fact school employees who either work in an instructional role or deliver direct service to students and/or their parents. They work under the supervision of teachers or other school personnel who have the ultimate responsibility for designing, implementing, and evaluating education programs and related service programs for students. Paraeducators are valuable to both general and special education teachers faced with the charge of delivering quality instruction to diverse student populations and the evaluation thereof. In the arena of instruction and assessment, the word *diverse* brings to mind the need for additional hands and help in the classroom.

BOX 8.2

Test Accommodation Planning Chart for Upcoming Tests

Test Accommodation Planning Chart					
Student Name	Class/ Teacher	Test Format	Needed Accommodation or Modification	Test Date	Actions

---

Once general and special educators have met to discuss the instructional needs, strengths, and accommodations necessary to allow students to be successful both in instruction and assessment, paraeducators are in the position to help carry out the plan of implementation. They may serve as supervisors of students taking tests, read the test to students, and/or modify or rework a classroom test. For example, some students simply need fewer problems or items per page, directions reworded, or the test given and supervised in a separate location. Paraeducators, under the supervision of a teacher, are fully capable of taking on these tasks. They also can be given the responsibility for organizing and supervising test administration. For example, every time a math test or quiz is scheduled, the paraprofessional knows what to modify and/or what accommodations specific students require.

Using a chart like that in Box 8.2, paraeducators can meet with teachers to learn the dates of class tests and testing formats and then accommodate or modify the tests for individual students. This, of course, is done in collaboration with, and under the supervision of, the classroom teacher. No test should be accommodated or modified until all parties are aware of each student's needs and strengths.

We recognize that not all schools are able to provide paraeducators for special needs children. In these cases, it becomes even more important for general and special education teachers to team up to plan and pool energies and resources.

Role of Related Service Providers

Related service providers are speech pathologists; school psychologists (counselors); occupational, physical, and art therapists; and social workers. Any or all of these related service personnel may be working with students with disabilities at one time or another. It is important to gather input from these personnel as well as from classroom teachers before making assessment and accommodation decisions. Each of these providers works with students for specific purposes, but all are working toward teaching the skills a student needs to be successful in his or her educational program and daily life. Related service providers can lend a different perspective and add information needed to make decisions about what accommodations could be used.

For example, a student with cerebral palsy may have physical and communication needs that can be addressed best by the physical therapist and speech pathologist who deliver direct services to the student. These related services personnel are in the position to suggest those assessment accommodations that are reasonable and functional, given the student's disability. Remember, a student with cerebral palsy may be quite capable of taking the traditional district or state assessment with accommodations. Alternate or partial assessment options may not be appropriate. The school psychologist may be in the position to help proactively plan for students with behavior disabilities. Often, these students receive counseling by a school psychologist. Together with teachers, the testing situation and potential reactionary behavior can be contained.

Coordination Among Service Providers

The need to coordinate all the team players for making decisions about any student is no small task. Scheduling meetings where all can attend is a major accomplishment, especially when many personnel travel and provide services in several sites. In many cases, each student with a disability has a lead special education teacher or a case coordinator who is responsible for the student's day-to-day and overall management. Typically, the responsibility of this teacher is to take the lead in communicating with all instructional teachers.

It is important that instructional teachers know a student's strengths and needs. Also, discussion about the need to identify or implement already identified accommodations must occur at the start of a new school year and enrolled class. Gathering input from all players, including service providers, can be simplified by using documentation forms. These can be placed in service provider mailboxes. When returned, input can be summarized and follow-up planned, if needed. The key is to gather as much information as necessary to determine that decisions to provide instructional accommodations are warranted. Once instructional accommodations are in place, continue the discussion for assessment accommodations. What does the student need to be able to show what he or she knows? What currently provided instructional accommodations need to flow to the assessment, and which do not? And, in the bigger picture, of those classroom assessment accommodations provided, which will be applicable to the district or state assessment? The worksheet in Box 8.3 is useful for identifying instructional and assessment accommodations for content area classes.

The process of identifying instructional accommodations, classroom assessment accommodations, and district/state accommodations is both important and necessary. It opens up communication among all service providers. It allows a student's strengths and needs to be known. It sets the tone for accommodations based on need and observation of classroom performance rather than on some committee (IEP team) handing down a decision.

We recognize that this process may not necessarily make the acceptance of providing accommodations to students with disabilities easier. However, we do know that the more people know, and the more they are involved in the process, the more likely they are to have a stake in it.

The Planning Process

In this section, we discuss the many facets of collaborative planning for the logistics of assessment at both the classroom and district levels. We provide you with variables and issues to consider and questions to ask.

Where to Start?

The range and severity of disabilities are vast. For example, you may know a student with disabilities who requires extra time to complete assignments due to a writing deficit (dysgraphia), another one who requires modifications in spelling or accommodations for math calculations, and still another student who is more physically involved and unable to hold a writing tool or one who requires a communication device. Students with behavior or emotional disabilities also present challenges. They may exhibit behaviors that promote their removal from a setting, often because they do not want to be there or take part in a particular activity or task. Medically fragile students or students with head

BOX 8.3

Worksheet for Identifying Instructional and Assessment Accommodations

Instructional and Assessment Accommodations Worksheet

Student:

Grade:

Teacher/Class:

Class/Content Area:

Service Provider:

Student's Strengths	Student's Needs

Based on student need, identify and list below the instructional accommodations that will be provided. Then list which of these naturally flow to classroom tests. Mark (**) those test accommodations that apply to the district/state assessment.

Instructional Accommodation(s)	Classroom Test Accommodation(s)

Comments:

injuries and visual and hearing impairments also present unique needs. Our point is that all students with disabilities are a part of our education system. They have, for the most part, been in our schools, whether segregated or integrated. Until now, unlike the situation for general education students, little interest or investment has been directed toward monitoring the learning, achievement, and progress of students with disabilities. With all the changes accompanying standards, accountability, and the "all students can learn" edict, it is time to put this familiar rhetoric into practice. For most states and schools, this means examining the current assessment and accountability systems.

Knowing the Purpose of Your District and State Assessment

Find out exactly the purpose of your district or state assessment. If students must take a reading test, find out what skills are measured on the test. For example, is the purpose of the reading assessment to find out how well students can read or decode words, comprehend what they read, or interpret the meaning of written language? The answer to this question will influence the kinds of accommodations that could be used and those that should be avoided to preserve the integrity of what the test is supposed to measure. For example, if the goal of a math assessment is to find out a student's ability to problem solve and apply algorithms and formulas, the use of a calculator is appropriate. The assessment goal in this example is the application of skills, not merely the ability to perform basic calculations. If the purpose of a writing assessment is to have students compose a piece of writing around a theme, then dictating thoughts to a scribe or a tape recorder for later transcription would also be appropriate.

Although we advocate strongly that assessment accommodations be provided on the basis of need, we know that in some cases the use of an accommodation may raise questions about the validity of assessment results. For example, the accommodation may interfere with the skills or constructs the test purports to measure. Perhaps the most controversial accommodation is reading a reading test to a student. If the test is measuring a student's reading comprehension, this accommodation would change what is being measured. However, if the reading test is measuring a student's ability to comprehend written language, then a reader for the test may indeed be appropriate. It is absolutely imperative that the purpose of the test be known. Decisions to provide reasonable accommodations that do not invalidate what the test is measuring cannot be made without this information.

The worksheet in Box 8.4 is useful for identifying reasonable accommodations specifically for your district or state assessment.

BOX 8.4

**Worksheet for Identifying District or
State Assessment Accommodations**

District/State Assessment Accommodations Worksheet

Use this worksheet to identify the skills measured on specific tests. Based on this information, identify reasonable accommodations that need to be provided. Keep in mind that these accommodations should be taken/recommended from those being currently provided during instruction.

Student:

Grade:

Date:

Test	**Skill(s) Measured**	**Reasonable Accommodation***

Comments/Further Action Needed:

*Will not invalidate the purpose of the test or the skill being measured.

Completed by:

Making Your Needs Known

Make requests of your district assessment personnel or administration to provide teachers, IEP teams, and any other persons involved in making these kinds of decisions with information about the assessments that are to be administered to all students. Often, students are excluded because surface decisions are made in reference to a required test. On the surface, the test appears too difficult for a particular student.

For example, José can't take the reading test because he is a poor reader. You must ask and answer the following questions: What is the purpose of the test? Could José take the test if provided an appropriate accommodation? Be careful. Often, not enough information is known about the purpose of assessment and/or assessment accommodations by everyone involved in the decision-making process. Some argue that any accommodation will invalidate test scores if these same accommodations were not used in the standardization or norming procedures. As pointed out in Chapter 4, little research currently exists on the impact of assessment accommodations and test results. When in doubt, include and accommodate students. For these and many other reasons, you, the IEP team, and your district must be prepared to educate those you work with on the purpose of specific assessments, accommodations, and inclusive accountability systems.

Deciding Who Takes What Test
With What Accommodation

Once you have secured all the necessary information about the purpose of the assessment, reasonable accommodations, needed test-taking skills, and any other details, it is time to decide which students take what test. Students receiving resource room and consulting services and working toward a diploma should automatically take the regular district or state test. Students not working toward a diploma require other considerations. Among these are how learning will be assessed and what assessment format is used (see Chapter 5). In Chapter 7, we provided checklists to guide these decisions. The answers to these questions need to be discussed and reviewed with teachers, parents, and IEP members.

Talking to Students

It is important to discuss with students the district- or state-level assessment well in advance of its administration. These discussions will vary in depth and breadth depending on students' cognitive, developmental, and chronological ages. Such discussions should occur with all students, but they are particularly important for students with disabilities. These can take place within the regular classroom as part of the larger class and/or independently to discuss any concerns about participation, expectation, and preparation.

It is important to work with older students so that they can begin to identify their own needs related to assessments. When they enter post-secondary training institutions or employment situations, they will need to take care of their own needs for participation in assessments and to advocate for themselves needed accommodations (see Chapter 3).

Discussing Recommended Accommodations

Students should be aware of accommodations recommended by the IEP team and the reasons for their selection. We have seen assessment situations in which accommodations provided to students were not used. For example, students often are provided extended time as an accommodation. Yet when they are sitting in a large group, say 50 students, they almost never make use of the extra time they are allowed. When asked, some students say it is because they do not need the extra time. Others indicate that they are embarrassed to continue working when all their classmates and friends have left the testing situation. In the latter case, unintended peer pressure affects students' motivation to show what they know. It is not difficult to understand this student behavior. However, if indeed extended time is an accommodation that the student needs to complete an assessment and there is hesitation about using it, this is the time to discuss it. Most students do not want to be different from their peers. However, each student has a different interpretation of what makes him or her appear different. By talking about each accommodation and its purpose and use, it is possible to identify ways to adjust the accommodation for students. For example, arrangements might be made for the student to take the assessment in a different setting.

Discussing Student-Desired Accommodations

Age and developmental level are key to the issue of student-desired accommodations. Students should be fairly knowledgeable about their own accommodations needs. This is more likely to be the case if they have been included in discussions about accommodations throughout their school careers. To guide these discussions, it may be wise to use a set of questions (see Chapter 3, Box 3.4). You may find that some students, usually older students, avoid using accommodations at all costs even though the IEP team has appropriately identified one (or more). These cases take more discussion. It is important to include or enlist parental support, if possible, in such cases. The role of a parent/guardian is an important one (see Chapter 10). Parents may help point out to their child what accommodations they see around the home (e.g., how they interact, carry out household tasks, and complete their homework).

Students may automatically accommodate themselves and be unaware of it. Of course, the ideal time to have this discussion is during the IEP conference.

Identifying Needed Student Preparation for Participation in Assessment

A student may not be prepared to take an assessment even though the decision has been made that the student is able and should participate. Given the history of excluding students with disabilities from assessments, it is likely that not enough thought or planning has been given to preparing these students to participate in testing. There are three things to keep in mind when talking with all students, including those with disabilities, in preparation for the assessment experience:

Tailor the conversation to the student's age, skills, and past testing experiences. Students will need to know why they are taking the assessment, the purpose of the assessment, and its importance.

Describe the test. Regardless of the student's background experiences, it is a good idea to describe the test. Review why the assessment is used, what it is like, and what can be done to prepare for it. Generate the understanding that students take these assessments to help people figure out whether school is doing what it needs to do to help all students learn. Do not assume that any of the students who take the assessment have this information.

Plan ways to prepare for the test. Over and above study skills and test-taking skills are other important variables in test preparation. They include eating meals, getting adequate sleep, and using relaxation techniques, among others. As simplistic as these sound, many students do not understand the impact that nutrition and sleep have on their ability to perform to their potential.

Teaching Test-Taking Skills

What skills do students need when taking specific assessments? Who teaches students these test-taking skills? Most of us have taken the Graduate Record Exam (GRE), the National Teachers Certification Exam (NTCE), or some other certification test. Think about your experience. What skills did you need to take the test? How difficult were the directions? How much time and frustration did you save or could you have saved by preparing for the test (e.g., being familiar with its format, knowing the directions for the test or subtest, and noting time limits)? If you went into the test cold without any preparation or completion of review

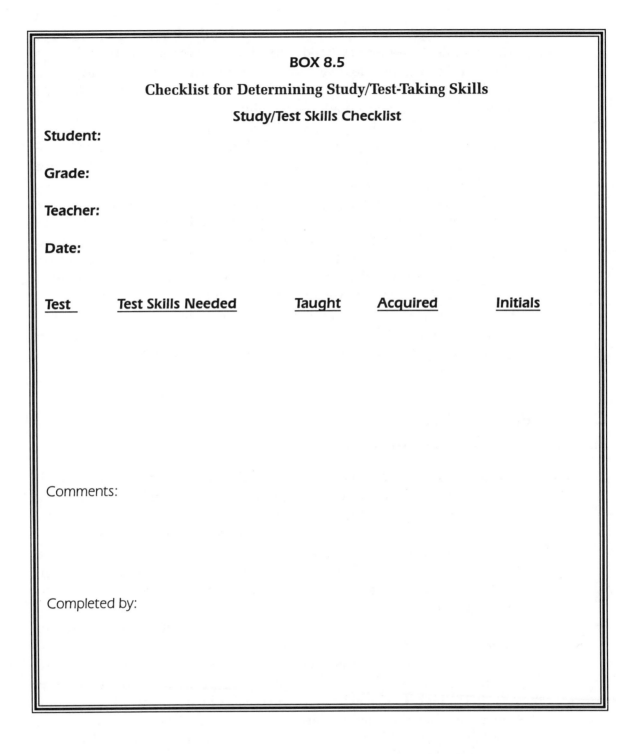

BOX 8.5

Checklist for Determining Study/Test-Taking Skills

Study/Test Skills Checklist

Student:

Grade:

Teacher:

Date:

Test	Test Skills Needed	Taught	Acquired	Initials

Comments:

Completed by:

books, how did you feel? Cold! If you were prepared for it, how did it feel when you found the format, time limits, and directions relatively close to what you expected?

These examples are what we mean when we refer to students having the necessary test-taking skills. Others include the ability to read and follow directions, complete specific sections of a test, stop at the end of the section, fill in bubble sheets so that marked answers correspond to questions, and so on. On the classroom level, think about the number of times students are told to "study" for the test. Who shows them how to do this? For example, do they know the format of the test? Are they emotionally prepared (e.g., understand the purpose of the test, relaxed)? Have they received adequate sleep and nutrition?

A checklist like the one in Box 8.5 should be completed at least once a year for each student. As noted, this form can be used for both classroom and district/state assessments. It is important to note which, since the timeline for preparation will differ for each.

Effective educators take the steps necessary to prepare students for classroom tests and find that students perform better when these steps are in place. It is also important to make sure the students are taught what they are expected to know. Students should be instructed in all the areas that will be on the assessment. We are not suggesting teaching to the test but, rather, making sure that what students are expected to know and do has been thoroughly instructed in the class. This goes for both classroom and district/state assessments. We also are not advocating replacing regular instruction with test preparation. A good balance must be obtained.

Coordinating the Logistics of Assessment Administration

Once decisions have been made about who takes what assessment with what, if any, needed accommodation, the logistics of who does what, when, and where must be mapped out. In Box 8.6, we provide an example of a timeline of planning that could be used for a spring cycle of testing. Months will vary. The key is to list all the things that must be completed to ready students, parents, teachers, and other school personnel for the upcoming assessment cycle. A timeline such as this keeps everyone informed about what is expected by whom and when.

As the spring or fall cycle of assessment gets closer, providing for students who are taking the regular assessment with accommodations, participating in an alternate assessment, or both, requires coordinated planning by several parties. Much of this planning depends on how many students (and teachers) are involved, the degree to which accommodations for the regular and partial assessment are needed, and the sophistication of the alternate assessment. Plans will look different for the three assessment options.

Regular Assessment

For those students with disabilities who participate in the district/state assessment without accommodation, it is important that they know where to report and what materials/instruments they need and are al-

```
┌─────────────────────────────────────────────────────────────────────┐
│                              BOX 8.6                                  │
│                                                                       │
│              Timeline for Planning the Assessment Cycle               │
│                                                                       │
│                   Timeline for Assessment Cycle*                      │
└─────────────────────────────────────────────────────────────────────┘
```

September	January	March	May
• IEP implemented	• Plan logistics of district testing	• Review test type	• Complete Final Arrangements for Assessment Accommodations Form
• Meet with teachers	• Review accommodations	• Complete Study/ Test Skills Checklist	
• Instructional accommodations reviewed	• Who will coordinate planning cycle?	• Complete Logistics and Strategic Plan for Providing Assessment Accommodations	
• Assessment accommodations reviewed			
• Complete Instructional and Assessment Accommodations Work sheet			

*Forms mentioned here are provided both in this chapter and in the Resources section.

lowed to use, especially if the instructional accommodation is one the assessment does not allow. For these students, their ability to take tests is important. Be sure to familiarize them with format and demands. If possible, use a previous version of the assessment to show students what to expect. Have them practice.

Regular Assessment With Accommodations

Along with the above provisions, students with disabilities needing accommodations require more coordination. Logistics of providing the actual accommodations (setting, timing, presentation, response, scheduling) must be planned. Who will arrange for the needed accommodations to be provided? A student requiring a reduced number of items per page will demand more advance planning than one who needs extended time or a separate environment. Accommodations that require use of assistive devices over and above what has been provided in classroom instruction must be arranged (e.g., Braille versions or enlarged print, increased spacing between items, reduced number of items per page).

These types of accommodation require that the assessment booklets be adapted. Of course, to do this you must obtain a copy of the assessment. These kinds of arrangements introduce the issue of test security, which rightfully creates concern. Therefore, test contractors, or the test company that provides your district or state with the assessment itself, need to know well in advance the accommodations required for some students. While this may introduce a cost issue, the result of a student not participating in an assessment who is capable of doing so with accommodation is discriminatory. The cost of a due process hearing or court appearance will no doubt outweigh that of providing the assessment accommodations that some students with disabilities are entitled to and need to participate in the assessment. Using the checklists in Boxes 8.7 and 8.8 will help you coordinate a plan for providing assessment accommodations.

It is not uncommon for members of the IEP team, most often special education teachers, to be given the responsibility for arranging, coordinating, and providing assessment accommodations for all students in the building who may need them, whether or not they have disabilities. These may be Section 504 students, those with special circumstances, or English-language learners. Often, special educators are seen as most qualified and knowledgeable about providing accommodations. While this may be true for classroom instruction and tests, district and state assessments introduce a variety of different variables. It is important to involve as many or as few personnel as needed to successfully plan for the logistics and provision of assessment accommodations.

Alternate Assessments

In Chapter 5, we discussed decisions surrounding students who need an alternate assessment. After decisions are made about which students will require an alternate assessment, the means to provide one must be broached. There are several scenarios to consider. We know that relatively few states or districts currently implement an alternate assessment. Although most believe they are a necessary addition to inclusive assessment and accountability systems, few have developed them. Your district and state may be in the process of exploring and developing alternate assessments, yet what do you do in the meantime?

Consider how these students can best be assessed according to their curriculum and what they are learning according to their IEP. The alternate assessment should align with what students are learning. And what students are learning should be aligned with a broader set of standards or learner outcomes that all students are striving toward. Regardless of whether a student takes the regular or alternate assessment or both, all students should be striving to achieve a similar set of broadly defined goals, also referred to as a common core of learning.

BOX 8.7

**Checklist for Logistics and Strategic Planning for
Providing Assessment Accommodations**

**Logistics and Strategic Plan for
Providing Assessment Accommodations**

Name: School Year:

Assessment: Special Education Teacher:

Day/Time of Test:

Case Coordinator:

Building Administrator:

Assessment accommodations student needs for this assessment and date
arranged:

1.

2.

3.

4.

Comments:

Person responsible for arranging accommodations and due date:

1.

2.

3.

4.

Comments:

Room Assignment for Assessment:

Planners for This Process (Signatures/Dates):

BOX 8.8

**Checklist for Making the Final Arrangements for
Assessment Accommodations**

Final Arrangements for Assessment Accommodations

Name: School Year:

Case Coordinator: Assessment:

Special Education Teacher: Date/Time of Test:

Building Administrator: Room Assignment:

The following assessment accommodations have been arranged (initial and date):

Setting:

Timing:

Scheduling:

Presentation:

Response:

Other:

Based on this premise, how can a student be meaningfully assessed? Consider the use of checklists that reflect daily living skills and their application in varied settings; mobility skills and demonstration of them; social skill checklists and opportunities for observation in real settings; performance-based tasks such as dressing oneself; use of a computer and production of a piece of work; vocational skills inventory; adaptive behavior scales; interviews with service providers, student, parents/guardians, and others involved in the student's life; and video-

---

BOX 8.9

Suggestions for Alternate Assessments

Below is a list of possible data sources for developing an alternate assessment.

Checklists for:
_____ Daily living skills
_____ Community mobility skills
_____ Social skills
_____ Self-help skills
_____ Adaptive behavior skills

Interviews:
_____ Service providers
_____ Parents/guardians
_____ Peers
_____ Employers

Observation:
_____ Note the frequency, intensity, and/or duration of target skill
_____ Informal observation of student in a variety of settings
_____ Formal or systematic observation using checklists, criteria, rubrics
_____ Videotaping of performance
_____ Application of skill(s) in varied settings (natural or staged)
_____ Demonstration of community mobility skills in real setting
_____ Use of technology (specify)

Tests:
_____ Portfolios
_____ Performance based
_____ Quantitative or qualitative

Record Review:
_____ School cumulative records
_____ Student products
_____ Anecdotal records (IEP objectives and general progress)

---

taping of the student (see Box 8.9). It is important to keep in mind that both the content and criteria of the assessment should be dictated by the student's IEP.

We know that some of you work with students who are medically fragile. The simple act of breathing and/or coordinating muscle groups to complete the task of rolling over on a mat is the level at which your students learn or function. All of your medically fragile students have IEPs and can be assessed or monitored according to what is on them. We want our point to be clear—all kids count!

Partial and Alternate Assessment

Students who are able to take part of the regular assessment but require an alternate one for the remainder of the assessment present similar considerations as those described above. Some students are able to take partial assessments without accommodations, whereas others need them. It is important to identify these and use the checklists to arrange for the logistics of providing them.

Evaluating the Planning and Assessment Process

Once the assessment cycle is complete, it is important to evaluate what worked, what did not, and how the students performed. Did they feel prepared? What went well? What needs work? It is important that feedback is solicited from students involved in all three types of assessment. And if there truly has been an effort devoted to the instruction-assessment process, these types of postevent data-gathering activities will be routine. It is important to gather similar information after tests or quizzes given at the classroom level to help better prepare the students for the challenges of the content and assessment. There are basically two parts to postassessment data gathering: debriefing the implementation and assessment procedures and interviewing students.

Debriefing

Along with the IEP team that began the decision process of participation and accommodation of special needs students, discuss how things went. Keep in mind that providing accommodations to students on three different types of tests in different content areas, most likely given at different times and days, can be a logistical nightmare. Celebrate the successes and rework rough spots. Refer back to the completed checklists and note any changes needed on the form(s) or additional information that must be included.

Interviewing Students

Find out from students what was helpful, easy, hard, confusing, and so forth about the assessment process. A form to use for doing this is presented in Box 8.10. To obtain specific information, you will likely need to ask specific questions. It may be of interest to gather information about their attitude toward taking tests, the usefulness of provided accommodation(s), and their feeling of preparedness. Encourage students to make suggestions for improvement.

BOX 8.10

Form for Obtaining Feedback From Students on the Assessment

Student Feedback/Interview Form

Student: **Grade:**

Assessment: **Case Coordinator:**

Date of Assessment: **Special Education Teacher:**

Date of Interview:

1. How did you think the test went? What was easy? What was hard?

2. How prepared were you for the

    Test format:

    Test content:

    Timing of the test:

    Any surprises?

    Other:

3. What (if any) testing accommodations did you use?

    a. Were they helpful?

    b. If so, how? If not, why?

    c. What, if any, other accommodations did you feel you needed?

(Continued)

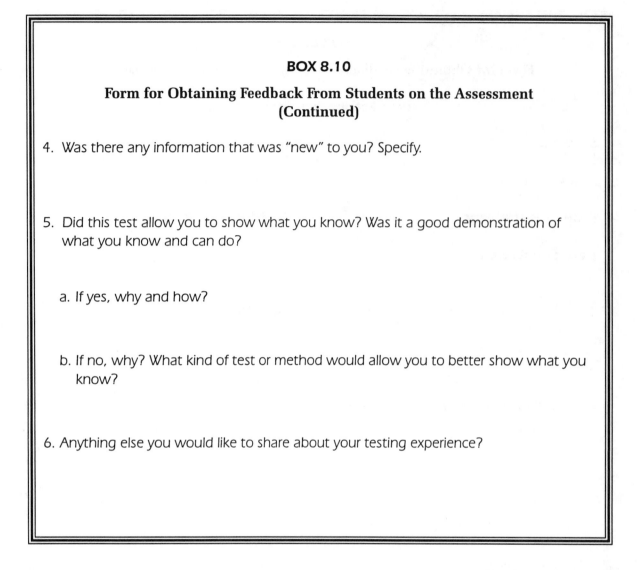

BOX 8.10

Form for Obtaining Feedback From Students on the Assessment (Continued)

4. Was there any information that was "new" to you? Specify.

5. Did this test allow you to show what you know? Was it a good demonstration of what you know and can do?

   a. If yes, why and how?

   b. If no, why? What kind of test or method would allow you to better show what you know?

6. Anything else you would like to share about your testing experience?

Summary

In this chapter, we discussed the role of the general educator, special educator, related services personnel, and paraprofessional. We also discussed the necessary steps to be taken for an inclusive assessment to take place, namely, (a) consider and decide on the purpose of the assessment, (b) decide on the type of assessment option for each student with a disability, (c) decide and delineate what accommodations, if any, are needed, (d) talk with the student to identify acceptance of accommodations and understanding of the assessment, and (e) plan for the logistics of the administration of the assessment.

Now check your knowledge about the myth/truth statements presented at the beginning of this chapter (see Box 8.11 for answers). Try to give an explanation for why each statement is correctly identified either as a myth or as the truth.

BOX 8.11

Myth or Truth Answers

TRUTH   There should be a link between accommodations provided during instruction and those provided for classroom and district/state assessments.
Explanation: Assessment accommodations should be those a student is familiar with prior to the test and not introduced at the time of the test. Therefore, the logical link is to that which is used during instruction. [See pages 120-121]

MYTH   Special education teachers are in the best position to make decisions about what accommodations students with disabilities need.
Explanation: Those who teach students with disabilities are in the best position together with other school personnel to make decision about accommodations. [See pages 121-122]

TRUTH   Paraprofessionals can be key players in the logistical planning and delivering of instructional and assessment accommodations.
Explanation: When available, paraeducators can be vital to the instruction and assessment process. [See pages 123-124]

TRUTH   Related services personnel (e.g., occupational and physical therapists, speech/language pathologists) can provide insight into what, if any, instruction/assessment accommodations are needed by a student they are delivering service to.
Explanation: Anyone who provides services to students with disabilities can provide valuable input during the process of making decisions about instruction and assessment accommodations. [See page 125]

TRUTH   In some places, all students are eligible for assessment accommodations.
Explanation: While a few states allow all students to be eligible for accommodations on the state performance test, most do not. This topic is being discussed with increasing frequency, however. [See page 123]

TRUTH   Students need to be taught test-taking skills for an assessment (e.g., format of test, time limits, directions).
Explanation: Levels of concern as well as anxiety can be dissipated by helping students become more familiar with the test and its format. [See pages 132-134]

Resources for Further Information

Archer, A., & Gleason, M. (1991). *Skills for school success.* North Billerica, MA: Curriculum Associates.

Archer, A., & Gleason, M. (1992). *Advanced skills for school success.* North Billerica, MA: Curriculum Associates.

Brolin, D. E. (Ed.). (1991). *Life centered career education: A competency-based approach* (3rd ed.). Reston, VA: Council for Exceptional Children.

Council of Chief State School Officers. (in press). *Questions and answers about assessment accommodations and students with disabilities: A guide for parents and teachers.* Prepared by the State Collaborative on Assessment and Student Standards, Assessing Special Education Students Project. Washington, DC: Author.

DeBoer, A. (1995). *Working together: The art of consulting and communicating.* Longmont, CO: Sopris West.

DeBoer, A., & Fister, K. (1995). *Working together: Tools for collaborative teaching.* Longmont, CO: Sopris West.

Dettmer, P., Thurston, L., & Dyck, N. (1993). *Consultation, collaboration, and teamwork for students with special needs.* Needham Heights, MA: Allyn & Bacon.

Friend, M., & Cook, L. (1996). *Interactions: Collaboration skills for school professionals* (2nd ed.). White Plains, NY: Longman.

Pickett, M. L. (1996). *State of the art report on paraeducators in education and related services.* New York: City University of New York, National Resource Center for Paraeducators in Education and Related Services, Center for Advanced Study in Education.

Sugai, G. M., & Tindal, G. A. (1993). *Effective school consultation: An interactive approach.* Pacific Grove, CA: Brooks/Cole.

Thurlow, M., Olsen, K., Elliott, J., Ysseldyke, J., Erickson, R., & Ahearn, E. (1996). *Alternate assessments for students with disabilities* (NCEO Policy Directions 5). Minneapolis: University of Minnesota, National Center on Educational Outcomes.

Gaining Support From Above: What Needs to Happen?

Topics

- ☐ Roles and Responsibilities
- ☐ Putting It All Together: Monitoring the Integrity of Implementation
- ☐ Organizing Staff Development

In this chapter, you will . . .

- – learn about the roles and responsibilities of boards of education, district- and building-level administrators, coordinators, and supervisors.

- – know what steps and procedures are needed to implement an inclusive assessment system districtwide.

- – learn about a model of staff development for training staff.

In Chapter 8, we discussed the roles of teachers, related service providers, and paraeducators. We also examined the logistics of planning, preparing the student, implementing assessment, and the need for coordinated collaboration. In this chapter, we discuss, in relation to the assessment of students with disabilities, the roles and responsibilities of the administrator, both building and district level; boards of education; district assessment coordinators; special education administrators; and department chairpersons. Although we address them individually, they are not necessarily mutually exclusive. And although there may be overlapping roles and responsibilities by different players

---

BOX 9.1

Myth or Truth? Do You Know?

Read each statement below and decide whether it is a myth or the truth about current practice.

- Most schools and districts have a mission statement for both learning and assessment.
- Staff development is provided to prepare staff for inclusive assessment, its purpose, and how to implement it with diverse student learners.
- Most administrators have a working knowledge of testing, assessment, and accountability and can distinguish among them within the broader context of inclusive accountability.
- There is uniform implementation of participation, accommodations, and reporting for students with disabilities from building to building and department to department within a school district.
- There are incentives for administrators to encourage the exclusion of students expected to do less well on assessments.

---

at the policy level, there most certainly is overlap in practice. The means by which inclusive accountability and assessment policy is brought into practice requires the work of several key players. In this chapter, we also describe how to plan staff development and make reference to the section of this book titled "Resources: Staff Development," which is full of materials for actually conducting staff development and engaging people in activities that will lead to inclusive assessment and accountability systems.

When you complete this chapter, you will be able to identify which of the statements in Box 9.1 are myths and which are the truth.

Roles and Responsibilities

As inclusive assessment programs and accountability systems continue to become the reality of school-based reform, state and local education agencies must work together to find ways to measure the learning progress of all students, including those with disabilities. The need for communication and joint planning for the ultimate goal of assessment and learner accountability is vital to the process and progress of implementation.

For inclusive assessment and accountability systems to evolve, we believe that several factors at minimum need to be in place (see Box 9.2).

BOX 9.2

Necessary Components for Inclusive Accountability Systems

Belief, mission, or vision statement about the learning and assessment of all students.

The development of assessment policy to include the following:

- Participation of all students, including students with disabilities, in the assessment program
- Accommodation of diverse learner needs on assessment
- Accounting for all test takers, including those who participate in an alternate or different assessment
- Reporting of the results of test takers to parents, teachers, and the community at large
- Observable and measurable benchmarks to mark progress toward inclusive accountability and assessment
- A plan for the implementation and use of assessment results
- A plan for staff development, technical assistance, information, dissemination, and exchange

---

We start from the premise that all kids count and must be accounted for. We begin the road of responsibility with the leaders at the state and school district levels and with professional organizations. Until recently, the idea of inclusive assessment and accountability has not been at the forefront of administrators' agendas. Their focus is on curriculum, instruction, leadership, testing programs, budget, and resource allocation, among many others. However, district and state testing programs have not necessarily required administrators to be equipped with a working knowledge of the broader issues of inclusive assessment and accountability.

The Superintendent

As leader of the school district, in conjunction with the board of education, the superintendent of schools is responsible for starting policy-level discussion about assessment and accountability. Discussions should be about mission and belief statements and the necessary components needed to foster information gathering and discussion at both the building and district levels. The role of the superintendent is to set a tone that communicates the importance of inclusive accountability—

what it looks like for students, teachers, parents, and the community and how this translates into shifts in beliefs and current practice at the district, school, and classroom levels.

Discussions about policy and guidelines for assessment practices are imperative. If you are in a state with strong local control, you may have more latitude to set these. However, for those of you in states where policy travels from the top down, it is important to converse with your state's assessment department to find out exactly what the statewide policy is for including students with disabilities in assessment.

Most states that have state assessment programs have written guidelines about their policies, but many of these guidelines are vague, in turn leading to wide and varied interpretation and implementation of the guidelines. In fact, such leeway in interpretation has resulted in some districts and school buildings leaving students with disabilities out of the assessment cycle to "look good" or rank high among other buildings and districts. This, however, makes equitable comparisons between school sites or states very difficult (even if the same test is used). If some states, districts, and schools follow the guidelines as suggested and others take latitude in implementation, the result usually is a competitive edge for those who exclude students with disabilities from assessment, creating the opportunity for dissonance among administrators, teachers, parents, and others.

We must begin to examine the practice of "looking good" versus being accountable for all students learning. Superintendents are in the position to streamline what state-level policy means across school districts and how it needs to be implemented (for guidelines, see Chapters 2 and 3). But superintendents too want to "look good" among peers. In fact, superintendents' salary increases (or decreases) are more and more being tied to the results of test scores in their districts. The temptation to put pressure on teaching staff and assessment personnel in a district to "make it happen" is prevalent at the district administrative level as well.

Although most districts and schools have mission statements and visions about learning, they lack the same for assessment. Mission statements for learning need to be grounded in the evaluation of student learning. Only then can we know whether all students are being provided the opportunity to learn as reflected in the school vision. A public mission statement about learning and assessment will help defer some of the temptation to test the best and baby-sit the rest. Public commitment holds us all accountable for our behavior. To heighten the discussion of these issues, superintendents' professional organizations, both regional and national, must make inclusive assessment and accountability central themes of conferences and publications so as to develop ways to address leveling the playing field for all superintendents, districts, and schools.

Boards of Education

Working in tandem with the superintendent of schools, the board of education (BOE) is in the position to approve, support, and operationalize policy into practice in the district. It is important that the BOE has a working understanding of the purpose and responsibility of an inclusive accountability system for all students residing in a district's attendance area. For example, include in the information packet that goes to the BOE national and state trends and practices in assessment, including participation, accommodation, and reporting of results. Help create a knowledge base of what leaders in the field of assessment are saying. Provide a balanced view of current practices.

The issue of inclusive accountability should be discussed not as a budgetary item but, rather, as one of ethics and responsibility. The role of the BOE is to make sure that decisions and discussions about inclusive assessment and accountability are proactive and aligned with the published mission/vision statement of the district. If the belief is that all students can learn to even higher levels than before, all students, especially those with disabilities, must be included in the discussion and in decisions about inclusive assessment.

Encourage BOE members to talk to state and national boards. Find out what is going on and how changes are being made. The BOE can create the policies that promote change for the betterment of all students. But until "all" does mean "all" for instruction, assessment, and accountability, vision and mission statements are nothing but words on paper.

District Assessment Coordinators

District assessment coordinators are becoming more a part of the current assessment scene. While we understand that many districts may not have a person in this position, or the job duties are assumed under another title (e.g., Assistant Superintendent for Curriculum and Instruction), involvement of personnel in charge of implementing the district assessment is key. However, it is important to find out what they know and understand about inclusive assessment and accountability. For example, even though most departments of education at the state level have assessment coordinators or directors of assessment, their work and efforts do not always reflect the inclusion of students with special needs. It is not uncommon for there to be no communication between state directors of special education and state directors of assessment. Hence, some policies and practices are created without knowledge or input from a very closely related department. This same scenario may be carried out at the local district as well. That is, policy and practices are implemented that do not reflect special populations.

Most often, special needs students are excluded because it is argued that any accommodation to the assessment provides an unfair advantage or skews the test results. Some argue that the provision of any accommodation that was not used during the standardization of the test invalidates the results. Currently, there are no adequate data on these issues. Counterarguments also raise issues: "How valid are the test results of a student with a disability who is not granted an accommodation?" "How will you validly assess these students?" "How will you account for those students you deem incapable of taking the assessment without an accommodation?" The answers to these questions are much less clear and less well thought out.

For years it has been too easy to justify the exclusion of special needs students from assessments. We now know too much about assessment and how to account for learning for all students to allow this discriminatory practice to continue. One of the roles of the district assessment coordinator is to make sure that "all" means "all."

It is important that assessment coordinators take part in assessment discussions held by the BOE and superintendent. Coordinators need to disseminate information about inclusive assessment practices. It is the role of the assessment coordinator to, if not already discussed, introduce the concept of an alternate assessment for those students who are unable to meaningfully participate in the general assessment administered to all students. Assessment coordinators need to be clear and reinforce the fact that an inclusive accountability system means that all students count and are accounted for. This means that all but a small percentage of students take the same test and that those comprising the small percentage take an alternate assessment.

It is the role of the assessment coordinator to meet with building administration and other personnel such as department chairpersons and other coordinators to disseminate and exchange information about inclusive assessment. This is no small task. There is often a strong reaction from teachers and administrators when the practice of inclusive assessment and accountability is introduced. We know that most teachers and administrators are put at ease when the "how to" about actual implementation of this innovation is explained. Start with small groups and be prepared to answer or defer until more information about an issue can be explored. The bottom line for all of this is alignment to the district and building vision/mission statement about learning and assessment. Backing up what was written—do you really believe that all students can learn?

Building Administrators

Building administrators are responsible for the integrity of the implementation of the assessment program in their buildings. That is, they are responsible for making sure that assessment decisions for students with special needs are informed decisions and that faculty and staff understand the meaning of inclusive assessment and accountability and what it looks like. It is important to avoid portraying the notion that this is a top-down decision, or one that makes no sense for students. It is not uncommon for ideas or policies that go against our own personal belief systems to be announced as "another idea from above" (and sometimes a few colorful adjectives are added). This portrays to faculty and staff that another bandwagon is coming through town. Be very clear and understand that this is not a bandwagon approach. Change for many comes slowly and with great trepidation. As leaders of instruction and curriculum, building administrators have as their charge to lead their staff into changes and implementation of inclusive accountability for the betterment of all students. Be sure to examine how and what you think about it before you present it to the staff. Remember, you are a role model for instruction and curriculum and assessment and responsible for student learning and the instruction delivered to them (see the section on Organizing Staff Development, and the Resources section that supports staff development efforts).

As a building administrator, you need to work with the team of personnel that makes the decisions about participation in and accommodation of needs during both classroom and district assessments. Most often, this is the Child Support Team (also known by other names such as Instructional Support Team and Teacher Assistance Team) or in some cases the IEP team. The Child Support Team (CST) usually has the charge of providing student-centered interventions, both academic and behavioral, in the classroom. The CST also makes direct recommendations about whether students need and/or qualify for additional services and remedial or special education. These recommendations are usually carried to the IEP team, which makes the final decision and approves an Individualized Educational Program for the student.

The place to start is with the team and other personnel who are making the decisions about assessment. It is not uncommon for districts to hold building IEP meetings during the annual review process. In other words, there may be a district IEP team that meets during the year at the central office and building IEP teams that function during annual review time because of the vast numbers of students whose programs need to be reviewed. Regardless of when or where the IEP teams meet, the members of this team must be equipped with information to allow them to make informed decisions about participation and accommodation during assessment. These personnel are those who decide what instructional accommodations are needed for a student (e.g., reduced assignments, extended time for projects, and outlines of lecture notes). It only makes sense that they use this information and the knowledge of the learner to make recommendations for accommodations in both classroom tests and district/state assessment. Instructional and assessment accommodations should be linked and flow naturally from one to another.

If little or no instructional accommodation is being delivered or provided in the classroom, a problem may be at hand. The accommodation should not be unveiled on the day of a test but should be familiar to the student through its use in the classroom. If a teacher does not make this provision during classroom instruction, then two things may occur: There may not be any flow in accommodations, natural or not, from instruction to assessment; and teachers may be reluctant to grant or see the need for an accommodation on an assessment because it is not provided during the instructional process.

Even though the best-case scenario is for the district to adopt an IEP form for all IEP teams to use, you do not need to wait for one to be developed. We offer a model format for documenting assessment accommodation needs that you can use and adapt for the IEPs in your district or building IEP (see Box 9.3). In this model are sections for both instructional and assessment accommodations that prompt people to think about and identify up front what instructional, classroom, and district assessment accommodations are needed. Identified are the needed instructional accommodations and what accommodations will be provided on which assessment. Keep in mind that if a student is to participate in the district assessment with accommodations, these accommodations are determined by the purpose of the test and a combination of three considerations: the needs of the student, what is allowed by the district, and whether the accommodation will invalidate the results of the test (see Chapters 3 and 4 for a discussion).

As the building administrator, it is important to initiate discussions with the person in charge of IEP teams, usually a special education administrator. The key is providing a vehicle that encourages personnel to think beyond the paperwork factor of the IEP to what the student sincerely needs to be successful in both the instructional and the assessment process.

Special Education Administrator

The role of the special education administrator in inclusive assessment is vast and important. You basically are "on call" to help problem solve, disseminate information, participate in discussions, and resolve implementation issues. However, as with other education innovations, this effort requires teamwork. We recommend the team approach. That is, there should be an assessment team assembled to work through all the issues listed above. Different personnel will be able to lend different areas of expertise—the power of the team approach. Your role is to meet with all special educators to introduce and explain the concept and practice of inclusive assessment and accountability.

BOX 9.3

**Model IEP Form for Documenting Assessment and
Needed Accommodations**

Instructional and Assessment Accommodations

Instructional Accommodations: List the accommodations this student needs during the instructional process to learn, perform, and participate on an equal footing with class peers.

Assessment Accommodations:

Classroom Tests: List the test accommodations this student needs to show what he or she knows and can do without impediment of the disability.

District Assessment Program:

Based on the above information, _____ will

_____ participate in district assessment _____ without accommodation.

_____ participate in district assessment _____ with accommodation.

- Based on current instructional practice, this student needs the following assessment accommodations:

- District assessment allows for the following above accommodations to be provided:

_____ participate in part of the district assessment and an alternate assessment as follows:

_____ not participate in the general assessment but will take an alternate assessment.

It has been our experience, and the experience of others, that special educators are often the most distressed by this shift. It requires a change in practice and the perception of protection of students. For years, common practice has been to exclude, often for altruistic reasons, students from taking district assessments simply because they have a special education label. This practice is moving into extinction. Special educators need to know that inclusive assessment and accountability means that, except for a very small number of students, all students with disabilities need to be included and participate in the same assessment program as their peers without disabilities.

Special educators may be the first ones to tell you how many of their students are unable to take "those" assessments. Listen carefully to those explanations and make note of the reasons. Are they due to access to curriculum? Student skill deficit? The reasons given may be the very ones that have kept students excluded based on decisions made by these teachers attending IEP meetings. However, another shift is required. For years, students with disabilities have been taught using parallel or different curriculum and material. If students with disabilities are to be included in the same assessment as their peers without disabilities, they need to learn similar or the same content. For those students unable to take the assessment, the role of the special education administrator, working with both special education and general education personnel, is to be sure these students are accounted for in the building and state accountability reports.

The concept and practice of alternate assessment for a small percentage of students must be introduced to special education teachers, especially those who work with students with more significant needs. In tandem with efforts to create an alternate assessment system for some students is the need to develop criteria or checklists that delineate which students are eligible for this assessment. The temptation may be strong to place more than a small number of students in this assessment for the same reasons they have been, in the past, left out of others. Be very clear that the alternate assessment is for those students who typically have more significant disabilities and who may not be working toward a high school diploma (see Chapter 5). With these stipulations set, it should become very clear to special educators that the majority of students in a district, including students with disabilities, will take the regular assessment. This same information must necessarily be presented to general educators as well.

Special education teachers will most likely be called on by those in their buildings to discuss the issues behind such a policy and help problem-solve building-based issues for special education students. It is important that these teachers have the knowledge and support to do so. Often, special educators feel ostracized already. Therefore, with the talk of inclusive assessment and accountability, these teachers may feel even more vulnerable than before. Your leadership, teamwork, and supportive networks will be imperative.

Department Chairpersons and Curriculum Coordinators

The role of chairpersons and curriculum coordinators is to help clarify and put into practice the policy of inclusive assessment and accountability. Stay informed and know what this means for the personnel with whom you work. The logistics of implementation is the area in which your help most likely is needed. Stay involved at the district level and volunteer to serve on assessment committees. Provide suggestions for needed staff development for all teachers and those you supervise. Create task forces to problem-solve implementation issues or any other areas in need of addressing. Work collaboratively with all teachers in the department as well as with those special education teachers who also teach students who attend classes in these departments.

Putting It All Together: Monitoring the Integrity of Implementation

With so many roles and so many players, it is easy for things to get lost in the mix. Therefore, it is important that there be a way to document the integrity of implementation. When most educators see the word *monitor*, they immediately associate it with compliance monitoring. We are not suggesting this interpretation. Instead, we are suggesting that there be a mechanism in place to supervise the integrity of the implementation of policy. For many reasons, there will be personnel who look for and find loopholes in the system. For example, some may talk to parents of special needs students to gain support for exclusion of their children from assessment. Parents do have the final say, but they must be fully informed of the purpose of the assessment program and accountability for all students.

We suggest the use of some sort of accountability system for the accountability system. It is not uncommon for practice to lag behind the development and implementation of policy. At the district level, there needs to be reporting on and/or a documentation format for practice and movement toward benchmarks connected to the goal of policy implementation. For example, what is or has been done to ready staff, parents, and the immediate community for inclusive assessment and the reporting of the results of all test takers? What is happening at the building level? What is being used to make decisions (e.g., checklists)? Who is involved in the decisions, and who signs off in agreement? How many students with disabilities are enrolled in the building? How many take the general assessment? How many took it without accommodation?

How many with accommodation? How many were excluded and why? And so on.

It would seem most logical for the building administrator to document this information and then forward it to the district assessment coordinator, who eventually sends it on to the superintendent and board of education. An example of an accountability implementation form that might be used is in Box 9.4. The flow of this process will, of course, depend on the organizational structure of your district. District statistics should be kept on this information and reviewed yearly.

Organizing Staff Development

Sustained and planned staff development and training is a key component of today's educational reform agenda that emphasizes *all students*, *high standards*, and the *alignment of assessment* and standards. It is clear that much of what is evolving from school reform needs to be addressed via staff development. Faculty and staff need to have input on what will make a difference in facilitating the needed shifts in practice and implementation. Unfortunately, all too often educational innovations are expected to be implemented immediately. Little or no training or staff development is provided for educators and administrators. Staff development, information exchange, and dissemination creates a more open-minded and accepting environment for change.

We offer in Box 9.5 a staff development survey that can be used districtwide or by building to find out and prioritize what personnel need and want to facilitate growth and development of the new practices. Concerns about the effect of change on current practices and the consequences attached to it result in educators approaching change with extreme caution and even misgiving. The purpose of the survey checklist is to obtain staff input regarding what they believe they need to meaningfully participate in the change process.

There are many ways to deliver and disseminate information about innovations, policy, and changes in practice. One way is through a faculty or staff meeting. It is common for the building administrator to both schedule and conduct them, but others may do so too. In this section, we provide you with an outline to use as a guide when planning a faculty meeting on inclusive assessment and accountability (also see Resources: Staff Development for the most important points that need to be made in each component and some specific activities in which people can engage).

The outline we provide will help you formulate information dissemination and awareness of the what, why, how and what-ifs of assessment programs and accommodation decisions. It is important that you be familiar with the requirements and practices of both your districtwide assessment program and your state assessment system.

BOX 9.4

Example of a Building Implementation Form

Building Implementation Document

Year/Test Cycle: Building:

Name/Form of Test: Grade Level:

Total number of students enrolled in building:
Number of students with disabilities enrolled in building:
Number of students taking assessment:
Number of students with disabilities taking assessment:
Number of students taking assessment with accommodation:
Types of accommodation provided:

Number of students excluded or exempted from assessment:
Reasons for exclusion or exemption (attach a separate sheet if needed):

Persons making exclusion and exemption decisions:

Last Year's Data
Total number of students enrolled in building:
Number of students with disabilities enrolled in building:
Number of students taking assessment:
Number of students with disabilities taking assessment:
Number of students taking assessment with accommodation:
Number of students excluded or exempted from assessment:

Submitted by:

Date:

BOX 9.5

Staff Development Needs Survey

Inclusive Assessment and Accountability Survey

We as a nation are moving toward an educational system that is more inclusive both in instruction and in accountability. As your district prepares for this process, we believe it is very important to survey your teachers and staff to find out what is needed to be prepared for this change. Our mission and belief is that all students can learn to higher levels than before. We believe all students must be included and accounted for in our efforts to educate all children for their future. With this in mind, complete the following survey:

Please indicate your position/role:

_____ General Education Teacher   _____ Special Education Teacher

_____ Administrator   _____ Related Service Professional

_____ Parent/Community Member   _____ Other _____

In the space next to each item, write one or more letters from A to E to indicate your anticipated need for staff development.

A. Need for **TRAINING** (in-service workshop, seminar)
B. Need for **MATERIALS** (literature, resources)
C. Need for **CONSULTATION**
D. Need for **IN-CLASS ASSISTANCE**
E. **OTHER** (please specify)

_____ 1. Overview of the "whys" of inclusive assessment and accountability
_____ 2. Recent laws and mandates that affect all students
_____ 3. Purpose and uses of the district/state assessment
_____ 4. Connection between instruction and assessment, especially as it relates to accommodations
_____ 5. Address the issue of how all students can participate in the district/state assessment program
_____ 6. Session on what kinds of assessment accommodations are allowed, who is eligible for them, and how these decisions are made
_____ 7. Hands-on session on how to decide and provide instructional accommodations to students who need them

(Continued)

BOX 9.5

Staff Development Needs Survey (Continued)

Inclusive Assessment and Accountability Survey

_____ 8. How to provide accommodations for both classroom tests and district assessments

_____ 9. Roles and responsibilities of teachers, administrators, and other staff in district assessment

_____ 10. Other (please specify) _____

Please write the numbers of your top three priorities on the lines below:

1st _____   2nd _____   3rd _____

Other questions, comments, or concerns:

This outline can be used to provide inservice to boards of education, central office and building administrative personnel, building faculty and staff, and community members. The overall components remain the same. The extensiveness of discussions will depend on the role and responsibility of the intended audience.

Goals of Staff Development

The staff development components that we have identified are designed to meet a set of goals. These are presented in Box 9.6. If your goals are different from these, the components of your staff development and the specific activities that you use should be altered to match your goals.

Components of Staff Development

The information on staff development provided here has nine components (see Box 9.7). The coverage of each component can vary, or you may want to present the information over two sessions. The content within each component is meant to afford you an overall understanding of the issues to help you when preparing for the meeting you will hold.

For each component, it is suggested that you investigate and prepare for how the information relates to your school district and/or state. This

---

BOX 9.6

Goals of Training Session

- Disseminate information to teachers and staff about district/statewide assessment and inclusive accountability programs
- Provide decisions makers (IEP teams, teachers, parents, etc.) with information they need to make thoughtful, thorough individualized decisions about student participation and accommodations on district/state assessments
- Provide an opportunity to evaluate current assessment practices of building(s) and the district
- Facilitate decisions about "next" steps needed to better align vision of learning, assessment, and accountability for all students
- Provide resources (e.g., where more information and training can be sought)

---

affords participants a grounded view of what is going on in their backyard as opposed to someone else's. The Resources section provides a brief overview of what should be explored and presented to participants. For more specific information, you can refer back to sections in the book. **Following each component's overview are suggested activities, handouts, and overheads** to help you get started planning your staff meetings. These materials are not meant to be exhaustive. Rather, they provide a springboard from which you can tailor your own sessions.

Summary

In this chapter, we highlighted several of the roles that need to be played by administrators as you move toward inclusive accountability systems. Of utmost importance are communication, stakeholder buy-in, and joint planning. Administrators play a leadership role in moving this forward. There necessarily must be a thoughtful process of planning and implementation with a cross-representative group of stakeholders. Much effort is required in the area of information dissemination and exchange. We also provided you with a plan for training and staff development, which we encourage you to review and modify to meet the needs of your situation.

Now check your knowledge about the myth/truth statements presented at the beginning of this chapter (see Box 9.8 for answers). Try to give an explanation for why each statement is correctly identified either as a myth or as the truth.

BOX 9.7

Components of Staff Training

Component 1: New Laws That Promote Educational Reform

Purpose: To briefly explain the provision of the new laws (Goals 2000, Improving America's Schools Act, School to Work Opportunity Act, IDEA), with an emphasis on assessment and accountability

Component 2: General Overview of Definition of Assessment, Its Purposes, and the Meaning of Inclusive Accountability

Purpose: To provide an overview of the purposes of assessment
To define and discuss what accountability is and its connection to assessment

Component 3: Why Assess?

Purpose: To provide an explanation for the variety of student and school purposes for assessment and the ways in which assessment results might be used

Component 4: Formats of Assessment

Purpose: To describe the variety of formats of assessments that might be used at the district or state and classroom levels

Component 5: Who's In, Who's Out?

Purpose: To provide information, based on inclusive accountability, about who participates in the district assessment program and how they participate
To provide reasons and documentation of past exclusionary assessment practices

Component 6: Who Makes the Decisions?

Purpose: To deliver information on who makes participation decisions and how they are made

Component 7: What Are Assessment Accommodations?

Purpose: To describe what assessment accommodations are, their purpose, and an understanding of what they might look like
To create a link between instruction and assessment accommodations, as well as understanding the range of accommodations that can be delivered for both

Component 8: Reporting of Results

Purpose: To provide an overview of how the results are reported
To provide an overview of how the results are used

Component 9: Next Steps

Purpose: To generate discussion on where to go from here
To identify what needs to be done to move forward (or share with personnel the direction in which the district is moving and the benchmarks that are in place to guide that movement)

BOX 9.8

Myth or Truth Answers

MYTH   Most schools and districts have a mission statement for both learning and assessment.
<u>Explanation</u>: Most schools have a vision or mission statement about student learning, but not assessment. [See page 147]

TRUTH   Staff development is provided to prepare staff for inclusive assessment, its purpose, and how to implement it with diverse student learners.
<u>Explanation</u>: Nationally, a plan is lacking for states and districts to provide sustained staff development for creating a system that is both accountable and inclusive. [See page 155]

MYTH   Most administrators have a working knowledge of testing, assessment, and accountability and can distinguish among them within the broader context of inclusive accountability.
<u>Explanation</u>: The nature of assessment programs has not necessarily required administrators or assessment coordinators to develop a working knowledge of tests or assessments. Inclusive accountability, until lately, has never really been at the top of the list of issues for administrators. [See page 146]

MYTH   There is uniform implementation of participation, accommodation, and reporting for students with disabilities from building to building and department to department within a school district.
<u>Explanation</u>: Due to the lack of or vagueness of guidelines about participation and accommodation, school personnel are left to interpret and implement them in their own way. [See page 147]

TRUTH   There are incentives for administrators to encourage the exclusion of students expected to do less well on assessments.
<u>Explanation</u>: More and more districts are creating rewards and sanctions for superintendents, basing salary increments and job security on district assessment performance. [See page 147]

Resources for Further Information

Allington, R., & McGill-Franzen, A. (1992). Unintended effects of reform in New York. *Educational Policy, 6*(4), 397-414.

Striking a balance between multiple choice and performance assessment. (1996, December). In *The School Administrator, 53*(11), 24-26.

Zlatos, B. (1994). Don't test, don't tell: Is "academic red-shirting" skewing the way we rank our schools? *American School Board Journal, 181*(11), 24-28.

Involving Parents in Testing Decisions

In this chapter, you will . . .

- learn how to better inform parents and other participants in the decision-making processes for participation and accommodation in assessment.

- find out what can be done to support the assessment cycle at home.

- learn where to obtain resources for parents in answering tough questions about assessing children with disabilities in both local and state assessments.

Parents must be active participants in making assessment and accountability decisions. They are powerful players in their child's education. After all discussion, it is the parent or guardian who has the final word in the implementation of a plan. Therefore, it is vital that parents be involved in and understand the discussions about assessment participation and accommodations. The focus of this chapter is on informing parents and those who work with them about assessment and accountability and how testing might affect their son or daughter. The information presented here also can be used to guide parent education programs in which the topics of assessment and accountability are addressed. While we understand the likelihood of a parent reading this entire book is slim, we encourage you to read this chapter and in turn share its information with parents.

We have found that most parents of students with disabilities think of testing as a process conducted to decide whether a child is eligible for services or can keep receiving services. There is little thought about the need for group assessments used for accountability. Accountability is a systematic method to assure those inside and outside the educational system that schools are moving in desired directions. We are referring to tests or assessments that not only measure achievement gains but also provide an accountability system for the school building, the district, and the state. It is important that these differences are made clear from the start of our discussion.

Currently, accountability for the education of students with disabilities is based on child count and compliance monitoring. Schools and school districts receive dollars based on the number of students with disabilities. Some states use a weighted-pupil funding. That is, different amounts of money are awarded to districts based on the students' severity of disabilities (e.g., mental retardation, autism, learning disability). Compliance monitoring is done by personnel from federal education agencies who visit states to see whether they are in compliance with federal laws and rules. Personnel from state education agencies, in turn, visit districts to audit compliance with state laws, rules, regulations, and guidelines.

These accountability mechanisms are no longer seen as adequate. Parents, community members, policymakers, and educators need and want to know how all students in America's schools, including students with disabilities, are learning and the extent to which education is working. It is no longer enough to base our investment in special education solely on the number of IEPs that have been completed on time, the description of services, or class size. Today, it is necessary to account for student performance and progress.

While there are many resources and networks for parents of students with disabilities, few if any deal with inclusive accountability systems. A system is accountable for all students when it makes sure that all of them count in the evaluation program of the educational system. This does not mean that all students need to take the same test but, rather, that all students' learning and progress are accounted for and included when reports about the education system are made.

For parents of students with disabilities, one of the central issues over the years has been gaining access to the general education system,

---

BOX 10.1

Myth or Truth? Do You Know?

Read each statement below and decide whether it is a myth or the truth about current practice.

- Parents can be powerful players in the decision-making process regarding participation in assessments and the provision of accommodations both for instruction and assessment.
- Most parents understand the concepts of accountability and assessment and the purpose(s) of district and state testing programs.
- Many parents have fought long and hard to gain access to general education curriculum and programs for their students; hence, inclusion in the district/state assessment program is not necessarily a priority at this time.
- Parents of students with disabilities assume that their child's district assessment results are included in the overall report of test results.
- When some students are excluded or exempted from the regular assessment, parents know to ask about what alternate assessment will be used to assess their child's learning.

---

with the result being the inclusive schooling movement or full implementation of education in the least restrictive environment. So, when asked about assessment decisions, many parents are thrilled with the programs their children are receiving and stop there. In our conversations about district or state large-scale assessment with parents of students with disabilities, common responses have been these:

- "Why should my child take that assessment? She is not in that curriculum and is not learning what is on that test."
- "My child attends a different school for his program. Why would he take that test?"
- "She could never take that test, it would be too hard."
- "Why would we put him through that test if he can get out of it?"

Using these questions as our guide, we discuss the issues, information, and resources that both IEP teams and parents need to know to make thoughtful decisions for individual students with disabilities.

When you finish this chapter, you will be able to identify which of the statements in Box 10.1 are myths and which are the truth.

Assessing Students With Disabilities: Should We or Shouldn't We?

"Why should my child take that assessment? She is not in that curriculum and is not learning what is on that test." This question, typically posed by parents, alone encompasses many of the current issues and beliefs about assessing students with disabilities in large-scale assessment. We must probe further to find out why the student is in a different curriculum and learning information that is not on the test. What are the standards or learning goals of the district? Are they aligned with the test given? If not, why not? What is the nature of the student's disability and how does the severity of the disability preclude this student from being included in the general assessment? And finally, if the student does not participate in this assessment, how are learning and progress assessed? More likely than not the answer to the last question is "There is no different assessment of student learning." In other words, if students do not participate in the regular assessment, there is no alternate form of assessment to monitor student learning and progress.

For those students who receive special education services in schools and classrooms outside their districts of residence, we hear parents comment, "My child attends a different school for his program. Why would he take that test?" We know that if that student does not take the test associated with his home district, he most likely will not take any assessment. No one is accountable for this student. Too often, when students are sent to other programs, the responsibility for their learning is shifted to the receiving school, but no accountability is required. In many cases, each educational institution has different rules and regulations it follows. A private or state-run facility may have different regulations from the sending district. For example, a residential facility may only be concerned with being in compliance and less concerned with student accountability systems per se. The school may be responsible for specific IEP goals that the district has sent forward or jointly developed, but it is not ultimately responsible for the student—the sending district is.

Conversely, the sending district often feels relieved of its responsibility for any student in an out-of-district placement. The sending district will re-enroll the student when it has been deemed appropriate, but until then, the student's education is delivered by the outside placement. The question remains—who *is* responsible for the student?

In states like Kentucky, the home school is assigned responsibility for out-of-district students. All students must take the test and the score is assigned back to the school the students would attend if in-district. If these students do not participate in the assessment, they are assigned the lowest score possible. If the school believes that it can educate students to achieve better than the lowest score possible, the incentive is to have students educated in their home school.

BOX 10.2

Facts That Parents Need to Know

Fact Sheet: Did You Know????

- 85% of students with disabilities can participate in general education assessments.
- There are three kinds of students with disabilities when it comes to assessments:
    1. Those who can participate without accommodation
    2. Those who can participate with accommodation
    3. Those who need an alternate assessment
- Less than 1% to 2% of the total school population should be deemed eligible for an alternate assessment.
- The National Center on Educational Outcomes has developed criteria for states and school districts to use to examine existing guidelines or to develop guidelines for inclusive assessment.
- It is not uncommon for students with disabilities to participate in the assessment but have their protocols destroyed, shared only with parents, or not reported at all.

Regardless of one's role (parent, teacher, administrator, etc.), it is important to find out who is responsible for monitoring and measuring a child's learning. Some of the facts that parents need to know about participation are presented in Box 10.2. Questions that parents and teachers might want to ask about their student's participation in assessments are included in Box 10.3.

Altruism: Not a Reason to Exclude

Often, we have heard parents say, "She could never take that test, it would be too hard. Besides, her teacher says it would cause too much frustration." It is not uncommon for parents to hear this reason and stop there. No one wants students to be in agony while taking a test. The cause for the agony must be teased out. Indeed, tests can be frustrating, especially if one is not prepared for the content and/or format. Who teaches students to take a test? When are they taught test-taking skills? Are they taught any at all? Teaching test-taking skills is one way to prepare students ahead of time for a test they will be taking. To exclude students based on the premise that it will cause too much frustration does not hold much weight; it is not a reasonable argument. Why will it be frustrating? If it is related to content, why aren't the students receiving the content? If it is due to test-taking skills, be sure these are taught. If it is due to needed assessment accommodations, provide them.

BOX 10.3

Look Further . . . Questions to Ask

Basic background questions that parents need to ask to gather information needed to make decisions about the participation of their child in assessment:

- What are the goals of instruction for my child?

- What is the common core of learning or standards that all students are working to achieve?

- Are these the same or reflected in my child's IEP? If not, why not?

- What is the district/state policy about the participation of students in the general assessment?

- Is there a broad set of standards for what all students should know and be able to do, especially for those students with significant or more severe disabilities?

- Does my child participate in the general education assessment? If not, why not?

- Could my child participate in the assessment if provided needed accommodations?

- Could my child participate in part of the assessment (with or without accommodations)?

- I hear that the assessment accommodation my child needs will invalidate the test results. If true, how will learning be assessed?

- Is it possible for my child to take the assessment with accommodations and have it reported as such? Total exclusion is not a better option.

- Given that my child's disabilities are significant enough to warrant exclusion from the assessment, how will learning be assessed? What alternate form of assessment is available to assess my child's learning progress?

- How are results of alternate assessments reported? Do my child's alternate assessment results count? If not, why not? If so, how?

Teachers and IEP teams must realize the importance of having all students, especially those with disabilities, in assessment and accountability systems and find ways to provide students the means to do so. Teachers and parents together must realize the importance of the participation of students with disabilities in both inclusive schooling and accountability. For too long, many students with disabilities have not been provided the opportunity to meet their full potential in the least restrictive environment. And too often, in places where they have participated, their educational results have not been included in reports. Sometimes, test protocols have been destroyed or shared only with the parents rather than being combined with the data on all other students and reported in aggregate.

BOX 10.4

Facts That Parents Need to Know

Fact Sheet: Did You Know????

- Less than 1% to 2% of the entire school population may need an alternate assessment.
- There is little research that indicates that using assessment accommodations invalidates test results. There is currently much research under way.
- The 1997 reauthorization of IDEA indicates that all students with disabilities are to be assessed and reported as a part of the general education assessment system. When needed, an alternate form of assessment must be provided to ensure that all students are included in the accountability system.
- The National Center on Educational Outcomes (NCEO) has a working list of assessment accommodations to consider for students with disabilities.
- Some states provide assessment accommodations for all students.

There is a strong parallel between the creation of an inclusive accountability system and the creation of the inclusive schooling movement. Initial reaction to inclusive schooling for many was disbelief or denial, but eventually acceptance of the benefits for students with and without disabilities occurs. A similar phenomenon is occurring in the area of assessment.

Relevant facts that parents need to know about accommodations are presented in Box 10.4. Questions that parents may want to ask are listed in Box 10.5.

Past Practice:
Needed Revisions, Needed Change

Finally, we know there are parents who refer their children for special education evaluation not only to find out what, if any, services they may be eligible for but also to secure testing accommodations for entrance exams such as the SAT and the ACT. In some states, assessment accommodations for classroom tests can be granted to any student by the building administrator. In this case, no evaluation is needed to secure testing accommodations for day-to-day testing. However, we have heard parents comment, "Why would we put him through that test if he can get out of it?"

We question the motivation for wanting to exclude any child from an accountability system that evaluates the effectiveness and impact of instruction. We believe that if there is a complete understanding of what

---

BOX 10.5

Look Further . . . Questions to Ask

Questions that parents need to ask about the facts leading to the decision of having their child participate in the general assessment:

- Will my child participate in the general assessment program? (Be sure your state has a state assessment. If it does not, find out what is used to monitor students' learning in your district.)

- If the facts and discussion lead to exclusion from the assessment, be sure to find out exactly why. These reasons for exclusion are important and should be grounded in valid beliefs. Remember, the ultimate accommodation is exclusion from the assessment itself. If the reason is this:

Different curriculum

- Find out why your child is in a different curriculum.

- Find out how this different curriculum aligns with the state assessment.

- District standards or common core of learning? Is there a direct correlation or link between the curriculum your child is in and the identified learning goals for all children?

- Find out how the school plans to evaluate your child's learning and progress. What alternate or different assessment is in place?

Test is too hard

- Find out why the test is "too hard" for your child (is it due to content, test-taking skills, time constraints, setting, and so on?)

- Find out what assessment accommodation would provide your child the opportunity to participate in the assessment.

- Find out what additional teaching (e.g., test and study skills) is needed to allow your child to participate in the assessment.

- Find out how this assessment differs from the classroom tests your child takes. What are the similarities? How can the gap be closed?

---

an inclusive accountability system is and its purpose, the question might be changed to "Why can students 'get out of' assessment?" On what grounds are they excluded? Who is eligible for exclusion?

In the past, it was students with disabilities who were excluded from assessment. In some states, students with disabilities can be excluded from testing and still receive credit or a high school diploma. In these cases, students need to meet their IEP goals to receive a high school diploma. Skyrocketing referrals to special education often are the product of this type of situation. The motivation behind these referrals is to not only secure services but also exemption from the assessment.

BOX 10.5

Look Further . . . Questions to Ask (Continued)

The accommodations your child needs are either not permissible or would invalidate the assessment results.

- Find out the basis for this (remind school personnel that there are minimal research data that support this).
- Regardless, insist that your child be provided needed accommodations to allow complete or partial participation in the assessment.
- Find out what instructional accommodations are used in classroom instruction and on class tests. Is there a natural flow of instructional accommodations to assessment accommodations?

We have never done this before—provided accommodations and had students with disabilities or those students in different programs participate in the assessment.

- Go for it! Now is the time to start the process of inclusive accountability and access to both programs and assessments for all students. All kids count and must be accounted for.
- Align service delivery and classroom instruction with assessment practices. Examine all the possibilities of providing your child the opportunity to participate not only in general education classes but also the assessment system.

Attitudinal—"It is not fair to provide accommodations to some but not others."

- Be sure to educate those who say or think these statements that "fair" means all students getting the services or provision they need to be successful—and that this looks different for different students.
- Be sure they understand that accommodations are for need, not advantage.

The purpose of assessment again must be made clear. Is it high or low stakes for students? For schools? What is driving the motivation to get students out of the assessment? Do parents and teachers really understand the purpose of assessment and the importance of having all students included in the accountability system? For the small percentage of students (no greater than 1% to 2% of the total school population) unable to meaningfully participate in the assessment, what is used to measure their learning?

Relevant facts for parents to know are presented in Box 10.6. Questions for parents to ask are listed in Box 10.7.

Parents should be informed partners and participants in the decision-making process about their child's participation in district and state

---

BOX 10.6

Facts That Parents Need to Know

Fact Sheet: Did You Know????

- Your child may be eligible for testing accommodations without needing to be classified as a special education student. Talk to your building administrator, director of special education, and/or state department of special education services.

- If you allow your child to be excluded from the standard assessment there may be no alternate means in place to assess your child's learning and growth. This means that your child may not be included in the broader accountability system for your school or district. However, by the year 2000, an alternate assessment must be used for every student not in the standard assessment.

- In some cases, the high-stakes nature of an assessment provides schools with incentives to exclude as many students as possible who are anticipated not to do well. In doing so, schools can look good when compared with others because the overall school building score represents students who are thought to achieve better than students with disabilities.

---

assessments as well as in the reporting of results. Are parents and IEP team members aware of the need for an alternate assessment for a small percentage of students with disabilities? Do they know and ask about it? The answer is usually no. We have reviewed some of the questions to ask and information to gather. In sum, be absolutely sure that parents know about the purpose of the assessment, the need for accountability assessments, the nature of the assessment, the goals of the student's instruction, and test preparation options.

BOX 10.7

Look Further . . . Questions to Ask

Before seeking ways to exempt a child from the district or state assessment, parents need to consider the following:

- What is the purpose of the assessment?
- What are the stakes involved (student, building, program)?
- How will my child benefit from participating in the assessment?
- How will the accountability system benefit from my child participating?
- How can my child participate? What, if any, accommodations are needed?
- What are other districts or states doing in this area?

Purpose of Assessment

What is the assessment used for: eligibility and reevaluation decisions for service delivery, classroom instruction decisions, or accountability? If the assessment is for the purpose of accountability, find out whether it is for system or student accountability. That is, does the assessment hope to gain information about how all students in a system or district are doing (system accountability) or how well an individual student is doing (student accountability)? The consequences attached to either one of these may be very different. For example, an assessment that evaluates system accountability could potentially result in the awarding of rewards or sanctions to the school. For student accountability, results on an assessment may mean certifying students for a high school diploma.

Need for Accountability Assessments

Be sure that all decision makers, including parents, are aware of the importance of knowing how all students are performing in school, not just whether they are in school. If needed, discuss the point that students who do not participate in the assessment tend to be left out of the educational reforms and changes in instruction that accompany assessment used for accountability.

Nature of the Assessment

Be sure that all parties know the following information about the assessment:

- Name of the test
- Content areas covered by the test
- Grades tested
- How the test is administered (over how many days, how long the testing sessions are)
- Nature of the items (multiple-choice, short answer, writing samples, performance-based)
- What is done with the students' scores

Everyone in the decision-making process benefits when more people know about what they are discussing.

Goals of Student's Instruction

Regardless of prior IEP planning meetings and discussions, be sure that everyone understands and can verbalize the purpose of each student's instruction and educational experiences. Parents need to understand whether their child is pursuing the same instructional goals as other students. If so, he or she should be in the general assessment system with the rest of the students. Of course, some students may need accommodations to participate. This is a different question from whether they should participate.

Preparation Options for Assessment

How are students being prepared for the assessment experience? Who is teaching and reviewing test-taking skills for the test? Do students know what to do if, say, they don't understand directions? What is being done?

Parents have their own history of experiences with assessments. Often, it can be beneficial to discuss these experiences with their child.

Guidelines and Policies for Assessment

In Chapters 2 and 3, we talked about guidelines and criteria for making participation and accommodation decisions. It is important to share with parents the policies, if any, that guide your district or state assessment. If needed, encourage parents to contact the state's assessment office in the department of education to obtain information on, for example, how scores of students who receive accommodations are reported. Are they included in the overall report or left out? Having guidelines and policies available for parents will help them in their role as participants in their child's education program.

We share with you the story of Beth (see Box 10.8) to make a point. The abilities of too many students with and without disabilities have been underestimated. Most students with disabilities are fully capable of participating in general education classes and assessment programs when accommodations and modifications to material have been provided. Don't be afraid to be a trailblazer. Beth's parents persevered and advocated strongly for her. Thinking and service delivery was pushed to greater breadth and depth. In working collaboratively with administration and the IEP team, many things are possible. However, we know that in some cases personnel need to be educated about what is possible and legally the right of the student. It is extremely important that parents be informed participants in their child's education program. Refer back to Chapter 7 for IEP forms and checklists that can be used in IEP team meetings.

BOX 10.8

A True Story About Beth

Beth was an extremely bright seventh grader who had gone on a ski trip with her best friend and her family. As the result of a ski accident, Beth sustained traumatic brain injuries so severe that she almost died. After spending months in a rehabilitative hospital and several brain surgeries, Beth returned home, not at all like she was when she left. Beth spent the next year learning to walk, talk, and make her needs known. Educational evaluations were performed, and learning levels and prognoses were discussed. In the summer before her freshman year in high school, a meeting was held with Beth's parents, her neuropsychologist, the school counselor, the school psychologist, and the building administrator. Information was exchanged and reports of progress distributed. As a result of this meeting, new directions for Beth's education as a high schooler began to be outlined. An IEP team meeting was convened and an IEP was written that incorporated all the reports and information about Beth's current condition. A reevaluation date was set for three months. This was due to the fact that the conditions of persons with traumatic head injury can change rapidly and require immediate modification.

Beth had lost her short- and long-term memory capacity as well as her ability to process auditory information, although some of these were making slow and minimal recovery. Therefore, information presented in class had to be modified to include visual presentation. All homework, reports, and other assignments had to be modified and accommodations provided to Beth so that she could participate in the educational process. Cosmetically, Beth looked no different from before. She looked like the average high schooler with no visible indication of her situation. She had learned to mask her gait, one result of the ski accident, and had learned to be resourceful in finding out information about what she needed to do. However, Beth would lose her way from class to class if not escorted by a friend.

Beth's IEP had to be modified tremendously for both class lectures, assignments, and tests, and day-to-day functioning. Beth lived in a state where students were required to take a minimal competency test to gain credit and graduate with a high school diploma. Where once Beth aspired to become a highly educated and skilled professional, she was now faced with the challenge of earning a high school diploma.

The then current IEP form did not have much room to record needed changes in her learning goals and modifications in her education program and had no place for the IEP team to note needed accommodations on class assignments, much less classroom tests and the mandated state competency exams. An addendum listing needed changes was attached to the IEP form. The state did provide a published list of accommodations that it allowed for classroom instruction and testing; however, there was no specific reference made to the statewide testing program. The IEP team was faced with figuring out how Beth would meaningfully participate in her general education curriculum and what accommodations were absolutely necessary.

(Continued)

BOX 10.8

A True Story About Beth (Continued)

After looking into existing policies and guidelines, they found that the only policy that existed for students with disabilities and the state testing program was that accommodations had to be noted on the IEP at least one year prior to the required exam. With this information as its guide, the IEP team tailored Beth's IEP with her best interests, both emotionally and educationally, in mind. Remember, Beth is a student for whom a general education program would not have been an option if it hadn't been for her parents (and their attorney). Beth maintained her classification of Traumatic Brain Injured while being educated in the least restrictive environment for her.

It clearly would have been much easier to have put her in a special education program. However, with strong work from the IEP team, Beth's program was made into one that was predominantly visual. Instead of reading books, she would watch videos; instead of writing assignments, she would dictate to a scribe or tape recorder. For book reports, Beth would make collages. Classroom tests were reformatted to be given orally with visual cues or use predominantly multiple-choice questions. This required the least amount of writing, which was needed as Beth had lost her capacity to spell or formulate written passages. For the minimal competency test, Beth was granted extended time. She took an average of eight hours to complete the test and scored 100 on every exam she took.

In the end, Beth met every requirement for a high school diploma except for one content area. This was because she physically was unable to take a full class load. Beth made the conscious decision to not pursue this final requirement because she did not have it in her to do so. It seemed too much to endure another year or two of the content course and then sit for the respective minimum competency exam. Instead, she graduated with an IEP diploma and went on to attend a private college where she audited art classes.

This true story illustrates in a very abbreviated form what is possible for students with disabilities even as severe and difficult as Beth's. She was capable of earning 100% on the competency exams, given accommodations she needed to participate (e.g., extended and frequent breaks, food ingestion, and a scribe). Beth was provided the opportunity to (a) make a choice as to the path her high school education would go and (b) participate in the accountability system and given the means (accommodations) to show what she knew. This is possible for almost all students who have disabilities.

Home Role and Responsibility in the Assessment Process

After the terms for participation in the accountability assessment system have been determined, there are many ways in which parents can facili-

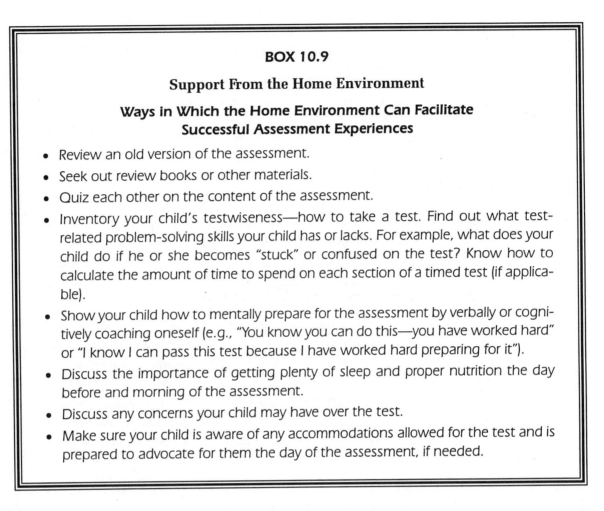

BOX 10.9

Support From the Home Environment

**Ways in Which the Home Environment Can Facilitate
Successful Assessment Experiences**

- Review an old version of the assessment.
- Seek out review books or other materials.
- Quiz each other on the content of the assessment.
- Inventory your child's testwiseness—how to take a test. Find out what test-related problem-solving skills your child has or lacks. For example, what does your child do if he or she becomes "stuck" or confused on the test? Know how to calculate the amount of time to spend on each section of a timed test (if applicable).
- Show your child how to mentally prepare for the assessment by verbally or cognitively coaching oneself (e.g., "You know you can do this—you have worked hard" or "I know I can pass this test because I have worked hard preparing for it").
- Discuss the importance of getting plenty of sleep and proper nutrition the day before and morning of the assessment.
- Discuss any concerns your child may have over the test.
- Make sure your child is aware of any accommodations allowed for the test and is prepared to advocate for them the day of the assessment, if needed.

tate student performance (see Box 10.9). This support can range from having parents ensure their children get the proper amount of rest to making sure they are mentally prepared for the task of assessment. It is important for students to have an anticipatory set for the assessment. That is, do they know the purpose of the test? Content covered? Format of the test (e.g., multiple-choice, short answer)? Length of the test, and so on? If possible, obtain an old version of the test and have parents walk through it with their child. Hopefully teachers will have already done this, but even so, familiarity can decrease the level of concern.

Summary

As you can see, the process of assessment is one that demands informed decisions and considerations of a student's needs, educational goals and experiences, and abilities. Parents are vital to the process. In this chapter, we provided you with a variety of questions to ask and information to share with parents for them to become informed participants in the assessment system of their child's school. Before decisions about partici-

---

BOX 10.10

Myth or Truth Answers

TRUTH   Parents can be powerful players in the decision-making process regarding participation in assessments and the provision of accommodations, both for instruction and assessment.
<u>Explanation</u>: Parents have the final say as to what can occur in their child's education program. [See page 163]

MYTH   Most parents understand the concepts of accountability and assessment and the purpose(s) of district and state testing programs.
<u>Explanation</u>: Most parents of students with disabilities are aware of assessment for eligibility purposes and the IEP team but not accountability or specific assessment programs. [See page 164]

TRUTH   Many parents have fought long and hard to gain access to general education curriculum and programs for their students; hence, inclusion in the district/state assessment program is not necessarily a priority at this time.
<u>Explanation</u>: Besides working for inclusion in the general education setting, many parents do not understand the concept of accountability or the importance of having their child participate in the district or state assessment. [See page 165]

TRUTH   Parents of students with disabilities assume that their child's district assessment results are included in the overall report of test results.
<u>Explanation</u>: For those students with disabilities who do participate in district assessments with peers, why would the parents think otherwise? Their child is taking the same test as his or her peers. [See page 168]

MYTH   When some students are excluded or exempted from the regular assessment, parents know to ask about what alternate assessment will be used to assess their child's learning.
<u>Explanation</u>: Both the parents and also many IEP team personnel are not aware of the need for, or importance of, providing an alternate assessment for students unable to participate in the regular assessment. [See page 172]

---

pation and accommodations can be made, it is imperative that both parents and the decision-making committees fully understand the following:

- Information about the assessment
- Its purpose
- The need for an inclusive accountability system

- Nature of the assessment
- The goals of student instruction
- The need for test preparation

Too often, it is easy to rationalize the exclusion of a student from an assessment and thus the accountability system. Although the reasons seem logical (e.g., test is too difficult, never provided these needed accommodations before), all students have the right to be counted and be accounted for in the overall accountability system.

Now check your knowledge about the myth/truth statements presented at the beginning of this chapter (see Box 10.10 for answers). Try to give an explanation for why each statement is correctly identified either as a myth or as the truth.

Resources for Further Information

Council of Chief State School Officers. (in press). *Questions and answers about assessment accommodations and students with disabilities: A guide for parents and teachers.* Washington, DC: Author.

Elliott, J. L., & Thurlow, M. L. (1997). *Opening the door to educational reform: Understanding assessment and accountability.* Berkeley, MA: National Center on Educational Outcomes, Parents Engaged in Educational Reform.

Elliott, J. L., & Thurlow, M. L. (1997). *Opening the door to educational reform: Understanding standards.* Berkeley, MA: National Center on Educational Outcomes, Parents Engaged in Educational Reform.

11

Implementation:
Where Reality Hits the Road

Topics

- □ From Corruption to Court Cases
- □ Inclusive Schooling Is Not Necessarily Inclusive Accountability
- □ Moving Forward

In this chapter, you will . . .

- find out about unintended outcomes of high-stakes accountability assessments.

- review recent cases of corruption in school-based assessment programs.

- learn about landmark court cases and rulings in the areas of providing accommodations, making modifications, and issues of "otherwise qualified."

In this book, we have discussed the issues surrounding inclusive assessment and accountability. The common theme throughout has been how students with disabilities have been underrepresented and left out of reforms, assessment, and reports on the progress of learning. Historically, educators have underestimated the potential of students with disabilities and their ability to participate both in the mainstream of the education process and in the assessment of that process. In this chapter, we provide a brief discussion of the realities and legalities of restructuring accountability systems that include all students and reflect

> ## BOX 11.1
>
> ### Myth or Truth? Do You Know?
>
> Read each statement below and decide whether it is a myth or the truth about current practice.
>
> - The inclusive schooling movement and inclusive accountability are aligned and in tandem with each other.
> - The education malpractice of tampering with test protocols has become a real issue in the evolving world of high-stakes testing.
> - There are court cases that rule in favor of the district not having to modify tests for students with disabilities who are otherwise not qualified to take them.
> - Inclusive assessment and accountability is potentially a very litigious area for education.

today's educational reforms. Once again, by the time you finish this chapter, you will be able to identify which of the statements in Box 11.1 are myths and which are the truth.

From Corruption to Court Cases

Historically, standardized tests have been the bogeyman of education. Unfortunately, this bogeyman has put pressures on schools and educators that has resulted, in some cases, in corruption. Some schools have been pressured to the point of doing whatever is necessary to improve scores or obtain higher scores. The most recent and notable manifestations of these pressures have involved tampering with test protocols. Some of these pressures stem from the following:

- More states are beginning to implement high-stakes tests for students and schools.

- Rewards and sanctions are being placed on schools as well as superintendents of school districts.

- Students must pass a test to be promoted to the next grade or graduate.

- Schools must show improvement to a preset level or risk sanctions and/or school takeovers.

- Teachers can be removed, administrators let go, and a state-based crisis team sent in to temporarily run the building.

Corruption

In the winter of 1996, Fairfield Connecticut's district officials became suspicious over a high number of erasures on students' Iowa test protocols (see Lindsay, 1996). Two central office administrators spent time reviewing the test protocols of Stratfield Elementary School students to find clues as to what other schools in the district could do to improve test scores. From 1990 to 1992, Stratfield had the unprecedented achievement of composite scores that had not dropped below the 98th percentile. What these administrators found instead was an unusually high number of erasures on the test protocols. By that spring, the test publisher concluded that indeed the test protocols in Stratfield Elementary School had been tampered with. In fact, most of the erased answers had been changed from incorrect to correct. Someone, possibly more than one person, had changed answers on answer sheets.

Stratfield Elementary happened to be the district's flagship school and had twice earned—in 1987 and 1994—the U.S. Department of Education's blue ribbon award for a school of excellence. In 1993, *Redbook* named this same school one of the best on the magazine's list of the top 177 elementary schools in the country. However, in the spring of 1996 when students at Stratfield and two other district elementary schools were retested, Stratfield's scores on some sections of the test were said to have dropped as much as 10 points. Further analysis by the test publisher showed that the number of erasures at the school was five times higher than other schools' tests—89% of the changed answers were from wrong to right at Stratfield, whereas 69% was the highest corrected rate shown at any grade in the other schools.

Dubbed "Erasuregate," the investigation continues in Fairfield, Connecticut—who committed the education malpractice? Is this the backlash created by lawmakers having placed so much emphasis on standardized tests as the yardstick of student and school achievement and progress? Test publishers are quick to point out that their products are not designed to be used as batting averages or to beguile teachers and administrators into forced change.

In March 1997, in the midst of the beginning of a legal procedure to investigate and remove Stratfield Elementary's principal, he voluntarily retired.

Another case of protocol tampering was uncovered in the fall of 1996 in the small upstate New York community of Barker. Third-grade teachers at an elementary school there were purportedly told by their principal to correct wrong answers on the state's Pupil Evaluation Program.

Yet another case appeared in November 1996 when a Chicago curriculum coordinator was suspended without pay after a test-tampering incident. A district investigation found that students at Clay Elementary School had been allowed to practice on the same version of the Iowa Test of Basic Skills they were later required to take as part of the district testing program. The same school's principal served a 10-day unpaid suspension for an even greater breach of test security. It was discovered that she had improperly kept old copies of the ITBS and the Illinois Goal Assessment Program (IGAP). Copies of the test had been made and distributed to teachers. Although the school's principal denies knowing of the cheating, it was thought that she should have taken action after hearing that students reported recognizing questions on the tests. Coincidentally, implementation had begun the previous spring of Chicago's new school board policy requiring third, sixth, and eighth graders to meet a preset cut score to be promoted to the next grade level.

Finally, in Hawaii in the spring of 1996, an elementary school principal directed her staff to fill in answers on students' uncompleted Stanford Achievement Tests. Corruption comes in various forms, and they continue.

In addition to these tragedies are those we mentioned earlier from an article by Zlatos (1994), a freelance education writer. He uncovered great discrepancies between school districts' test-taking policies and aggregate test scoring reports. Zlatos found that school districts artificially inflated their test scores by excluding students with disabilities and English-language learners from the test or from the reports published for the public. He determined that the percentage of students who were tested and whose scores were reported in the aggregate of scores ranged from 66% to 93%.

Referrals to special education and grade retentions kept many eligible students from participating in the district assessment programs. However, in one case where Zlatos factored in all the students who had intentionally been excluded, the passing rate of one school dropped from 96% to 78%.

So, with all this in mind, we ask, which is more corrupt—changing answers on bubble sheets or excluding students who are expected to do less well from tests? We rank them as equal.

Court Cases

A number of court cases have been judged over the past several years to be directly related to assessment accommodations and the high-stakes nature of tests (for a detailed discussion of the legal implications of both, see Phillips, 1993, 1995, 1996). The new frontier of inclusive assessment and accountability presents itself as a potentially litigious one in many ways.

In 1984, the landmark case *Debra P. v. Turlington* held that a diploma is a property right protected by the Fourteenth Amendment. *Debra P.* found that procedural due process required adequate notice of the testing requirement to pass the state test to earn a diploma for graduation. Although this case did not specifically address the rights of students with disabilities, it has generated at least two major questions: First, can diplomas be denied to students with disabilities who complete their IEPs but are unable to pass a required graduation test? Second, if students require an accommodation to take the test that the school or state disallows, and such action results in failure on the test and consequent denial of a diploma, what criteria should be used for making testing accommodation decisions?

Another notable court case, *Brookhart* (1983), involved a minimum competency test mandated by a local school district. Students who failed the test were granted school completion certificates instead of regular diplomas. Students with IEPs who did not pass the graduation test challenged the requirement. These students had varying physical and cognitive disabilities. The court ruled that all students, including those with disabilities, could be required to pass such a test; however, both parents and educators would need sufficient time to determine whether the skills tested should become part of the student's IEP. Finally, the court ruled that assessment administrators must provide accommodations for students with disabilities as long as their use does not "substantially modify" the test.

In *Southeastern Community College v. Davis*, a 1979 case, the Supreme Court ruled that the college was not required to modify its nursing program to exempt a profoundly hearing-impaired applicant from the clinical training. The Court's ruling indicated that an educational institution is not required to lower or substantially modify its standards to accommodate a disabled student and is not required to disregard the disability when determining an applicant's eligibility or fit for a program. In this case, the Court agreed with the college that the student was not "otherwise qualified" for the clinical program because her hearing impairment would introduce communication problems with patients and physicians, especially in a surgical environment where facial masks preclude lip reading.

The 1991 *Anderson v. Banks* case involved a mentally retarded student who was denied a diploma based on a graduation test. The court looked at the issue of "otherwise qualified" and ruled that if a person's disability is extraneous to the skills needed for the test, that person is otherwise qualified, but if that disability prevents that person from demonstrating the required skills the person is not otherwise qualified. Therefore, the court held that the school district should not be prevented from establishing academic standards for a diploma. The fact that these standards have an adverse impact on students with disabilities does not make the test unlawful.

Board of Education v. Rowley reviewed the intent of the Education for All Handicapped Act (EHA), enacted in 1975 and renamed in 1991 the Individuals with Disabilities Education Act. The court ruled that the Act mandated specialized and individualized education but did not guarantee any specific educational outcome. In fact, the court stated that "the intent of the Act was more to open the field of public education to handicapped children on appropriate terms than to guarantee any particular level of education once inside." Therefore, the denial of diplomas to students with disabilities who are unable to pass a minimum competency test, given proper notification and instruction, did not constitute the denial of a "free and appropriate public education."

The Hawaii decision in the spring of 1996 involved an OCR (optical character recognition) ruling in which a student with a learning disability that affected his writing was denied a reader for the statewide graduation test. The state's policy guidelines allowed for a reader only for nonreading portions of the test and only for students with visual impairments. These students were required to take the reading portion of the state test in Braille. Although requests for exceptions could be filed for other students with disabilities, these requests were usually denied. The Court in this case ruled that providing a reader for the reading portion of the test would be in direct conflict with the construct being tested. However, not providing one for portions of the test not designed to measure reading competency constituted unlawful discrimination.

These are but a few of the most recent and applicable court cases dealing with accommodations for and high-stakes assessment of students with disabilities. As inclusive assessment and accountability become more the norm and the recognized right of all students, including those with disabilities, we will likely see more court cases. We have learned from these and other such cases that (a) assessment accommodations cannot be denied, (b) assessment coordinators or administrators must process each request for an accommodation carefully and individually, (c) accommodations that do not change or modify the skill to be measured should be granted, (d) accommodations that invalidate the test constructs or construe a score that misrepresents the student's actual ability may not be granted, and if granted, the reporting of the score needs to indicate the use of such accommodation, and (e) the high school diploma is a protected property under the Fourteenth Amendment, thus, students and parents must have adequate notice of the requirement to pass the test to graduate with a diploma.

Inclusive Schooling Is Not Necessarily Inclusive Accountability

Today, a nationwide initiative of inclusive schooling has been raising awareness levels about the potential, capabilities, and means of educating students with disabilities. More and more students with disabilities are being educated side by side with their peers without disabilities. Students who once would have been educated in a self-contained classroom for special education students are now being integrated and succeeding in the general education mainstream. Likewise, students with more significant cognitive disabilities are integrated into the general education process with their IEPs driving the instruction they receive. More students with disabilities are receiving their education in schools and classes they would attend if they had no disability. We know that implementation of the inclusive schooling model is all over the map, just like inclusive assessment.

However, when you stop to think about it, the inclusive schooling movement does not align or match the current accountability system. That is, although more students with disabilities are being educated in the least restricted environment or an inclusive education setting, these same students are not accounted for in the larger system of student accountability. On one hand, people have advocated, to varying degrees, and achieved integration and inclusion of students with disabilities in the general education setting; on the other hand, these same students are not accounted for even when they are there.

Let us be unequivocally direct. You do not necessarily have accountability when you have inclusive schooling, just as you do not necessarily have inclusive schooling when you have accountability. That is, including students in assessment does not mean that inclusive schooling is taking place. Conversely, to tout inclusive schooling as a model of educating students with disabilities without accounting for their learning is equally unacceptable.

Moving Forward

As the catchy saying goes, there has been a paradigm shift. Over the past 10 years, major educational changes have been afoot (see Box 11.2). We know more about the business of educating students, including those with disabilities, than we ever did before. We have more tools and technology for assessing learning and progress than ever before. We have rules, regulations, mandates, and court cases to show for these efforts. So where do we go from here?

The reality of standards-based reform is here to stay, as is assessment and accountability. A perspective shift in many arenas has resulted in more, not less, money being allocated for research and development in instruction, assessment, and efforts to create broad-based accountability systems at the local, state, and national levels. We must work hard to make this shifting system one that benefits and includes all students, first in accountability and then in life.

Summary

We must continue our effort of standard-based reform and be sure it reflects all students. We must provide the means to help all students meet higher goals and standards. We must provide sustained staff development and training to educators and parents and fortify the collaboration

---

BOX 11.2

Perspective Shift: The Emerging Paradigm

POLICY

From an emphasis on	To an emphasis on
Viewing special education exclusively	Viewing special education inclusively
Segregation	Integration/inclusive schooling
Labeling	Functional language

ADMINISTRATION

From an emphasis on	To an emphasis on
Centralization	Decentralization
Teachers' responsibilities	Teachers' rights
Bureaucracy	Child centeredness
Applying pressure	Applying resources
Surrendering responsibility	Participating in decision making

IDENTIFICATION, ASSESSMENT, AND PLACEMENT

From an emphasis on	To an emphasis on
Medical model	Educational-needs model
Standardized assessment tools	Individualized/performance assessment tools
Reactive assessment and remediation	Proactive assessment, prevention, and intervention

---

CLIENTELE

From an emphasis on	To an emphasis on
Unilingualism	Multilingualism
The dominant culture	Diverse cultures
Predictable and limited needs	Needs over the life span
Homogeneity	Diversity of clients

CURRICULUM AND INSTRUCTION

From an emphasis on	To an emphasis on
Central design control	Local design control
Teacher directedness	Child centeredness
Conformity in learning	Diversity of learning styles
Excellence for a few	Excellence for all
One curriculum for all	Individualized curriculum
Access to facilities	Access to quality programs
Individual teachers taking responsibility	Collaborative teams taking responsibility for all
Academic learning	Developing habits and attitudes

SUPPORT SERVICES

From an emphasis on	To an emphasis on
Federal supports	Local supports
Minimal use of technology	Maximum use of technology
Student-focused resources	Trainer-focused resources

BOX 11.3

Myth or Truth Answers

MYTH   The inclusive schooling movement and inclusive accountability are aligned and in tandem with each other.
Explanation: Perhaps the only thing aligning inclusive schooling and inclusive accountability is the fact that both have met with tremendous resistance. [See pages 185-186]

TRUTH   The education malpractice of tampering with test protocols has become a real issue in the evolving world of high-stakes testing.
Explanation: The pressures of standardized tests and incentives to look good have caused corruption in some testing programs. [See page 181]

TRUTH   There are court cases that rule in favor of the district not having to modify tests for students with disabilities who are otherwise not qualified to take them.
Explanation: Courts have ruled that students who, because of their disability, do not have the skills needed to take and pass a test for graduation do not have the right to demand that a district or state modify its academic standards. [See page 184]

TRUTH   Inclusive assessment and accountability is potentially a very litigious area for education.
Explanation: Many recent court cases are the signs of things to come as states raise standards and stakes of assessment. [See page 185]

---

between home and school in the name of student school success. We must do a better job of communicating and involving a wide selection of stakeholders in school-based decision making and other reforms affecting school change. We must take a serious look at reallocating resources to do a better job of providing needed support in delivering services to students. We must never lose sight of the importance of all students achieving their best and thus must take into consideration individual needs. We must create a school culture that recognizes and celebrates diversity. And we must always put children first!

One last time, check your knowledge about the myth/truth statements presented at the beginning of this chapter and attempt an explanation for each answer that you gave. Correct answers and possible explanations are given in Box 11.3.

Resources for Further Information

Lindsay, P. (1996, October 2). Whodunit? Someone cheated on standardized tests at a Connecticut school. And it wasn't the students. *Education Week, 16*(5), 25-29.

Phillips, S. E. (1993). *Legal implications of high-stakes assessment: What states should know.* Oakbrook, IL: North Central Regional Educational Laboratory.

Phillips, S. E. (1995). *All students, same test, same standards: What the new Title I legislation will mean for the educational assessment of special education students.* Oakbrook, IL: North Central Regional Educational Laboratory.

Phillips, S. E. (1996). Legal defensibility of standards: Issues and policy perspectives. *Educational Measurement: Issues and Practice, 15*(2), 5-19.

Zlatos, B. (1994). Don't test, don't tell: Is "academic red-shirting" skewing the way we rank our schools? *American School Board Journal, 181*(11), 24-28.

Resources:
Reproducible Forms

Reproducible Forms

A. Participation Decision-Making Form

B. Alternate Assessment Case Study

C. Checklist of Criteria for Making Decisions About Participation and Needed Accommodations for Classroom, District, and State Assessments

D. Checklist for Deciding Assessment Type

E. IEP Form for Identifying Accommodations

F. IEP Form for Identifying Accommodations, With Examples

G. Accommodations Case Study

H. Test Accommodation Planning Chart

I. Instructional and Assessment Accommodations Worksheet

J. District/State Assessment Accommodations Worksheet

K. Study/Test Skills Checklist

L. Logistics and Strategic Plan for Providing Assessment Accommodations

M. Final Arrangements for Assessment Accommodations

N. Suggestions for Alternate Assessments

O. Student Feedback/Interview Form

P. Instructional and Assessment Accommodations

Q. Building Implementation Document

R. Inclusive Assessment and Accountability Survey

Participation Decision-Making Form

1. Is the student working toward the same   [ ] YES   [ ] NO
    standards as other students in the classroom?

    (If answer to 1 is YES, student should participate in the regular
    assessment)

2. If NO, is the student working on a modified   [ ] YES   [ ] NO
    set of standards (many are the same, but some
    are modified slightly)?

    (If answer to 2 is YES, student should participate in the regular
    assessment)

3. If NO, is the student working on an alternate   [ ] YES   [ ] NO
    set of standards?

    (If answer to 3 is YES, student should participate in an alternate
    assessment)

4. If the student is working on an alternate set   [ ] YES   [ ] NO
    of standards, are there any areas of unique
    skills that could be assessed through the
    regular assessment?

    (If answer to 4 is YES, student should participate in both the regular
    and an alternate assessment)

Copyright © 1997 by Corwin Press, Inc.

Alternate Assessment Case Study

BACKGROUND INFORMATION:

Paulita is an intellectually impaired 10th grader. Her verbal IQ is 50; performance IQ is 72; full scale is 61, math grade equivalent is 5.3; reading grade equivalent is 3.7; and written language is 3.0. Paulita exhibits expressive speech and language difficulties. Paulita attends a regular school in a special education class. She is integrated for art and wood technology.

INSTRUCTIONAL INFORMATION:

Paulita requires extra processing time (extra wait time). Directions must be presented multiple timeS and in stages. Paulita has a short attention span but works well in a small group. She is working on her own individualized goals and objectives according to her IEP and is not expected to graduate with a regular high school diploma.

Based on the information above, suggest some instructional accommodations for Paulita.

How will you assess Paulita's learning and progress? Suggest alternate ways to assess her learning and achievement of her goals and objectives. Consider the following categories:

Observation: **Interviews/Checklists:**

Testing: **Record Review:**

Copyright © 1997 by Corwin Press, Inc.

Checklist of Criteria for Making Decisions About Participation and Needed Accommodations for Classroom, District, and State Assessments

Student Name: *Grade:*

School/Program: *Date of Meeting:*

Our goal as the IEP team of _____ school is to include all students with disabilities in district and state assessments. The decisions for participation and accommodation of _____ (student's name) are based on the following process:

Use the checklist below to guide decisions about accommodations.

The following decisions were made by person(s) who know _____'s learning needs and skills. These decisions were based on _____'s current level of functioning and learning characteristics as follows:

Yes   No

SETTING

____ ____   **1.   Can work independently**

____ ____   **1a. Can complete tasks with assistance or with the following accommodation(s):**
        ____One-to-one assistance to complete written tasks
        ____On-task reminders
        ____Directions repeated and/or clarified
        ____Other _____

____ ____   **2.   Can complete tasks within a large group but quiet setting**

____ ____   **2a. Can complete tasks if provided the following accommodation(s):**
        ____Test administered in a separate location with minimal distractions
        ____Test administered in a small group, study carrel, or individually (circle one)
        ____Special lighting
        ____Adaptive furniture—specify _____
        ____Noise buffer (e.g., earplugs, earphones, other _____)
        ____Other _____

TIMING

____ ____   **1.   Can work continuously for 20- to 30-minute periods; if not, specify the average length of time student is able to work continuously.**

____ ____   **1a. Can work in a group without distracting other test takers**

Copyright © 1997 by Corwin Press, Inc.

Yes   No

SCHEDULING

____ ____ 1. **Can complete tasks if provided periodic breaks or other timing consideration(s)/ accommodation(s):**

___Test administered over several sessions, time per session not to exceed _____ minutes

___Allowed to take breaks as needed, not to exceed _____ breaks per 20- to 30-minute period

___Test administered over several days, each session not to exceed _____ minutes in duration

___Test administered in the morning, early afternoon, late afternoon (circle one)

___Extended time to complete the test in one session

___Other _____

PRESENTATION

____ ____ 1.   **Can listen to and follow oral directions given by an adult or on audiotape**

____ ____ 1a. **Can listen to and follow oral directions with assistance or the following accommodation(s):**

___Visual cues or printed material to facilitate understanding of orally give directions

___Directions repeated, clarified, or simplified

___Directions read individually

___Visual magnification device

___Auditory amplification device

___Other _____

____ ____ 2.   **Can read and comprehend written directions**

____ ____ 2a. **Can comprehend written directions with assistance or the following accommodation:**

___Written directions read

___Directions repeated, clarified, or simplified

___Key words or phrases in written directions highlighted

___Visual prompts (e.g., stop signs, arrows) that show directions to start, stop and continue working

___Written directions presented in larger and/or bold print

___Written directions presented with one complete sentence per line of text

___Visual magnification device

___Auditory amplification device

___Other _____

____ ____ 3.   **Can read, understand, and answer questions in multiple-choice format**

____ ____ 3a. **Can understand and answer questions in multiple-choice format with assistanc or the following accommodation(s):**

___Reader to read the test*

___Pencil grip

___Access to prerecorded reading

Copyright © 1997 by Corwin Press, Inc.

Yes   No

    ___Test signed
    ___Test presented in Braille or large print
    ___Visual magnification device
    ___Auditory amplification device
    ___Increased spacing between items and/or limited items presented per page
    ___Templates or masks to reduce visible print
    ___Papers secured to desk (e.g., magnets, tape)
    ___Other _____

RESPONSE

____ ____ 1. Can use paper and pen/pencil to write short answer or paragraph-length responses to open-ended questions

____ ____ 1a. Can respond to open-ended questions when provided assistance or the following accommodation(s):
    ___Pencil grip
    ___Word processor
    ___Scribe (someone to record verbatim oral responses to questions)
    ___Brailler
    ___Copy assistance between drafts of writing
    ___Write an outline to a question and, using a tape recorder, dictate the body of the response, per the written outline
    ___Dictate answer into a tape recorder
    ___Visual magnification devices
    ___Touch Talker or other communication device
    ___Calculator*
    ___Abacus
    ___Arithmetic tables*
    ___Spell checker or spelling dictionary*
    ___Other _____

____ ____ 2. Can use pencil to fill in bubble answer sheets

____ ____ 2a. Can use pencil to fill in bubble answer sheets with assistance or the following accommodation(s):
    ___Pencil grip
    ___Bubbles enlarged
    ___Bubbles presented on the test itself next to each question
    ___Bubbles enlarged and presented on the test itself next to each question
    ___Scribe
    ___Calculator*
    ___Abacus
    ___Arithmetic tables*
    ___Spell checker or spelling dictionary*
    ___Other _____

Copyright © 1997 by Corwin Press, Inc.

Use the following section to guide decisions about participation in assessments.

Yes   No

> ### LEVEL OF PARTICIPATION
> ____ ____ 1. _____'s current level of skill and noted accommodations allow him/her to meaningfully participate in all/part (circle one) of the following assessments:
> ___Classroom
> ___District—specify which one(s)
> ___State/national—specify which one(s)

If partial participation is considered more appropriate, specify which part of the assessment. The decision for partial participation on the assessment is based on the following:

> ____ ____ 2. _____ is incapable of meaningfully participating in the _____ assessment, regardless of accommodation. This decision is based on the following:

> ____ ____ 3. Consideration has been given to how _____'s learning will be assessed. A different or alternate assessment of learning will be conducted as follows:

> ____ ____ 4. The consequences of exclusion and/or use of accommodations (if applicable) have been discussed with _____'s parent/guardian.

> ____ ____ 5. Proactive planning is under way to provide _____ the opportunity to meaningfully participate in the assessment cycle (either entire or partial) next year as follows (specify who is involved in the planning process):

> ____ ____ 6. _____'s parent/guardian is fully aware of these participation and accommodation decisions and has been a part of the process. Explain, if necessary.

Your signature on this form indicates that you were a part of the participation and accommodation decision-making process for _____. You are in agreement with the decisions.

IEP Team Chair	**Building Administrator**	**Student**

Parent/Guardian	**Student's Teacher(s)**	**Others**

Assessment Coordinator	**Director of Special Education**

Date of Meeting: _____

*Careful consideration must be given to the purpose of the test for which these accommodations are provided.

Copyright © 1997 by Corwin Press, Inc.

Checklist for Deciding Assessment Type

Name: *School Year:*

School: *Special Education Teacher:*

Grade: *Date:*

The purpose of this checklist is to facilitate and justify what district or state assessment program _____ will be a part of. Three options are being considered: regular (or the name of the district/state assessment), alternate, or both (regular/alternate) assessments. The final decision must be justified and validated by several parties including, but not limited to _____ (student, if deemed appropriate), parent/guardian, special and general education teachers, and involved related personnel.

On _____ (date), the IEP team, after much discussion and consideration, has decided that _____ is a candidate for:

____ ____ 1. Regular assessment (or the name of the district/state assessment)
    ____ a. Without accommodation
    ____ b. With the following accommodation(s):
____ ____ 2. Alternate assessment (student is not working toward diploma)*
____ ____ 3. Regular/Alternate.* List the content areas_____
_____

*This decision is based on the following (list any and all factors that led to the above decision—be specific):

While this decision was made based on the above factors, we recognize that the decision is not a permanent one and may change, if warranted and appropriate, at another scheduled IEP meeting.

Parent/Guardian _____   **Other** _____

Administrator _____   **IEP Chair** _____

Special Educator _____   **General Educator** _____

Related Service Providers: _____

_____

_____

Copyright © 1997 by Corwin Press, Inc.

IEP Form for
Identifying Accommodations

Name: *Grade:*   *School/Teacher:*

Date:

Instructional Accommodations:

List the accommodations needed for general instruction.

List instructional accommodations needed for each applicable content area.

Copyright © 1997 by Corwin Press, Inc.

IEP Form for Identifying Accommodations, With Examples

Name: *Grade:*   *Date:*

Use the following checklist to guide decisions about what instructional accommodations are needed by this student.

INSTRUCTIONAL ACCOMMODATION CHECKLIST:

SETTING
____ Distraction-free space within classroom (e.g., doorway, windows, other students, front of class, back of class)
____ One-to-one assistance to complete written tasks
____ On-task reminders
____ Several verbal prompts to initiate a task
____ Verbal encouragement, praise, or recognition to continue a task
____ Directions repeated and/or clarified
____ Small group or partner instruction, especially when learning or practicing new facts, concepts, and strategies
____ Adaptive furniture
____ Other _____

TIMING
____ Periodic breaks during work sessions (specify)
____ Other _____

SCHEDULING
____ Extended time to complete class/homework assignments
____ Length of assignments shortened to complete as overnight homework assignments
____ A daily assignment sheet
____ A weekly quick strategic assignment meeting
____ A weekly or monthly assignment calendar
____ A weekly or monthly assignment calendar with check-in and due dates posted

PRESENTATION
____ Visual cues or printed material to facilitate understanding of orally given directions
____ Directions repeated, clarified, or simplified
____ Directions read individually
____ Visual magnification device
____ Auditory amplification device
____ Written directions read

Copyright © 1997 by Corwin Press, Inc.

____ Key words or phrases in written directions highlighted

____ Visual prompts (e.g., stop signs, arrows) that show directions to start, stop, and continue working

____ Written directions presented in larger and/or bold print

____ Written directions presented with one complete sentence per line of text

____ Reader to read the text

____ Pencil grip

____ Access to a prerecorded reading

____ Test presented in sign language

____ Written information presented in Braille or large print

____ Increased spacing between items and/or limited items presented per page

____ Templates or masks to reduce visible print

____ Papers secured to desk (e.g., magnets, tape)

____ Calculator*

____ Abacus

____ Arithmetic tables*

____ Spell checker or spelling dictionary*

____ Manipulatives

____ Other _____

RESPONSE

____ Text-talker converter

____ Speech synthesizer

____ Pencil grip

____ Word processor

____ Scribe (someone to record verbatim oral responses to questions)

____ Brailler

____ Copying assistance between drafts of writing

____ Option to write an outline to a question and, using a tape recorder, dictate the body of the response, per the written outline

____ Option to dictate answer into a tape recorder

____ Visual magnification device

____ Touch Talker or other communication device

____ Calculator*

____ Abacus

____ Arithmetic tables*

____ Spell checker or spelling dictionary*

____ Other _____

*Based on the purpose of the assignment and what and how the skill(s) will be assessed.

Additional Instructional Accommodations Needed for Specific Content Areas

List content area and any additional instructional accommodations needed.

Copyright © 1997 by Corwin Press, Inc.

Accommodations Case Study

STUDENT: IMA TRYUN

Ima Tryun is an eighth grader who was retained in first grade. Ima has been identified as a student with a learning disability in the area of written communication/basic reading skills. Ima attends school regularly. Ima has an integrated special/regular instruction schedule. He receives resource room services and in-class support for mathematics. Science and social studies are taken in the general education classroom.

Ima reads on a third-grade level. His writing is hampered by his inability to spell. He has wonderful ideas and communicates them well. With the use of a tape recorder, Ima is able to record his ideas. His writing skills are improving with his reading skills. Ima shows excellent auditory comprehension, and his attention to task is above average. He actively participates in class activities and discussions.

Ima exhibits low self-esteem toward school. However, he will ask for and accept help from teachers. Ima is well accepted by his peers and is "looked up to" within the school context.

INSTRUCTIONAL ACCOMMODATIONS

Using the above information, suggest instructional accommodations for Ima.

ASSESSMENT ACCOMMODATIONS

Now that you have identified possible instructional accommodations, suggest accommodations that would be needed for assessment

Setting: **Presentation:**

Timing: **Response:**

Scheduling: **Other (specify):**

Copyright © 1997 by Corwin Press, Inc.

Test Accommodation Planning Chart

Test Accommodation Planning Chart					
Student Name	Class/ Teacher	Test Format	Needed Accommodation or Modification	Test Date	Actions

Copyright © 1997 by Corwin Press, Inc.

Instructional and Assessment Accommodations Worksheet

Student:

Grade:

Teacher/Class:

Class/Content Area:

Service Provider:

    Student's Strengths   *Student's Needs*

Based on student need, identify and list below the instructional accommodations that will be provided. Then list which of these naturally flow to classroom tests. Mark (**) those test accommodations that apply to the district/state assessment.

Instructional Accommodation(s)   *Classroom Test Accommodation(s)*

Comments:

Copyright © 1997 by Corwin Press, Inc.

Form J

District/State Assessment Accommodations Worksheet

Use this worksheet to identify the skills measured on specific tests. Based on this information, identify reasonable accommodations that need to be provided. Keep in mind that these accommodations should be taken/recommended from those being currently provided during instruction.

Student:

Grade:

Date:

Test	*Skill(s) Measured*	*Reasonable Accommodation* *

Comments/Further Action Needed:

*Will not invalidate the purpose of the test or the skill being measured.

Completed by:

Copyright © 1997 by Corwin Press, Inc.

Study/Test Skills Checklist

Student:

Grade:

Teacher:

Date:

Test	*Test Skills Needed*	*Date Taught*	*Date Acquired*	*Initials*

Comments:

Completed by:

Copyright © 1997 by Corwin Press, Inc.

Logistics and Strategic Plan for
Providing Assessment Accommodations

Name: *School Year:*

Assessment: *Special Education Teacher:*

Day/Time of Test: *Case Coordinator:*

Building Administrator:

Assessment accommodations student needs for this assessment and date arranged:

1.

2.

3.

4.

Comments:

Person responsible for arranging accommodations and due date:

1.

2.

3.

4.

Comments:

Room Assignment for Assessment:

Planners for This Process (Signatures/Dates)

Copyright © 1997 by Corwin Press, Inc.

Final Arrangements for Assessment Accommodations

Name: *School Year:*

Case Coordinator: *Assessment:*

Special Education Teacher: *Date/Time of Test:*

Building Administrator: *Room Assignment:*

The following assessment accommodations have been arranged (initial and date):

Setting:

Timing:

Scheduling:

Presentation:

Response:

Other:

Copyright © 1997 by Corwin Press, Inc.

Suggestions for Alternate Assessments

**Below is a list of possible data sources for developing an alternate assessment.
Checklists for:**

   ____ Daily living skills
   ____ Community mobility skills
   ____ Social skills
   ____ Self-help skills
   ____ Adaptive behavior skills

Interviews:

   ____ Service providers
   ____ Parents/guardian
   ____ Peers
   ____ Employers

Observation:

   ____ Note the frequency, intensity, and/or duration of target skill
   ____ Informal observation of student in a variety of settings
   ____ Formal or systematic observation using checklists, criteria, rubrics
   ____ Videotaping of performance
   ____ Application of skill(s) in varied settings (natural or staged)
   ____ Demonstrate community mobility skills in real setting
   ____ Use of technology (specify)

Tests:

   ____ Portfolios
   ____ Performance based
   ____ Quantitative or qualitative

Record Review:

   ____ School cumulative records
   ____ Student products
   ____ Anecdotal records (IEP objectives and general progress)

Copyright © 1997 by Corwin Press, Inc.

Student Feedback/Interview Form

Student:

Grade:

Assessment:

Case Coordinator:

Date of Assessment:

Special Education Teacher:

Date of Interview:

1. How did you think the test went? What was easy? What was hard?

2. How prepared were you for the

   Test format:

   Test content:

   Timing of the test:

   Any surprises?

   Other:

3. What (if any) testing accommodations did you use?

   a. Were they helpful?

   b. If so, how? If not, why?

   c. What, if any, other accommodations did you feel you needed?

4. Was there any information that was "new" to you? Specify.

5. Did this test allow you to show what you know? Was it a good demonstration of what you know and can do?

   a. If yes, why and how?

   b. If no, why? What kind of test or method would allow you to better show what you know?

6. Anything else you would like to share about your testing experience?

Copyright © 1997 by Corwin Press, Inc.

Instructional and Assessment Accommodations

Instructional Accommodations: List the accommodations this student needs during the instructional process to learn, perform, and participate on an equal footing with class peers.

Assessment Accommodations:

> *Classroom Tests:* List the test accommodations this student needs to show what he or she knows and can do without impediment of the disability:

District Assessment Program:

> Based on the above information, _____ will

> ____ participate in district assessment _____ without accommodation.

> ____ participate in district assessment _____ with accommodation.

> > • Based on current instructional practice, this student needs the following assessment accommodations:

> > • District assessment allows for the following accommodations to be provided:

> ____   participate in part of the district assessment and an alternate assessment as follows:

> ____   not participate in the general assessment but will take an alternate assessment.

Copyright © 1997 by Corwin Press, Inc.

Building Implementation Document

Year/Test Cycle: *Building:*

Name/Form of Test: *Grade Level:*

Total number of students enrolled in building:

Number of students with disabilities enrolled in building:

Number of students taking assessment:

Number of students with disabilities taking assessment:

Number of students taking assessment with accommodation:

Types of accommodation provided:

Number of students excluded or exempted from assessment:

Reasons for exclusion or exemption (attach a separate sheet if needed):

Persons making exclusion and exemption decisions:

Last Year's Data

Total number of students enrolled in building:

Number of students with disabilities enrolled in building:

Number of students taking assessment:

Number of students with disabilities taking assessment:

Number of students taking assessment with accommodation:

Number of students excluded or exempted from assessment:

Submitted by:

Date:

Copyright © 1997 by Corwin Press, Inc.

Inclusive Assessment and Accountability Survey

We as a nation are moving toward an educational system that is more inclusive both in instruction and in accountability. As your district prepares for this process, we believe it is very important to survey your teachers and staff to find out what is needed to be prepared for this change. Our mission and belief is that all students can learn to higher levels than before. We believe all students must be included and accounted for in our efforts to educate all children for their future. With this in mind, complete the following survey:

Please indicate your position/role:

____ General Education Teacher	____ Special Education Teacher
____ Administrator	____ Related Service Professional
____ Parent/Community Member	____ Other _____

In the space next to each item, write one or more letters from A to E to indicate your anticipated need for staff development.

A. Need for *TRAINING* (in-service workshop, seminar)
B. Need for *MATERIALS* (literature, resources)
C. Need for *CONSULTATION*
D. Need for *IN-CLASS ASSISTANCE*
E. *OTHER* (please specify)

____ 1. Overview of the "whys" of inclusive assessment and accountability
____ 2. Recent laws and mandates that affect all students
____ 3. Purpose and uses of the district/state assessment
____ 4. Connection between instruction and assessment, especially as it relates to accommodations
____ 5. Address the issue of how all students can participate in the district/state assessment program
____ 6. Session on what kinds of assessment accommodations are allowed, who is eligible for them, and how these decisions are made
____ 7. Hands-on session on how to decide and provide instructional accommodations to students who need them
____ 8. How to provide accommodations for both classroom tests and district assessments
____ 9. Roles and responsibilities of teachers, administrators, and other staff in district assessment
____ 10. Other (please specify) _____

Please write the numbers of your top three priorities on the lines below:

1st _____   2nd _____   3rd _____

Other questions, comments, or concerns:

Copyright © 1997 by Corwin Press, Inc.

Resources:
Staff Development

Conducting Staff Development

Staff development and training are key components of today's educational reform agenda. This is true for all kinds of reform, not just those associated with standards and assessments. But the need for staff development and training is particularly critical when it comes to topics that have not been addressed before, such as the participation of students with disabilities in district and state assessments.

This section is designed to help you deliver and disseminate information about the what, why, how, and what-ifs of assessment programs and accommodations decisions for students with disabilities. It includes information on some of the most important points that need to be made in each of nine components and on some specific activities in which people can engage. Reproducible handouts and overheads are provided as well.

The information included here can be used to provide in-service to boards of education, central office and building administrative personnel, building faculty and staff, and community members. The components can be altered to meet the needs of different groups, as can the materials and activities within components.

Overview

There are nine components to this informational session on inclusive assessment and accountability. The coverage of each one can vary, and/or you may want to present the information over two sessions. The content within each component is meant to provide you with an overall understanding of the issues to help you as you prepare for the meeting you will hold. For each component, we suggest that you gather relevant information on how the issues under discussion have had an impact on your school district and/or state. This provides participants with relevant information to which they can relate.

Considering Staff Development Stages

Before starting the process of staff development on inclusive assessment and accountability, it is wise to consider the levels of awareness or development about the topics or activities you are about to present. The Concerns-Based Adoption Model (CBAM) by Hall, Wallace, and Dossett (1973) provides you with the opportunity to get a feel for an individual or group and help guide staff development for a particular topic.

The CBAM proposes that people differ tremendously in their readiness to accept major changes, such as inclusive accountability. As staff members become ready, they move through various stages. We have adapted CBAM to identify various stages of staff development activities for promoting inclusive accountability and assessment, no matter what stage of readiness individuals may be at. The following are the adapted stages:

Awareness—Very low level of involvement. These are staff members who act as though they have not even heard of accountability or inclusive assessment.

Informational—General awareness and interest but still relatively uninvolved. These are staff members who realize that something to do with inclusive accountability and assessment is going on in the building or district but do not believe it will affect them.

Personal—Staff members begin to consider the impact of the innovation on themselves. They worry that they may be asked to include students with disabilities in their classroom, provide needed accommodations for both instruction and classroom assessment, and be involved in decisions concerning participation in the district assessment.

Management—Concern focuses on efficient and effective methodologies. These are staff members who have been informed about the policy and practice changes about assessment and accountability and now are extremely concerned to find out what to do and how to do it.

Consequence—Here, attention is on student outcomes and accountability. These are staff members who, after learning more about inclusive assessment (participation, accommodation, and reporting of results), begin to raise questions about outcomes about learning results, fairness, progress, evaluation, and/or resources to make it happen.

Collaboration—Here, the focus is on working with others and becoming involved with change. These are staff members who recognize that colleagues, especially those with inclusive schooling and assessment experience, may be able to help.

Refocusing—Interest here is in refinement, improvement, and innovation. These are staff members who, with some successful experience behind them, are ready to make the situation even better for all students.

For each stage, we offer some suggestions to consider if you have staff members who may need additional information on inclusive assessment and accountability according to their stage of CBAM development.

Stage	Activity
Awareness	• Overview or brief workshop • Awareness-level information explaining the whys and whats about inclusive assessment and accountability • Easy-reading professional or newspaper articles on the state of assessment and inclusive accountability systems • Ongoing staff meetings
Informational	• Full-day workshops based on needs assessment • Presentations from other districts' personnel on what they are doing in the area of assessment, accommodation, participation, and reporting of all student learning • Easy-reading professional or newspaper articles on the state of assessment and inclusive accountability systems
Personal	• Topical sessions that provide for group discussions on areas of concern or interest • Presentations and question-and-answer sessions by personnel most familiar with what it takes to create and facilitate the development of inclusive assessment and accountability systems

Management
- Practical strategies for approaching "how to's"
- Problem-solving sessions with a group or consultant
- Networking with other districts and/or states working on similar efforts and initiatives
- Visits to other districts and various personnel in charge of district assessment program and inclusive accountability system

Consequence
- Professional and information-based articles depicting the consequences of exclusion or selective accountability systems
- Articles and information showing past practice and the unanticipated outcomes or results
- Aligning efforts with intended outcomes and mapping action steps to get there
- Study groups and support groups

Collaboration
- Research projects and grants within the district
- Staff meeting updates on progress and efforts
- Assessment and accommodation committees
- Peer support groups that focus on improvement

Refocusing
- Reading alert club—highlight and distribute key articles that lend valuable information to the process
- Conferences
- Revisiting where you began, where you currently are, and where you are going next
- Creation of independent study or progress plans to promote better practice for meeting both instruction and assessment needs of all students

You may want to consider making a CBAM needs assessment that covers each stage of the model. First, you would provide a brief explanation of the model and the stages (as shown above). Then you could develop questions depicting current situations or directions your district is planning on taking and ask your staff to rate each item from 1 to 7, where 1 is awareness and 7 is refocusing. For example,

1   2   3   4   5   6   7   I am aware of the reporting procedures of our district assessment. That is, I know who is included and reported in the results.

SOURCE: Hall, G., Wallace, R., & Dossett, W. (1973). *A developmental conceptualization of the adoption process within educational institutions.* Austin: University of Texas, Austin Research and Development Center for Teacher Education.

Component 1
New Laws That Promote Educational Reform

Purpose

- To briefly explain the provisions of the new laws (Goals 2000, Improving America's Schools Act (Title I), School to Work Opportunity Act, IDEA), with an emphasis on assessment and accountability

Background Information

The information in this section covers the key points to be made for this component of staff development. The facilitator of staff development sessions must decide how much of the information is needed by the targeted audience. It is important to relate the background information to the local situation in which the facilitator is working.

What Is Educational Reform All About?

Reform usually means "change for the better." Today, our education system is undergoing major changes in response to concerns about its adequacy. Why are we concerned?

- International comparisons suggest that in some areas U.S. students do not perform as well as students in many other countries.

- Colleges and universities are having to give remedial work to more and more students before they are ready for college-level classes.

- U.S. businesses have complained that high school graduates in our country do not have the skills needed to be good workers in today's global economy.

While some may disagree about whether these statements are true, most people do agree that we should support our educational system and, at the same time, push for it to improve. Thus, we are always interested in changing education for the better. In many states and across the nation, policymakers, educators, and parents alike are pushing harder than usual for reforms in education.

Educational reform has implications for students with disabilities, especially now when the focus is on producing workers who can help the United States compete in a global economy. Too often, students with disabilities are not thought about in discussions of educational reform.

217

Yet we want all individuals to be contributing members of our society, including those with disabilities. We want our educational system to be *accountable* for all children.

What Are Some Common Educational Reforms?

There are many reforms in the news today. Most of them are said to be "systemic"—occurring throughout the system. Systemic reform can occur in local schools, school districts, or states. You may have heard about site-based management, cooperative learning, teaming, collaboration, and other reform strategies.

Although many reforms are being promoted, different people push different reforms because there is disagreement about which are the best approaches. Yet there remains a strong push for schools to help students learn at a high level—that is, to challenging standards. Schools must show that their students meet these challenging standards through assessments that now are more varied and real-world based and that result in better information about student learning. These reform themes are reflected in several federal education laws and in the education laws of many states. They are themes that have significant implications for students with disabilities.

What New Laws Promote Educational Reform?

Three federal education laws enacted in 1993 and 1994 are important steps toward helping states in their reform efforts: *Goals 2000: Educate America Act,* the *Improving America's Schools Act,* and the *School-to-Work Opportunities Act.*

Goals 2000: Educate America Act (Public Law 103-227)

Goals 2000 was signed on March 31, 1994 to provide states with funds for school reform. It encourages setting high standards of learning for students and the use of better assessments to evaluate progress toward the standards. *Goals 2000* is very clear in its definition of "all students" and in the requirement that students with disabilities be considered in all aspects of reform.

Goals 2000 identifies eight national education goals that are designed to be inclusive of *all* students. These goals are to be reached by the year 2000:

(1) SCHOOL READINESS   All children in America will start school ready to learn.

(2) SCHOOL COMPLETION   The high school graduation rate will increase to at least 90%.

(3) STUDENT ACHIEVEMENT AND CITIZENSHIP All students will leave Grades 4, 8, and 12 having demonstrated competency over challenging subject matter including English, mathematics, science, foreign languages, civics and government, economics, arts, history, and geography, and every school in America will ensure that all students learn to use their minds well so that they are better prepared for responsible citizenship, further learning, and productive employment in our nation's modern economy.

(4) TEACHER EDUCATION AND PROFESSIONAL DEVELOPMENT The nation's teaching force will have access to programs for the continued improvement of their professional skills and the opportunity to acquire the knowledge and skills needed to instruct and prepare all American students for the next century.

(5) MATHEMATICS AND SCIENCE U.S. students will be first in the world in mathematics and science achievement.

(6) ADULT LITERACY AND LIFELONG LEARNING Every adult American will be literate and possess the knowledge and skills necessary to compete in a global economy and exercise the rights and responsibilities of citizenship.

(7) SAFE, DISCIPLINED, AND ALCOHOL- AND DRUG-FREE SCHOOLS Every school in the United States will be free of drugs, violence, and the unauthorized presence of firearms and alcohol and will offer a disciplined environment conducive to learning.

(8) PARENTAL PARTICIPATION Every school will promote partnerships that will increase parental involvement and participation in promoting the social, emotional, and academic growth of children.

"All students" is specifically defined in *Goals 2000* as "students . . . from a broad range of backgrounds and circumstances, including . . . students . . . with disabilities, limited-English proficiency, [dropouts], migratory students . . ., and academically talented students and children."

Improving America's Schools Act (Public Law 103-382)

This used to be the *Elementary and Secondary Education Act* until it was revised and signed into law on October 20, 1994. The *IASA* authorizes funding for Title I programs (what used to be called Chapter 1 programs) as well as several others (e.g., Title VII).

Title I programs provide students extra help in math and reading. If states have already developed new "challenging standards" in math and reading to receive *Goals 2000* monies or as part of their already ongoing reform efforts, they can use those same standards to get additional Title I money. Like *Goals 2000*, the *Improving America's Schools Act* clarifies that *IASA* money is for all students, including those with disabilities.

As described in the law, the *Improving America's Schools Act* promotes the following schoolwide reform strategies:

   (i)   Provide opportunities for all children to meet the State's proficient and advanced levels of student performance

  (ii)   Are based on effective means of improving the achievement of children

 (iii)   Use effective instructional strategies, . . . that (I) increase the amount and quality of learning time, . . . (II) include strategies for meeting the educational needs of historically underserved populations, . . .

  (iv)   (I) address the needs of all children in the school . . . [and] (II) address how the school will determine if such needs have been met. . . .

   (v)   Are consistent with, and designed to implement, the state and local improvement plans, if any, approved under Title III of *Goals 2000: Educate America Act.*

School-to-Work Opportunities Act (Public Law 103-239)

The critical time of transition from school to work is the target of this national education law, signed on May 4, 1994. The intent of the law is to help schools combine classroom lessons and workplace training. As with *Goals 2000* and the *IASA*, this law makes it clear that students with disabilities are to be included in the initiatives undertaken as part of its funding.

The specific purposes of the *School-to-Work Opportunities Act*, as defined in the law, are these:

 (1)   Establish a national framework within which all States can create statewide School-to-Work Opportunities systems

 (2)   Facilitate the creation of a universal, high-quality school-to-work transition system that enables youths in the United States to identify and navigate paths to productive and progressively more rewarding roles in the workplace

 (3)   Utilize workplaces as active learning environments in the educational process by making employers joint partners with educators in providing opportunities for all students to participate in high-quality, work-based learning experiences

 (4)   Use federal funds under this Act as venture capital to underwrite the initial costs of planning and establishing statewide School-to-Work Opportunities systems that will be maintained with other Federal, State, and local resources

        . . . .

(11)   Motivate all youths, including low-achievers, school dropouts, and those with disabilities, to stay in or return to school or a

classroom setting and strive to succeed by providing enriched learning experiences and assistance in obtaining good jobs and continuing their education in postsecondary educational institutions

(12) Increase opportunities for minorities, women, and individuals with disabilities by enabling these individuals to prepare for careers that are not traditional for their race, gender, or disability

In the *School-to-Work Opportunities Act*, the term "all students" means "both male and female students from a broad range of backgrounds and circumstances, including . . . students with disabilities."

Individuals With Disabilities Act (IDEA, Public Law 105-117)

The reauthorized IDEA (June 1997) continues to provide federal funds to assist states and school districts in making a free, appropriate public education available to students who have been identified as having a disability. Some of the changes in the law address IEPs and state/district assessments. IEPs must now document how a student's disability affects involvement and progress in the general curriculum; individual modifications needed for students to participate in state and district assessments; and, if the student is unable to participate in the general assessment, why and how learning will be assessed. Public reporting requirements are also included in the reauthorization of IDEA: (a) the number of students with disabilities assessed (by July, 1998), (b) the performance of students in the general education assessment (by July, 1998), and (c) the performance of students with disabilities in an alternate assessment (by July, 2000).

Activity

Use the Myth or Truth Worksheet on the next page to warm up people in the training session. Most people are willing to guess at the extent to which each statement is the truth or a myth. Answers to the statements are as follows:

1) M	4) M	7) M	10) M	13) T
2) T	5) M	8) M	11) T	14) M
3) M	6) M	9) M	12) T	15) M

Handouts and Overheads

Use the handouts and overheads presented on the pages following the Myth or Truth Worksheet to convey information on educational reform. Add others that are relevant to your situation.

Myth or Truth Worksheet

Assessment and Accountability: Where Are Students With Disabilities?

The statements below represent current myths or truths about educational reform and students with disabilities. Read each and write M (myth) if you think the sentence describes an inaccurate statement about current practice and T (truth) if you think the statement describes an accurate statement.

____   1.   A well-established accountability system is one where all students take the same tests.

____   2.   Providing accommodations to students with disabilities is an attempt to "level the playing field."

____   3.   The majority of students with disabilities participate in district and state assessments.

____   4.   There is agreement about the purpose of assessment accommodations.

____   5.   There is a common set of assessment accommodations allowed by states.

____   6.   The scores of students with disabilities typically are included in reports of district and state scores.

____   7.   Parents are fully informed about their child's participation in all assessments.

____   8.   Administrators are aware of the importance of an accountability system for all students, including those with disabilities.

____   9.   Teachers are aware of the importance of an accountability system for all students, including those with disabilities.

____ 10.   State and local directors of assessment and special education, in general, inform each other about what is occurring in their departments.

____ 11.   Criteria exist for developing policy about participation, accommodation, and reporting of assessment results so that students with disabilities are included.

____ 12.   The IEP is one of the critical links in providing students with disabilities the opportunity to participate in assessments.

____ 13.   Parents are key players in putting into play the participation and accommodation pieces in assessment.

____ 14.   There is a significant amount of research indicating that when students with disabilities are allowed to participate in assessment, with or without accommodation, the results are skewed.

____ 15.   Educators and administrators have little impact on establishing guidelines or criteria for standards and assessment that reflect "all" students.

Copyright © 1997 by Corwin Press, Inc.

Educational Reform: What Is It? Why Do We Need It?

What: Educational reform

✓ **"Change for the better"**

✓ **"Mechanism to bring about change"**

Why: Dissatisfaction with the quality of high school graduates

✓ **Need for remedial work in post-secondary school settings**

✓ **U.S. business concern over lack of skills to compete in a global economy**

✓ **Poor performance in international comparisons**

Copyright © 1997 by Corwin Press, Inc.

Educational Reform History 1989 Summit—Six Goals

Goals 2000: Educate America Act (PL 103-227)

1. Ready to Learn
2. Graduate Rates = 90%
3. Academic Focus
4. First in World in Math and Science
5. Teacher Training
6. Literacy and Lifelong Learning
7. Safe and Drug-Free Schools
8. Parent Involvement

School-to-Work Opportunity Act (PL 103-239)

Improving America's School Act (PL 103-382)

Individuals with Disabilities Education Act (PL 105-117)

Copyright © 1997 by Corwin Press, Inc.

Component 2
General Overview of Definition of Assessment, Its Purposes, and the Meaning of Inclusive Accountability

Purpose

- To provide an overview of the purposes of assessment
- To define and discuss what accountability is and its connection to assessment

Background Information

The information in this section covers the key points to be made for this component of staff development. The facilitator of staff development sessions must decide how much of the information is needed by the targeted audience. Remember to relate the background information to the local situation.

Assessment

What is assessment? Assessment is the process of measuring learning against a set of standards. Assessment and the notion of using new forms of assessment are integral parts of new legislation such as *Goals 2000* and the *Improving America's Schools Act (IASA)*. One of the characteristics most apparent in current school reforms is a shift from documenting the process of educating students to measuring the results of the educational process.

There are many purposes to assessment. To develop a coordinated assessment system, the purposes for which assessment information are needed and at what level(s) such information is needed must be determined. The primary functions of state and district assessment programs include the following:

- Accountability (describing the educational status)
- Instructional improvement (making decisions on what and how to teach)
- Program evaluation (effectiveness of programs and curricula)
- Student diagnosis (eligibility for service/programs)
- High school graduation (certification of mastery or accomplishment)

Accountability

What is accountability? Accountability is typically defined as a systematic means of assuring those inside and outside the educational system that schools are moving in desired directions. *Accountability* is a more encompassing term than *assessment*. It can include more than the collection of data via test, record review, and other performance assessments. Rather, a system is accountable for all students when it makes sure all students count or participate in the evaluation program of the educational system.

Accountability has a number of layers. These layers include the classroom, building, district, and state.

- *Classroom accountability* can focus on the individual student as well as on the group as a whole. Individual student accountability examines the degree to which a student is learning what she or he is supposed to be learning and the extent to which the student is moving through the curriculum at the expected rate of progress. Classroom accountability looks at the degree to which students as a group are learning and progressing through the curriculum. Both individual student and classroom accountability provide teachers and administrators with information they can use to make teaching decisions for individual students and groups of students.

- *School building accountability* provides information to both building and central office administration about the overall picture of student learning. It must include all students in the building. Every student enrolled in the school building must be accounted for. Only then can there truly be an inclusive accountability system for the school. Using this information, administrators and policymakers can make programmatic decisions about curriculum and instruction. Support for adoption of new materials or programs, as well as staff development, typically is gleaned from information rendered from assessment and accountability reports.

- *School district accountability* allows the state to examine how it is doing in providing an education to those enrolled in schools throughout the state. It provides a crude comparison of districts across the states. The estimate is crude because many variables (e.g., the number of students enrolled, socioeconomic status, the number of children excluded from assessments) create an uneven level with which to accurately measure how states compare with each other.

- *State-level accountability* allows for national comparisons. That is, one state may be compared with another in terms of test scores, number of school-age students, and percentages of English-as-a-second-language learners and special education students, to mention a few.

Relationships Between Assessment and Accountability

Assessment and accountability are closely related. Whereas assessment provides information about student and system growth and progress toward a set of standards, accountability provides those inside and outside the education system information about how students in America's schools are learning.

Assessment and accountability results tell us how students are doing against a set of learning goals or standards. Accountability systems tell you how students in the classroom, school building, and state are achieving. The important thing is that all students are included in the accountability system so that accurate information about all students is reported. Inclusive accountability systems are those that account for all students in the district or state, regardless of what kind of test they take (general assessment or alternate assessment).

Activities

Use either or both of the following activities to promote the involvement of participants in this component's content.

Activity 1

This activity can be done by individuals or in small groups. Or the entire activity can be completed first individually and then processed in small and then large groups.

Take a minute to brainstorm the purposes of testing, assessment, and accountability. Then identify similarities or differences among the three. Mark items similar to testing with a **T,** those similar to assessment with an **A,** and those similar to accountability with **AC.**

Activity 2

In small groups, have participants discuss the following statement: *Educational accountability has a number of layers.* Identify and discuss the layers of accountability in education.

Handouts and Overheads

Use the handout/overhead on the following page to convey information on assessment and accountability. Add others that are relevant to your situation.

Accountability

What Is It?

A means to show those both inside and outside the education system how students in America's schools are learning.

Why Do Accountability Systems Exist?

Accountability systems are meant to provide student-based information about curriculum, instruction, and learning. They are a means of providing information about return on the public's investment (tax dollars).

Copyright © 1997 by Corwin Press, Inc.

How Do They Work?

There are at least four layers of accountability, each of which may organize information in different ways:

- *Classroom*: by individual or group

- *Building:*   by classroom and grade level

- *District:*   by school building, curriculum, and instruction

- *State:*   by school district

What If We Do Not Have Inclusive Accountability Systems?

All students enrolled or residing in each layer of the accountability system must be accounted for. No student may be left out or not reported. If so, an incomplete picture of performance and learning is portrayed and decisions are made that do not have the best interest of all students in mind.

Copyright © 1997 by Corwin Press, Inc.

Component 3

Why Assess?

Purpose

- To provide an explanation for the variety of student and school purposes for assessment and the ways in which assessment results might be used

Background Information

We have identified some of the key points for this component; however, the facilitator of staff development should decide how much of the information is needed by the targeted audience. Relate the background information to the local situation.

Purposes of Assessment

Educational assessments are conducted for a variety of reasons. In schools, assessments commonly are used for screening purposes, for determining eligibility for programs/services, for evaluation of programs and service delivery, and for program planning. Another useful distinction is the one between two broad types of assessment: individual and large-scale. For our purposes, we will focus on large-scale assessment, including performance-based tests. Important points to know about large-scale assessments include the following:

- Large-scale assessment is a form of testing in which large groups of students are tested across a broad domain in a relatively short period of time.

  ✓ Typically, it is administered under uniform conditions so that results can be compared across groups of students within districts, states, and the nation.

  ✓ Its main purpose is to document how students are performing (and thus may be used to push for instructional change), but generally it is not useful for individualized decisions about instruction or diagnosis.

- Performance-based large-scale assessment is considered by many to be a new form of assessment.

✓ It is a multifaceted approach to measuring knowledge and competencies in ways that tap higher-order thinking skills as well as content knowledge.

✓ It takes a variety of forms, ranging from essays, open-ended problems, hands-on science, the production of artwork, and portfolios of student work to computer simulations.

Assessment programs can provide a plethora of information about individual students and systems at a variety of levels. The kinds of information range from monitoring to allocation of resources. Below is a list of the types of information that can be gathered using assessment systems.

Monitoring

- *Individual student level:* Provide periodic measurements of student progress in order to determine the education "growth" of a student from year to year

- *System performance:* Provide a periodic measure of the performance of groups of students to track performance over time

Information and Accountability

- *Parents and students:* Inform parents and students about performance so as to encourage students or teachers to improve performance

- *Public:* Provide the public with information about the performance of groups of students so as to encourage schools to improve the system

Improving Student Performance

- *Individual student level:* Provide data to teachers and students to encourage effective instruction geared to the needs of individual students to help them achieve at high levels

- *System level:* Provide information to educators on groups of students, such as at the school level, that can be used to review current instructional strategies and materials at one or more grade levels and to make improvements

Allocation of Resources

- *Human:* Use information to determine where additional staff are needed

- *Financial:* Determine where financial resources should be used

Selection/Placement of Students

- *Selection:* Help determine the eligibility of students for various education programs or services
- *Placement:* Determine the program or service most appropriate for the instructional level of the student

Certification

- *Individual student level:* Provide a means to determine the competence level of individual students (e.g., basic skills, grade promotion, graduation)
- *System level:* Provide data to certify the acceptability of an education system, such as in accreditation programs

Program Evaluation

- Provide the information needed to determine the effectiveness of an education program or intervention

Activity

Use the following Think-Pair-Share activity. The procedures for this activity are provided in Steps 1 through 5. Use these steps for either or both of the two information stems provided below and/or come up with your own stems.

1. Have participants individually THINK about one of the information stems (see below). When in the THINK step, there should be no eye contact or talking. Encourage participants to write things down if they choose.

2. After a period of about 3 to 5 minutes, have participants PAIR up and tell each other about what is on their lists.

3. After about 4 minutes, have pairs get together with other pairs (to form groups of 4) to SHARE their collective information.

4. Have each group select a spokesperson who will summarize the group's findings or highlights for the entire group.

5. Be sure to record the overall themes of the group. You can then return to them anytime during the session, as needed or relevant.

Information Stems

> ✓ Brainstorm as many types of tests as you know. Then identify their respective purposes.
>
> ✓ Identify the types of information that can be gathered using assessments.

Handouts and Overheads

Use the handouts and overheads on the next two pages to convey information on educational reform. Add others that are relevant to your situation.

Why Assess?

- **New emphasis on higher educational standards**

- **Two general types of assessment**
    - ✓ **Individual**
    - ✓ **Large-scale**
- **Large-scale assessment**
    - ✓ **Not necessarily useful for making individualized decisions about instruction**
- **Performance-based**
    - ✓ **Multifaceted approach to measuring knowledge**
    - ✓ **A variety of forms**

Copyright © 1997 by Corwin Press, Inc.

Purposes of Assessment

Monitoring

- ✓ Student level
- ✓ System performance

Information and Accountability

- ✓ Parents and students
- ✓ Public

Improving Student Performance

- ✓ Student level
- ✓ System level

Allocation of Resources

- ✓ Human
- ✓ Financial

Copyright © 1997 by Corwin Press, Inc.

Selection/Placement of Students

- ✓ **Selection**
- ✓ **Placement**

Certification

- ✓ **Student level**
- ✓ **System level**

Program Evaluation

- ✓ **Provide information needed to determine the effectiveness of an education program or intervention**

Copyright © 1997 by Corwin Press, Inc.

Component 4
Formats of Assessment

Purpose

- To describe the variety of formats of assessments that might be used at the district or state and classroom levels

Background Information

The information in this section covers the key points to be made for this component of staff development. The facilitator of staff development sessions must decide how much of the information is needed by the targeted audience. It is important to relate the background information to the local situation in which the facilitator is working.

Assessment Formats

The format of an assessment can refer to either the type of items used within an assessment (e.g., multiple-choice, essay) or the type of test overall (e.g., norm referenced, criterion referenced). Another distinction has been whether assessments are on-demand (requiring performance immediately, during a defined time frame) or are extended-time assessments. Until recently, most large-scale assessments were multiple-choice tests, with essays used on occasion. Similarly, most large-scale assessments were norm referenced, and most were on-demand assessments.

Because the nature of the skills that educators consider important is changing, the manner is which these skills are assessed is also changing. For example, to see whether students are capable of defining an issue, determining what information is needed to respond to the issue, and providing a rationale for their response to the issue, students need to be assessed in a way that allows them to set up the problem, select the information needed, and then provide their unique and extended responses to it. Different kinds of assessment formats are needed.

Some alternative formats that might be used are extended-response formats (including essays), the use of an interview, hands-on performance exercises, group performance exercises, and the like. Different types of formats are categorized and described in different ways. Some of the types of assessments that might be used within the two broad categories of on-demand and extended-time are summarized here.

On-Demand Assessments

- *Selected response exercises:* Here students select one or more answers from a list of suggested responses. These exercises have the advantage of speed, which may make them well suited for assessment of a broad set of content goals. The disadvantage is that it is difficult to develop selected-response exercises that tap student thinking.

- *Short answer, open ended:* In these exercises, students write in an answer to a question. The response is usually a phrase, sentence, or quick drawing or sketch. Less guessing is involved here, but these exercises do not tap much student thinking.

- *Extended response, open ended:* Students are required to compose a response that may be several pages in length. Much thought is required on the part of the student. Remember, this is only first-draft student work and thus may not represent what students could do given additional time and encouragement in which to compose a final draft.

- *Individually administered interview:* The assessment is given to each student on a one-on-one basis. This may be because the exercise requires special equipment, such as science equipment, or requires the individual student to perform or the observation of the student in the process of responding to the question. This format permits the interviewer to ask each student questions about the topic being assessed. It has the advantage of tapping important skills often desired of students. However, keep in mind that this process is both time-consuming and expensive to administer and score.

- *Individually administered performance events:* These are exercises that are completed by individual students within a class period and involve some type of performance on the part of the student. Tasks may range from hands-on exercises in a content area to playing a musical instrument, completing a drawing in visual arts, or writing an essay in a writing assessment.

- *Group-administered performance events:* These are exercises to which groups of students respond. These may be existing groups or those made up just for assessment purposes. For example, students in a band or orchestra are considered an existing group, while a group of five students assessed for teamwork skills is not. Here, students typically perform as a group, and the group interaction and/or performance is scored as a whole.

Extended-Time Assessments

- *Individual performance tasks:* Here students may work for several days, weeks, or months to produce an individual student response. For example, a science experiment may include designing and planting a garden and making observations of it over time.

- *Group performance tasks:* These exercises are ones on which groups of students may work for several days, weeks, or months to produce a group and/or an individual student response. An example could be a health education task where students are to design a school lunch menu for a month that is nutritious, affordable, and that would be appealing to students.

- *Portfolio assessment:* These assessments include an assembly of a collection of the best work of individual students. Portfolios provide the opportunity to document students' improvement over time and their ability to achieve important learning outcomes designated by state or national goals.

- *Observations:* Structured observations are those that are prearranged in perhaps a classroom setting and provide students the opportunity to choose from several activities in which to participate. Unstructured observations are the events that occur in the day-to-day classroom that teachers choose to record for the future. For example, a teacher may observe a student struggling with the writing process during instruction and therefore not picking up on the knowledge needed to take the assessment.

- *Anecdotal records:* There are other sources of information about students, such as notes from teachers, parents, and other people involved in the student's education.

Activity

On an overhead or chart paper, draw a box and divide it into quadrants. Below the box write the following statement stem: "Learning about types of assessment is like (a) _____ because. . . ."

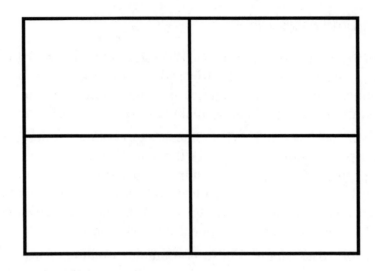

Learning about types of assessment is like

(a) _____ **because . . .**

Cover up the statement stem and solicit four nouns—any words—from the participants. One word for each quadrant. The words can be about anything. The more fun the words, the more fun the activity.

After you have written a word in each quadrant, instruct the participants to get into groups of 4 or 5 and complete the sentence stem. They should choose a recorder and have four sentences, one for each word, at the end of the activity.

You can use any statement stem you would like. The sky is the limit. Try to keep the sentence stem closely related to the upcoming discussion. This activity helps you get a read on the participants' knowledge and attitudes as well as engaging them in a fun-related activity.

Handouts and Overheads

Use the handouts and overheads on the following pages for this component on the formats of assessment.

Formats of Assessment

On-Demand Assessments

- ✓ Selected response exercises
- ✓ Short answer, open ended
- ✓ Extended response, open ended
- ✓ Individually administered interview
- ✓ Individually administered performance events
- ✓ Group-administered performance events

Extended-Time Assessments

- ✓ Individual performance tasks
- ✓ Group performance tasks
- ✓ Portfolio assessment
- ✓ Observations
- ✓ Anecdotal records

Copyright © 1997 by Corwin Press, Inc.

Free Association: Let It Flow!

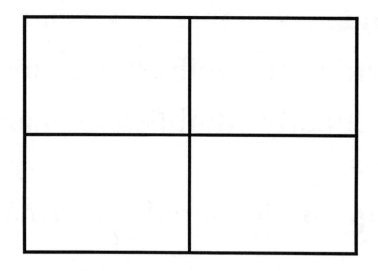

Learning about types of assessment is like

(a) _____ because . . .

Copyright © 1997 by Corwin Press, Inc.

Component 5
Who's In? Who's Out?

Purpose

- To provide information on who participates in the district assessment program and how they participate
- To provide information on typical reasons for exclusion and documentation of past exclusionary assessment practices

Background Information

This section covers the key points for this component. The staff development facilitator decides how much of the information needs to be presented and relates it to the local situation.

Participation in Assessments

Educators and policymakers have decided that it is important to assess the extent to which students have accomplished the goals of education. Schools are being held accountable for all students attaining those skills. Key questions to ask are these: How do we assess the accomplishment of desired skills? How will schools be held accountable for attainment of those skills? How will diverse learners, including students with disabilities, be assessed?

What do we know about current practice in the assessment of what we want students to know and be able to do when they leave school and at various points along their educational careers? There are several key things that we know:

- First, it has been the diverse learners, particularly students with disabilities, who have been left out of assessment activities. If one of the purposes of assessment is to describe the status of students in the educational system, why would any child be excluded?

- One implication of exclusion from assessment is that students who are left out of assessments tend not to be considered during reform efforts. Educators, parents, policymakers, and the general public want and need to know the extent to which all students, including those with disabilities, are profiting from their educational programs and schooling experiences.

- Despite improvement over the past few years in the knowledge that states have about the participation of students with disabilities in state assessments, relatively few states are able to report the number of students with disabilities included in their state-wide assessments.

Why should we be concerned about the participation of students with disabilities in assessments? Because out of sight is out of mind. Those individuals excluded from assessments are not likely to be considered in policy decisions that affect all students. Students with disabilities must be considered and included in the process of assessing what they know and can do.

Past Practice: Reasons for Excluding Students With Disabilities

Students with disabilities have been excluded from assessment for a variety of reasons. Among those most frequently identified are the following:

- ✓ *Lack* of written policy *guidelines*
- ✓ *Vagueness* of wording in guidelines, which leads to different interpretation and implementation
- ✓ *Lack* of successful *monitoring* of the extent to which the guidelines are followed
- ✓ Test administration that *does not include students who are in separate schools or who are not in graded programs* (e.g., residential placements, juvenile homes, hospitalized or home-bound students)
- ✓ *Lack* of available *accommodations* in the actual tests themselves as well as the procedures
- ✓ *Incentives* created by the desire to have a school or state look good in comparison with others in the state or nation
- ✓ *Altruistic motivation*, such as lessening the emotional distress to the student who is either not expected to do well or does not perform well under test conditions (e.g., anxiety ridden)

For there to be an inclusive accountability system, an assessment system must be in place that accounts for and assesses all students. This does not mean that all students must take the same test but that all students must be accounted for. A small number of students will require an alternate way to assess what they know and can do. The bottom line is that all students residing in a school district and attending a school will be assessed and results accounted for.

Activities

Use one or more of the following activities to promote the involvement of participants in this component.

Activity 1

Have participants turn to their neighbor to brainstorm all the reasons they think students are excluded from district and state assessments.

Activity 2

In small groups, have participants discuss and decide how decisions should be made about who participates in or is excluded from district and state assessments.

Activity 3

Use either one or both of the worksheets on the following pages for participants to reflect on their feelings about exclusion and the current status of assessment in their own school or district.

Handouts and Overheads

Use the handouts and overheads on the pages following the worksheets to present the information for Component 5.

Exclusion Worksheet

Too often in today's society, people are included in or excluded from different events and life experiences for a variety of reasons. Take a minute to jot down how it feels to be included in an activity or society at large.

Now take a minute to think how it would feel to be excluded from the same activity or social situation.

How does it feel to be INCLUDED?   How does it feel to be EXCLUDED?

How would these feelings make you act?

What changes would make a difference in your feelings and behavior?

Copyright © 1997 by Corwin Press, Inc.

Educational Accountability
and Reform Survey

Use this survey to briefly inventory the current status of your school or situation related to educational accountability. Please take a minute to respond to the following items.

One of the greatest challenges related to educational reform for students in my school is . . .

One of the greatest challenges related to educational reform and students with disabilities in my school is . . .

Some immediate needs I see in my school for students with disabilities related to standards and assessment are . . .

One thing I can contribute to the process of all students and issues of standards and assessment is . . .

Copyright © 1997 by Corwin Press, Inc.

Systemic Reform and Special-Needs Students

✓ How can special-needs students, specifically students with disabilities, be included in general education reforms while still preserving what is "special" in special education?

✓ How can we focus more on the results of education and still protect compliance and procedural safeguards?

✓ How can education be individualized to the needs of students and still be oriented toward the achievement of high standards?

✓ How can we develop assessments that can measure the progress of students with disabilities in the same way that they measure the progress of students without disabilities?

Copyright © 1997 by Corwin Press, Inc.

Assessment Issues

✓ **WHO PARTICIPATES?
(Participation)**

✓ **How do they participate?
(Accommodation)**

✓ **How are they counted?
(Reporting)**

Copyright © 1997 by Corwin Press, Inc.

Reasons for Exclusion

- *Lack* of written policy *guidelines*

- *Vagueness* of *guidelines*

- *Lack* of successful *monitoring*

- *Not including* students who are in *separate schools* or *ungraded programs*

- *Lack* of available *accommodations*

- *Incentives* to look good

- *Altruistic motivation*

Copyright © 1997 by Corwin Press, Inc.

Component 6
Who Makes the Decisions?

Purpose

- To deliver information on who makes participation decisions and how they are made

Background Information

The information in this section covers the key points for this component. The facilitator should decide how much of the information is needed by the targeted audience and should adapt the information to the local situation.

Decisions About Who Participates and How They Participate

For some students, meaningful participation in assessments requires the use of testing accommodations. What do we know about accommodations in large-scale assessments?

- States and districts vary considerably in the policies they may have, both for making decisions about the participation of students with disabilities in assessment and for deciding the kinds of accommodations and adaptations that are used during assessments.

- Many state and district assessment guidelines defer decisions to the team that develops the student's IEP. Other state guidelines recommend that participation and accommodation decisions be based on the student's category of disability. Some states recommend decisions based on the percentage of time the student spends in the general education curriculum.

Each of the options just described is problematic. Leaving the decision to the IEP team is problematic because the team often allows too much slippage in the team decision-making process. It is not uncommon for all students with IEPs to be excluded from testing. Members of IEP teams must be trained in the purpose and use of inclusive assessment and accountability systems.

Using the percentage of time spent in the general education curriculum to decide on assessment participation also is a questionable practice. The percentage of time does not reflect the student's instructional program, level of skill development, or ability. There are too many other considerations that are more important (e.g., student goals).

Recommendation

A better indicator than any of the previously identified criteria is the alignment between what the test is intended to measure and the student's curriculum. The type of curriculum, rather than the setting or category of disability, should be the factor that determines the nature of the assessment. Instead of referring to the IEP, it is a better practice to identify skills needed to take the assessment and then teach them if need be. This is *not* "teaching to the test." Rather, it is teaching the skills needed to take the test.

Activity

Using the following scenarios, have participants make participation decisions for each student—should the student participate in assessment? Have participants be specific in their recommendation, designating what assessment the student will take (e.g., regular assessment, regular assessment with accommodations, partial assessment, or alternate assessment).

Scenario 1: Chester

Chester is an eighth-grade student with a learning disability who receives resource room services once a day. His area of learning disability is written expression. Chester is enrolled in general education classes. The state that Chester resides in has mandated a writing test for all eighth graders.

What test should Chester be required to take?

What is the basis for your decision?

What additional information may you need?

Scenario 2: Keri

Keri is a ninth-grade student who has been classified as having mental retardation since kindergarten. In the state where Keri lives, students must pass mandated tests in reading, writing, math, science, and history in order to graduate with a high school diploma. Keri is instructed in a curriculum that focuses on vocational and life skills.

What test should Keri be required to take?

What is the basis for your decision?

What additional information may you need?

Scenario 3: Aaron

Aaron is a fourth grader who has a reading disability and is reading two years below level. In Aaron's district, all fourth graders are required to take a reading test. His Title I reading teacher claims that the required reading test is too hard for Aaron and will cause undue stress on him.

What test should Aaron be required to take?

What is the basis for your decision?

What additional information may you need?

Handouts and Overheads

Use the handouts and overheads on the following pages as you present the information from this component.

Three Types of Students With Disabilities in Assessment

Those who

. . . are able to participate without accommodations

. . . are able to participate with accommodations

. . . will need to take a different or alternate assessment

Copyright © 1997 by Corwin Press, Inc.

Issues of Participation

- **Who participates?**

- **Who decides?**

- **In what assessment?**

- **Responsibility for results?**

- **Unanticipated consequences?**

Copyright © 1997 by Corwin Press, Inc.

Reported Practices in Deciding Who to Include

- **The IEP team makes all the decisions**

- **Based on category of disability**

- **Based on percentage of time spent in the mainstream**

- **Any student with an IEP is automatically excluded**

- **Type of curriculum**

Copyright © 1997 by Corwin Press, Inc.

Component 7
What Are Assessment Accommodations?

Purpose

- To describe what assessment accommodations are, their purpose, and what they might look like
- To create a link between instruction and assessment and to identify the range of accommodations that can be delivered for both

Background Information

Key points of this component are covered here. Remember to adapt the information to the audience and local needs.

Purpose of Accommodations

Assessment accommodations provide students the means to show what they know without being impeded by their disability. Accommodations provide equal footing for students (i.e., level the playing field), not an advantage. Most states have made provisions for students with disabilities to use accommodations during statewide tests, probably because both statutory law and constitutional law imply that policies should provide students with disabilities the opportunity to participate in assessments with appropriate accommodations. Providing assessment accommodations should be based on what the student needs, not what the student would benefit from.

Accommodations fall into several categories (e.g., timing, scheduling, setting, presentation, and response). There are a number of accommodations that can be provided within each category.

Eligibility for Accommodations

Depending on state and district policy, any student with a disability is eligible for an assessment accommodation if in fact it is needed to show what the student knows. Some places are beginning to examine accommodations for all students in need, not just students with disabilities.

Decisions About Accommodations

Decisions about who receives what kinds of accommodations are important ones. Most often, these decisions are left to the building or district IEP teams. It is imperative that these decision makers understand the purpose of a district's assessment program and the appropriateness of granting accommodations. For example,

- If a reading test is given to evaluate a student's ability to decode, providing a reader for the test (i.e., someone who reads the test to the student) is inappropriate. However, if the same test is given for the purpose of measuring a student's understanding of written text, a reader is appropriate.

- Often, the use of calculators is controversial. If the test purports to measure a student's ability to calculate numbers, providing a calculator is inappropriate. However, if we are interested in evaluating whether a student understands when to use a formula to derive an answer, a calculator is an appropriate accommodation.

Decisions to provide individual students with assessment accommodations and reasons given for their use need to be documented.

Current Practice

There is much activity centered on accommodations policies and the provision of assessment accommodations. The use of assessment accommodations has been one of great controversy for test developers and measurement people.

- Many argue that the introduction of an accommodation contaminates or changes what the test intends to measure. However, most of these statements are made on the basis of opinion, not fact. Those based on data are from assessments unlike those we are discussing.

- Currently, research is under way that examines the impact of assessment accommodations on test integrity for large-scale accountability assessments.

- Until we have a better understanding of the impact of the use of assessment accommodations, to deny their use to students who need them raises legal questions—especially if there are high stakes attached for the student. If there is a question about the provision of an assessment accommodation, it is usually best to provide the accommodation.

- It is important to remember that not all students with disabilities need accommodations during assessment. But for those who do need them, assessment accommodations should not be introduced for the first time during the administration of a test but, rather, should align with those provided during the instructional process.

- Providing accommodations to students who need them increases the number of students with disabilities who can take district and state assessments and thus be included in the accountability system.

Activities

Activity 1

Using the information presented in the case study in Handouts, suggest instructional and assessment accommodations for Rosa.

Activity 2

Using the chart below, generate examples of the types of accommodations that could fall under each category.

Handouts and Overheads

Use the handouts and overheads on the following pages as you present the information for this component.

ACTIVITY 1

Background:

Rosa is an eighth grader who has lived in the United States for three years. Her primary language is Hmong. Rosa had limited education in her home country. She has been identified as having a learning disability with severe language disabilities. Areas in need include receptive/expressive language, written communication, basic reading, basic math (computation and problem solving), prior knowledge in many areas, and social-emotional skills.

Instructional Needs:

Rosa is at the first-grade level for reading, writing, and mathematics, She is able to work independently and in groups of two or three but with the assistance of an adult. She likes to work in workbooks. In general, Rosa works well with a buddy and in cooperative learning groups. Rosa does not accept school authority or routines well. She requires frequent breaks during instruction. Given specific teacher direction and close proximity, Rosa is able to write in her daily journal. Use of a computer and a tape recorder do not improve performance.

Suggest Instructional Accommodations for Rosa:

Suggest Assessment Accommodations:

Setting   Timing

Scheduling   Presentation

Response   Other

ACTIVITY 2

Accommodations:

Timing   Scheduling

Setting   Presentation

Response   Other

Assessment Issues

✓ **Who participates?
(Participation)**

✓ **HOW DO THEY PARTICIPATE?
(ACCOMMODATION)**

✓ **How are they counted?
(Reporting)**

Copyright © 1997 by Corwin Press, Inc.

Issues in Accommodation

- What is a "reasonable" accommodation?

- Available for ALL?

- Disability specific?

- The "fair" argument

- Linkage to instruction

- Validity of results

Copyright © 1997 by Corwin Press, Inc.

Accommodations

Timing   Scheduling

Setting   Presentation

Response   Other

Copyright © 1997 by Corwin Press, Inc.

Component 8
Reporting of Results

Purpose

- To provide an overview of how results are reported
- To provide an overview of how results are used

Background Information

This section covers key points for this component. Actual staff development sessions should reflect the information needs of the targeted audience and the local situation.

Reporting and Use of Results

It is not uncommon for students with disabilities to be excluded when reporting assessment results. In fact, some students with disabilities are allowed to take the assessment, but their test protocols are destroyed or shared only with those students' parents. Test scores of these students are not included in building, district, or state reports. Often, there is no record of any district or state assessment in the student's cumulative file. There are several reasons why this practice is inappropriate.

- What accountability system do students with disabilities belong to if they are not in the one that all students belong to? All students count and need to be accounted for. Student learning, regardless of the test, must be reported in the results of district and statewide accountability systems.

- Students who, for any reason, do not participate in traditional assessment must be accounted for. The manner in which this is done will vary by the types of assessment program (e.g., traditional or alternate forms). Documentation of these decisions, reasons for them, and their results must be done on an individual student basis. However, all student performance must be reported to better decipher program effectiveness and learning trends and to make instructional decisions.

- The issue of reporting has vast impact on school buildings and districts. Many bond issues are won or lost based on how well students do on the assessments. Districts and states are constantly compared with each other, and the media often shows no mercy in its front-page display of results. Therefore, there are incentives for school buildings, districts, and states to selectively report the results of assessment.

Participation Rates Key to Reporting

The issue of reporting is centered around who is included when the participation rate for the assessment is calculated. It is not uncommon for students with disabilities to be excluded from this calculation, accommodated or not. Others exclude only those students who receive accommodations.

Some states start with the number of students with disabilities who are eligible to participate in the assessment and use this number to reflect all students with disabilities. For example, District A has 500 students with disabilities. After participation decisions are made (usually by the IEP team), only 150 students with disabilities take the assessment. District A then reports that 90% of students with disabilities passed the assessment. Using these results, District A appears not only inclusive in its assessment program, but programmatically meeting the needs of students with disabilities. However, a closer look begs the question "90% of what number?" The reality is that approximately one-third of all students with disabilities in the district actually took the test. What about the 350 students with disabilities who did not take the assessment?

Considerations

Determining an accurate number of students with disabilities who currently are participating in district and state assessments must begin with creating a means to account for them. Many states and districts are collecting this information by adding demographic descriptors to student answer sheets. To do this successfully requires collaboration and coordination between general and special education personnel. Because general educators may not always be aware of which students are receiving special education services, it is essential that these educators verify assessment rosters.

- Policy and procedural guidelines need to be identified to standardize the calculations of participation rates. Because of their inclusiveness, some suggest December 1 child counts of students with disabilities. However, this number does not take into account those students who become eligible for special education services between December 1 and a spring testing cycle or those who discontinue services. The result can be an exaggerated or underestimated rate at which students with disabilities participate in assessment.

- Keep lines of communication open. Much of the current confusion about who the students with disabilities are and how they get reported can be resolved through better and more open communication between departments within both state and school district education agencies.

Failure to include students with disabilities in assessment and accountability systems leads to failure to assume responsibility for all students, for included in "all" are students with disabilities. Policymakers, community members, and parents need and want to know how students in America's schools are learning. Inclusive accountability systems is a means to that end.

Activities

Activity 1

In a small group or dyad, discuss the following:

- What is the purpose of reporting assessment results?
- What gets reported?
- Whose scores are reported in school/district reports?

Activity 2 (Use this activity when deemed appropriate)

In a small group or dyad, discuss the following:

- How is the reporting of assessment results useful?
- How could they be more useful?

Activity 3

Think about the pluses, minuses, and interesting (PMI) aspects of including all students in the overall reporting of assessment results. Jot down some of the pluses (positives), minuses (potential negatives), and interesting thoughts (things you may need more information about).

When directed, gather into a small group and collectively share your Ps, Ms, and Is. Make a list for each category. Then, using consensus, identify the top three Ps, Ms, and Is that represent your group's ideas about the topic of reporting. Select a spokesperson to report to the entire group (see handout).

Handouts and Overheads

Use the handouts and overheads on the following pages as you present the information on this component.

Assessment Issues

✓ **Who participates?**
(Participation)

✓ **How do they participate?**
(Accommodations)

✓ **HOW ARE THEY COUNTED?**
(REPORTING)

Copyright © 1997 by Corwin Press, Inc.

Issues in Reporting Results

- **How are the results used?**

- **Who sees them?**

- **Are all test scores included in the accountability report?**

- **Are results reported together or separate?**

- **Where are scores assigned?**

- **What kinds of scores are used?**

Copyright © 1997 by Corwin Press, Inc.

PMI

Reporting Assessment Results of All Students

Pluses (What are the pluses? What are the positives?)

Minuses (What are the minuses? What might be negative?)

Interesting (What could be interesting? Something we need more information about is . . .)

Copyright © 1997 by Corwin Press, Inc.

Component 9
Next Steps

Purpose

- To generate discussion on where we go from here

An Action Plan

In less than a decade, there has been a dramatic increase in the amount of attention that our nation pays to assessments given both in and outside the classroom.

- Assessment and accountability have moved to the forefront of restructuring efforts.

- It is imperative that special-needs students, including those with disabilities, be considered in the process of planning and development as states and school districts strive to rework existing curricular frameworks and corresponding assessments.

- Building a system that is accountable for all students should be a goal of our education system. If we begin our planning and development of assessments with the end in mind, we can proactively address the issues of accountability for all students' learning.

We recognize that many states have local control. That is, the school districts and schools have autonomy in setting selected practices and policies. Furthermore, we recognize that even within a school district, autonomy is granted to school buildings. Despite this, policy is policy. The overall assessment policy should be firm even though the ways in which districts and schools ready themselves for implementation and train their staff may differ.

Without policy and/or guidelines for assessment participation, accommodations, and reporting of results, it will be virtually impossible to level the accountability playing fields of school buildings, districts, and states. We encourage you to set policy at both the state and local district levels so as to provide a framework from which implementation can occur on a relatively consistent basis.

Actions Steps at the School District Level

- Conduct meetings on specific issues or topics that your school, district, and state face. Gather information from a stratified stakeholder group composed of parents, general and special education teachers, administrators, and even students, if appropriate.

- Be sure that both general and special education personnel are present and participate.

- Hold information-gathering meetings with central office and building administrators.

- Provide training for personnel involved in the assessment decision-making process. These include, but are not limited to, members of the IEP team and building administrators.

- Provide a public forum or hold informational meetings that allow for dissemination and information exchange on assessment issues such as participation, purpose, accommodation, and reporting of results. Parents and community members need to be informed up front about changes in or alterations to the assessment program.

- Develop a vision for learning and assessment for all students. Make sure that they are aligned and include accountability for all learners.

- Develop and/or revise assessment policies and practices to reflect an inclusive assessment and accountability system, including participation, accommodations, and reporting.

- Create a task force or team to train the trainers or answer any questions that may arise from changes in the assessment program.

- Develop a monitoring system to ensure that policy and guidelines are implemented correctly.

- Make connections with state education personnel and include them when needed and appropriate.

Activity

Use the chart below to have participants summarize their learning and to identify next steps or directions. This activity can be done alone or in small or large groups.

Handout and Overhead

Use the handout and overhead on the following page to work through possible action steps.

Using the chart below, record any questions, concerns, or challenges you may have as the result of the assessment session(s). What do you see as immediate and long-term needs for our district in the area of inclusive assessment and accountability? Suggest some action steps that could facilitate meeting those needs.

Concerns, Questions, and Challenges	Needs	Action Steps

Action Steps: Where Do We Go From Here?

Options and Considerations

- Topical meetings with a stratified group of stakeholders

- Develop criteria or policy guidelines on participation and accommodation of students with disabilities in large-scale assessment

- Training for assessment process decision makers

- Informational and public forum meetings

- Develop a vision and mission statement for learning and assessment

- Task force to plan training and staff development and information dissemination on the assessment, learning, and accountability connection

- Develop a system to oversee implementation

Copyright © 1997 by Corwin Press, Inc.

Resources: Technical Assistance and Dissemination Networks

For more information on research and development efforts in the areas of instruction, assessment, and accountability, contact:

Office of Educational Research and Improvement (OERI)
U.S. Department of Education
555 New Jersey Avenue NW
Washington, DC 20208
Fax: 202-219-2135

Office of Special Education and Rehabilitative Services (OSERS)
U.S. Department of Education
330 C Street SW
Mary E. Switzer Building
Washington, DC 20202-2500
Telephone: 202-205-5465
Fax: 202-205-9252

National Center on Educational Outcomes
University of Minnesota
350 Elliott Hall
75 East River Road
Minneapolis, MN 55455
Telephone: 612-626-1530
Fax: 612-624-0879
Web: http://www.coled.umn.edu/nceo

National Center for Research on Evaluation, Standards, and Student Testing
UCLA Graduate School of Education
405 Hilgard Avenue
Los Angeles, CA 90024-1522
Telephone: 310-825-8326
Fax: 310-206-6293
Web: http://cresst96.cse.ucls.edu/index.html

For a state and local policy perspective, contact:

National Association of State Boards of Education
1012 Cameron Street
Alexandria, VA 22314
Telephone: 703-684-4000
Fax: 703-836-2313
email: boards @nasbe.org

Consortium for Policy Research in Education (CPRE)
Graduate School of Education
University of Pennsylvania
3440 Market Street, Suite 560
Philadelphia, PA 19104-3325
Telephone: 215-573-0700
Fax: 215-573-7914

National Association of State Directors of Special Education (NASDSE)
1800 Diagonal Road, Ste. 320
King Street Station I
Alexandria, VA 22314
Telephone: 703-519-3800
Fax: 703-519-3808

For state-based regional resource centers, contact:

Federal Resource Center for Special Education (FRC)
Academy for Educational Development
1875 Connecticut Avenue NW, Ste. 900
Washington, DC 20009
Telephone: 202-884-8215; TTY: 802-860-1428
Fax: 202-884- 8443
web: http://www.aed.org/special.ed/frc.html

Region 1: Northeast (Connecticut, Maine, Massachusetts, New Hampshire, New Jersey, New York, Rhode Island, Vermont)

Northeast Regional Resource Center (NERRC)
Trinity College of Vermont
McAuley Hall
208 Colchester Avenue
Burlington, VT 05401-1496
Telephone: 802-658-5036
Fax: 802-658-7435
web: http//interact.uoregon.edu/wrrc/nerrc/index.html

Region 2: Mid-South (Delaware, District of Columbia, Kentucky, Maryland, North Carolina, South Carolina, Tennessee, Virginia, West Virginia)

Mid-South Regional Resource Center (MSRRC)
Human Development Institute
University of Kentucky
126 Mineral Industries Building
Lexington, KY 40506-0051
Telephone: 606-257-4921; TTY: 606-257-2903
FAX: 606-257- 4353
email: msrrc@ihdi.ihdi.ukt.edu
web: http://www.ihdi.uky.edu/projects/msrrc/index.html

Region 3: South Atlantic (Alabama, Arkansas, Florida, Georgia, Louisiana, Mississippi, New Mexico, Oklahoma, Texas, Puerto Rico, U.S. Virgin Islands)

South Atlantic Regional Resource Center (SARRC)
Florida Atlantic University
1236 North University Drive
Plantation, FL 33322
Telephone: 954-473-6106
Fax: 954-424-4309
email: sarrc@acc.fau.edu
web: http://www.fau.edu/divdept/sarrc

Region 4: Great Lakes (Illinois, Indiana, Michigan, Minnesota, Ohio, Pennsylvania, Wisconsin)

Great Lakes Area Regional Resource Center (GLARRC)
Center for Special Needs Populations
Ohio State University
700 Ackerman Road, Ste. 440
Columbus, OH 43202
Telephone: 614-447-0844
Fax: 614-447-9043
web: http://www.osu.edu/csnp/glarrc.html

Region 5: Mountain Plains (Colorado, Iowa, Kansas, Missouri, Montana, Nebraska, North Dakota, South Dakota, Utah, Wyoming)

Mountain Plains Regional Resource Center (MPRRC)
Utah State University
1780 North Research Parkway, Ste. 112
Logan, UT 84341
Telephone: 801-752-0238 TTY: 801-753-9750
Fax: 801-753-9750
web: http://www.edu.drake.edu/rc/rrc/mprrc.html

MPRRC
Drake University
2507 University
Memorial Hall, 3rd Floor
Des Moines, IA 50311
Telephone: 515-271-3936
Fax: 515-271-4185

Region 6: Western (Alaska, Arizona, California, Hawaii, Idaho, Nevada, Oregon, Washington, American Samoa, Federated States of Micronesia, Commonwealth of the Northern Mariana Islands, Guam, Republic of the Marshall Islands, Republic of Palau)

Western Regional Resource Center (WRRC)
University of Oregon
Eugene, OR 97403-1268
Telephone: 541-346-5641; TTY: 541-346-0367
Fax: 541-346-5639
email: dls@oregon.uoregon.edu
web: http://internet.uoregon.edu/wrrc/wrrc.html

Other technical asistance and dissemination networks to contact:

National Center to Improve the Tools of Educators
College of Education
University of Oregon
805 Lincoln
Eugene, OR 97401
Telephone: 503-683-7543
Fax: 503-683-7543
email: douglas_carnine@ccmail.uoregon.edu
web: http://darkwing.uoregon.edu~ncite/

Technology, Educational Media, and Materials Program
Chesapeake Institute
1000 Thomas Jefferson Street NW, Ste. 400
Washington, DC 20007
Telephone: 202-342-5600
Fax: 202-944-5454
email: dosher@air-dc.org

National Clearinghouse for Professionals in Special Education
Council for Exceptional Children
1920 Association Drive
Reston, VA 22091
Telephone: 703-264-9476, 800-641-7824; TTY: 703-264-9446
Fax: 703-620-2521
email: ncpse@cec.sped.org

National Information Center for Children and Youth With Disabilities (NICHCY)
Academy for Educational Development
P.O. Box 1492
Washington, DC 20031-1492
Telephone: 202-884-8200; Voice/TTY 800-695-0285
Fax: 202-884-8441
email: nichcy@aed.org
web: http://www.aed.org/nichcy

Council for Exceptional Children
1920 Association Drive
Reston, VA 22091-1589
Telephone: 703-264-9479, 800-224-6830
Fax: 703-264-1637
Web: http://www.cec.sped.org/

Inclusion:

Consortium on Inclusive Schooling Practices (CISP)
National Association of State School Boards of Education
1012 Cameron Street
Alexandria, VA 22314
Telephone: 703-684-4000
Fax: 703-836-2313
email: michaelc@nasbe.org
web: http://www.asri.edu.cfsp/brochure/abtcons.html

Transition:

National Transition Alliance for Youths With Disabilities (National
Transition Network, Academy for Educational Development,
Transition Research Institute)
Transition Research Institute at Illinois
University of Illinois
113 Children's Research Center
51 Getty Drive
Champaign, IL 61820
Telephone: 217-333-2325 (Voice/TTY)
Fax: 217-244-0851
email: leachlyn@uxl.cso.uiuc.edu
web: http://www.aed.org/transition/alliance/nta.html

National Transition Network (NTN)
Institute on Community Integration
University of Minnesota
430 Wulling Hall
86 Pleasant Street SE
Minneapolis, MN 55455
Telephone: 612-626-8200
Fax: 612-626-7956
email: guyxx002@maroon.tc.umn.edu
web: http://www.ici.coled.umn.edu/ntn/

Parents:

Parents Engaged in Educational Reform (PEER)
Federation for Children With Special Needs
95 Berkeley Street, Ste. 104
Boston, MA 02116
Telephone: 617-482-2915
Fax: 617-695-2939
email: cromano@fcsn.org
web: http://www.fcsn.org/peer/

Technical Assistance for Parent Programs (TAPP)
Federation for Children With Special Needs
95 Berkeley Street, Ste. 104
Boston, MA 02116
Telephone: 617-482-2915
Fax: 617-695-2939
email: mzeigler@fcsn.org
web: http://www.fcsn.org/tapp

Early Childhood:

National Early Childhood Technical Assistance System (NECTAS)
Frank Porter Graham Child Development Center
University of North Carolina at Chapel Hill
500 Nations Bank Plaza
137 East Franklin Street
Chapel Hill, NC 27514
Telephone: 919-962-2001
Fax: 919-996-7463
email: nectasta.nectas@mhs.unc.edu
web: http://www.nectas.unc.edu

Other:

ERIC Clearing House on Assessment and Evaluation
O'Boyle Hall, Department of Education
Catholic University of America
Washington, DC 20064
Telephone: 800-464-3742
Fax: 202-319-6692

Education Commission of the States
707 17th Street, Ste. 2700
Denver, CO 80202-3427
Telephone: 303-299-3600
Fax: 303-296-8332
email: ecs@ecs.org

U.S. Department of Education
600 Maryland Avenue SW
Washington, DC 20202
Telephone: 800-USA-LEARN
Web: webmaster@inet.ed.gov

National Center to Improve Practice
Education Development Center, Inc.
55 Chapel Street
Newton, MA 02158
Telephone: 617-969-7100, x2387
Fax: 617-969-3440
email: ncip@edc.org

Selected Web Sites:

Education Newsletters
http://www.newsletteraccess.com/subject/edu.html
Connects to over 135 education newsletters within a directory of over 5,000

Federal and State Education Organizations
http://www.ezonline.com:80/parss/edorg.html
Links to national and state education organizations

Goals 2000 Legislation and Related Items
http://www.ed.gov/g2k/
Provides information about Goals 2000

Improving America's Schools Act of 1994 (IASA)
http://www.ed.gov/legislation/ESEA/index.html/
Presents the law for the act

National Clearinghouse for Bilingual Education (NCBE)
http://www.ncbe.gwu.edu/index.html
Addresses critical issues dealing with education of linguistically and culturally
    diverse students in the United States

Other Assessment Resources:

http://www.firn.edu/doe/sas/othrhome.html
Links to 14 assessment/educational resources

Thomas: U.S. Congress on the Internet
http://thomas.locgov/home/thomas.html
Reports on floor activities of the week, status of major legislation,
    committee reports, and more